T0204147

THE FIRST IDIOT
IN HEAVEN

Secrets of the Apostle Paul
(And why the meek merely inherit the Earth)

martin zender

THE FIRST IDIOT IN HEAVEN

Secrets of the Apostle Paul
(And why the meek merely inherit the Earth)

Starke & Hartmann, Inc.

The First Idiot In Heaven
© 2012 by Martin Zender

Published by Starke & Hartmann, Inc.
P.O. Box 6473
Canton, OH 44706
www.starkehartmann.com
1-866-866-BOOK

Printed in the United States of America

Editor: Rebecca E. Tonn

Cover: © Can Stock Photo Inc. / dundanim

Publisher's Cataloging-In-Publication Data
(Prepared by The Donohue Group, Inc.)

Zender, Martin.
  The first idiot in heaven: secrets of the Apostle Paul, and why the meek merely inherit the earth / Martin Zender.

    p. : ill. ; cm.

  ISBN-13: 978-0-9709849-9-9
  ISBN-10: 0-9709849-9-5

  1. Paul, the Apostle, Saint. 2. Bible.--N.T.--Epistles of Paul--Criticism, interpretation, etc. 3. Christian saints--Turkey--Tarsus--Biography. 4. Jesus Christ--Teachings. I. Title.

BS2506.3 .Z46 2012
225.9/2   2011942888

Contents

To J.H. Tonn,
who was deeply interested in
God's Word

"I have been entrusted with the evangel
of the Uncircumcision, according as
Peter of the Circumcision."

—the apostle Paul
Galatians 2:7
Concordant Literal New Testament

ACKNOWLEDGEMENTS

First of all, I would like to thank the apostle Paul—formerly the Pharisee Saul—who was doing his own thing one day a couple of thousand years ago, when the resurrected Christ U-turned his life and told him celestial secrets no human had ever heard—and then said, "Broadcast them!"

Paul did not ask for this call, and yet my life has been enriched because of Paul's faithfulness to it. I thank this man, especially, for keeping the celestial message pure against all those wishing to taint it and mix it with the Circumcision gospel of Israel.

I would like to thank, secondly, the small handful of fellow-workers who helped Paul broadcast the celestial secrets, and who suffered along with him. Thanks to Timothy, Apollos, Epaphras, Barnabas, Onesimus, Tychicus, Priscilla, Aquila, Luke, and Archippus. I also wish to thank those who opened their homes to Paul for meetings and Bible studies, including Nympha, Mary, Gaius, Phoebe, Tryphena, and Tryphosa. An especial thanks to Lydia, of Thyatira, who financed Paul's first journey into Europe, and to all those in the small group at Philippi, who continually sent Paul money to keep him eating, traveling, and writing. We are forever indebted to your generosity.

Speaking of writing, a big "thank you" to Tertius, Paul's scribe, to whom Paul dictated many of the letters that God has preserved for over 2,000 years.

I am grateful for the small groups here in Colorado that help keep me in the Word and encouraged in the grace of God. Thanks to Gerald and Illa Visser of Monument, for the meetings in their home, and to DeLois Carleton of Denver, who opens her home twice a month for teaching, at the same time refreshing the saints. These small bodies of Christ gather not only for fellowship, but to gain light for living from the Scriptures. Along that line, thanks to our teacher Sean Marting, who labors in the Word, bringing it alive each Thursday night, and gives me a regular lift to Denver in his Honda.

I quote liberally from the *Concordant Literal New Testament*, the most accurate translation in print. Thanks to A.E. Knoch who, in 1909, got the idea to translate Scripture with an actual method, giving each Greek word its own English equivalent and then refusing to use that English word for any other Greek word, avoiding the "cross-wiring" and confusion of other versions. Whenever Scriptural accuracy is not compromised, I like to quote from *The Message*, which brings Paul's words alive to the modern reader.

Thanks to Tony Smith and J.D. Fine for their mastery of InDesign and Photoshop, respectively. You guys are magicians.

I am indebted to Kelly Stokoe, of Starke & Hartmann, Inc., who, when she heard of this project, simply said, "What a great idea. Go for it." Thanks, Kelly!

I would still only be *thinking* about writing this book were it not for the love, support, and encouragement of my wife, Rebecca Tonn. Rebecca is not only my life-partner and fellow-laborer in the gospel of God's grace, but one hell of an editor. In instances too numerous to count, she has made me sound smarter than I actually am. Rebecca has labored many hours over this manuscript (chewing much peppermint gum), for me, for you, and for her Lord and Savior, Jesus Christ. *I love you, Babe!*

Finally, "Thanks be to God for His indescribable gratuity" (2 Corinthians 9:15), and for the ability to attempt to describe such an amazing grace.

1.

INTRODUCTION

INTRODUCTION

You want to live like Jesus, you really do. You're sincere as can be, but it's an uphill climb. You love people and you love God, so maybe today will be the day you can finally imitate His Son. Maybe today you can finally be meek, turn the other cheek, and rejoice while getting mud thrown in your face.

Think how good it would feel to be pure—to have no sin and no guilt. Think how good it would feel to wake up calm each morning, love everyone during the day, and rest your head at night with a prayer for your enemies.

If only.

And yet it never quite works out that way. In the darkness of your bed each night, you know who you are. Jesus was Jesus, but you are you. When you curl up beneath the covers, you face the terrible truth: It has been another day of failure and frustration.

If only there were a gospel in the Bible for common, ordinary human beings. Or even mediocre people. It seems the gospel of Jesus that tells us to live like Jesus sets the bar just a little too, um, *high.*

I know all about it. I was raised Catholic. The nuns told me all I had to do was be meek and mild like Jesus (plus do everything else like Jesus) and I would go to heaven. It seemed like a tall order for someone with cartoons on his underpants. What did I know? All I wanted was to play football and eat candy.

I remember asking one of the nuns tormenting me if *she* was meek and mild; I asked her if *she* did everything like Jesus. My mistake. She fingered her rosary, made threatening gestures with a yardstick, and said of course she did everything like Jesus; she did it for a living. I wasn't so sure. None of the drawings I saw of Jesus ever showed Him holding a green yardstick.

Nonetheless, when Jesus was on Earth, He said some difficult things. He told the rich to give away all their money and follow Him (Mark 10:21). He told sophisticated people to become as children (Matthew 18:3). If confidence was your thing, you had to lose it. Were you happy? Sorry to hear that; you needed to become sorrowful instead. Here was the prescription: Give up joy for mourning—and call me in the morning.

All you have to do is obey all the commandments (Matthew 28:20). If your hand makes you stumble, simply cut it off (Matthew 5:30). If your eye wanders, it's not a problem—as long as you pluck it out (Mark 9:47). Quit whining; it's better to enter the kingdom maimed and blind than to keep making fatal mistakes. If you walk a mile with someone, tough luck—you must walk another mile (Matthew 5:41). If someone sues you for the shirt off your back, it's still not enough; you must give away your coat as well (Matthew 5:40). Throw in your shoes and socks while you're at it. Better to be safe (and naked) than sorry.

Be watching and praying—or else (Luke 21:36). If the Bridegroom arrives and your lamp has no oil, you will be cast into the outer darkness, where there will be weeping, gnashing of teeth (Matthew 25:30), and a pathetic lack of adult beverages.

Now go in peace, love and serve the Lord—*and have a good day.*

No wonder a friend of mine, after reading the four gospels, said, "I want to live like Jesus, Martin—I really do—but can I start Monday? I'd like to enjoy the weekend."

Obviously, the words of Jesus are perfect. His commandments are pure and holy, refined seven times—*and meant for Israelites.* Jesus Himself said, "I was not sent except to the lost sheep of the house of Israel" (Matthew 15:24, *New King James Version*).

Why have we not believed these simple words? Is it too shocking to think that—while on Earth—Jesus preached a national rather than a universal message? Too tough to admit that Jesus emphasized the law of Moses (the law given to Israel), rather than grace?

Wouldn't we be honoring Jesus by believing His own declaration? Or do we think we are doing Him a favor by ignoring this plain sentence, supposing we know better than He does? Are we afraid of limiting Him? Why? While on Earth, Jesus purposely limited Himself:

"I was not sent except to the lost sheep of the house of Israel."

Am I a lost sheep from the house of Israel? I'm Dutch and English, actually—with a little French mixed in. Does that mean Jesus was not sent to *me*? The shocking answer is: *That's exactly what it means.* While Jesus was on *Earth* (this is the key), He preached a national message to Israelites. Period. Which means the words in red are not meant for men and women (nor kids with cartoons on their underpants) of the other nations. Nor were the Ten Commandments meant for any non-Israelites.

Don't shoot the messenger. I will back myself up with Scripture every step of the way. ("Those of the nations have no law"—Romans 2:24.) Keep reading, and you will be delivered from the cycle of failure and guilt that has dogged you for months or years. There is another message (gospel) in the New Testament that *is* for you. It's infinitely easier (you get more for doing less) and Jesus approves of it 100 percent. Why wouldn't He? Jesus invented it. But Jesus did not divulge *this* gospel until He returned to heaven and traded in His dusty robe for blinding beams of light.

The gospel that Jesus preached while on Earth has a name. It's called, "The Gospel of the Circumcision" (Galatians 2:7). This gospel is not for losers. Idiots need not apply. It *is* for sinners, yes, but the sinners better shape up quickly before Jesus returns and finds them slacking. These sinners have to repent. They have to be baptized. It helps if they cry a lot. They definitely need to "produce fruit worthy of repentance" (Matthew 3:8). All they need to do, really, is behave themselves constantly or at least try like crazy. And wiping those silly grins off their faces wouldn't hurt, either.

Why do we have such a difficult time shaping up and producing fruit worthy of repentance? Maybe better to ask: Why do we instinctively know we *can't* do these things? Why do we give up *trying* to do them? Is it because we are lazy? Ungodly? Satanic? Because we think we deserve nothing more than to be crushed beneath God's fist? Or could it be that, deep down, we think God doesn't really expect us to weep and wail, repent, and be practically perfect in every way? But if He doesn't expect all that, what do we do with all the Bible verses saying He does expect it? Could it be there are *other* Bible verses that say *different* things?

Are you bold enough to entertain a new thought? What if we, who are not Israelites, have a different gospel—*in the Bible*—than the one meant for Israel? What if this other gospel even has a different name? What if it has a different set of requirements (and a different outlook on run-of-the-mill people or hapless nincompoops) than the gospel given to Israel? And—think of this—what if this gospel promises an enormously better destiny than the one promised to Jewish believers?

Were faithful Israelites ever promised heaven? Not once. Jesus Himself said, "The meek shall inherit the *Earth*" (Matthew 5:5). Wouldn't Jesus have known what He was talking about? Israelites never dreamed of getting lifted from Terra Firma. Why would they? Jesus never spoke to them of such a thing. And neither did their prophets. Faithful Israelites were promised that they would rule and reign over the other nations of Earth. This was the promise God made to Abraham.

Back to my question. What if this different gospel I have been referring to (the easier one; the kinder and gentler one; the one that caters to those of us who are not-so-perfect) *does* take people to heaven? Wouldn't that be mind-boggling? It would mean that Sister Mary Yardstick was all wrong. Imitating the walk of Jesus would not have gotten me to heaven—as she insisted it would—but would, instead, have kept me on Earth to rule the other nations. What *would* get me to heaven would be giving up trying to be like Jesus and embracing a gospel for regular folks—assuming such a gospel actually exists.

Wouldn't that be something God would do? Bless the socks off average, ordinary people? Doesn't it align with everything we know about His penchant to stun loser-types (fishermen, prostitutes, tax-collectors) with draughts of favor? So God gives reformed sinners (obedient Israelites) what He promised them—namely, Earth—but then later announces a *different* gospel that seats unworthy people (those who haven't a prayer of being like His Son) at His right hand in the highest regions of heaven.

Would this be a gospel you'd like to learn about?

What if—after all these years of struggling and failing to be like the meek and mild Jesus—you have been laboring upon someone else's path? Reading someone else's mail? Straining to pay someone else's bill? What if you have been sweating up someone else's Mount Sinai, while misguidedly condemning yourself for not only losing your way, but repeatedly falling? And what if ceasing all these struggles will actually land you a *better* destiny than the one you'd have had if you'd done everything right?

The entire Bible is *for* us, but what if not all of it is *to* us? While on Earth, Jesus Christ directed His words to the descendants of Abraham. Several hundred years later, someone got the brilliant idea of taking everything Jesus said and printing it in red ink. Red is the color of "do this or else," so we who are not descendants of Abraham assume these words are *our* marching orders.

What if they aren't? What if Jesus Christ did have a special message for all humanity, but He saved *that* message until He had traded in His earthly sandals for more glorious heavenly footwear?

Several months after Jesus Christ left this Earth from the Mount of Olives, He appeared as a beam of light brighter than the sun to a hate-crazed sinner (read: idiot) en route to Damascus to kill Christians. The glorified Christ gave this man (the apostle Paul, then known as the Pharisee Saul) a message so different than the one the humbled Christ gave Israel (it was grace instead of law; rest instead of works; joy instead of dread, heaven instead of Earth), that even the Jews who believed in Jesus as their Messiah—when they got wind of this new gospel—wanted the messenger dead.

Today, these two messages—or gospels—are so completely opposed that people wonder: *How can such a strict, hardcore Messiah who barely talked to Gentiles when He was on Earth, suddenly be telling all kinds of people: "I love you no matter what you do; you are completely perfect in spite of your behavior or nationality. And you know what? Leave Earth to Israel; I am taking you to heaven"? And why are both messages side-by-side in the same Bible?*

Not even I, Martin Zender—The World's Most Outspoken Bible Scholar—have the audacity to pit the words of Jesus Christ (printed in religious red) against the words of the apostle Paul (printed in standard, boring black). I don't have to. These words are not at odds; they are purposely distinct. Besides, the words of the apostle Paul *are* the words of Jesus Christ—albeit the glorified Christ Who revealed things to Paul which God kept hidden while His Son walked among Israelites.

Peaches and pears go together fine in a salad, but we mix the fruit from disparate spiritual trees at our own peril.

Does the thought of plucking out your eyes make you queasy?

Are you too tired to go the extra mile? Loathe to climb one more mountain? In short, are you frustrated at not being able to live like the sandal-wearing Messiah?

Rejoice! Not even Jesus expects you to live like Jesus. He, Himself, brought a new, non-Jewish message to the most hateful, self-righteous jerk ever to walk the planet. If God's grace can save such a loser, then what are you worried about?

These are Paul's secrets.

I commend to you this new—yet very old—adventure.

Martin Zender
Colorado Springs

2.
WHO IS THIS IDIOT?

WHO IS THIS IDIOT?

Of all the Bible writers, Paul was the trouble-maker. If Bible writers were a class of eighth graders in a Catholic grade school, then Paul was the one making paper airplanes, passing notes during math class, and asking for a bathroom pass so he could climb out the window and escape his status quo. I liked him because of that. (Well, I could relate to him.)

Paul had a thing for radical statements and for taking the highest viewpoint possible. Because of this, I used to call him "Mr. Radical" and "Mr. Absolute." To me, Paul's revelations on the big themes went a giant step further than those of every other Bible writer.

For instance, while the others wrote about how sin could screw up my safety in God, Paul wrote, "Where sin increases, grace superexceeds" (Romans 5:20, *Concordant Literal New Testament*). While the others pressured me to keep law, Paul said, "We are reckoning humanity to be justified by faith, apart from works of law" (Romans 3:28, CLNT). Everyone else noted their pedigree and bragged about it. *This* man said: "I was a Hebrew of the Hebrews ... but I've counted it as dung" (Philippians 3:4-8). While the others anticipated a future reward on Earth, Paul said, "We are now seated in heavenly places" (Ephesians 2:6).

"YOU'RE FINISHED, ZENDER."

Let us now consider works. Everyone in the Bible demanded works—except Paul. Concerning salvation, *he* said: "If it's works, then it's no longer grace. And if it's grace, then it's no longer works" (Romans 11:6). Those were plain words that even I—ex-Catholic window-jumper—could understand. But were they too radical to believe? They clashed with everything else in the Bible. Reading Paul was like wandering through a fun house where every mirror somehow made you look better than you were:

Warning: Objects in mirror are more righteous than they appear.

The rest of the Bible—with what appeared to be an endless list of do's and don'ts—set me up for failure. Only Paul, it seemed, cut me slack. How did this radical messenger of grace make it into Scripture? God inspired Paul, did He not? Or did Paul finagle his way into Holy Writ like I finagled my way out that bathroom window in grade school? How was I supposed to make Paul fit with the other Bible writers? Or was it possible that Paul was God's radical, and he wasn't *meant* to fit?

The other writers exhorted me to change myself; I considered them reformers. Paul, on the other hand, had given up on me. To Paul, I was beyond reforming. Usually when someone says, "You're hopeless, kid," it's bad news. But when Paul said it—it spelled relief. I could never be acceptable to God—at least not by following all the rules. So Christ accomplished things I could never have accomplished for myself. I could never make myself righteous, so Christ did it for me. All Christ now wanted from me was thanks and a sigh of relief.

That, I could do.

My quirks never alarmed Paul. I pictured myself approaching him like I used to approach the priests once a month in those shadowy confessionals. I would tell Paul my sins. But unlike the priest, Paul would yawn and say:

> Well, duh, Zender. That's the old humanity; what would you expect it to do? I'm surprised you're as good as you are. You're probably worse than you're telling me. In any case, it doesn't matter. Now you are to think of yourself as having died with Christ (Romans 6:8). News flash: The old humanity has been crucified, Zender (Romans 6:6). God isn't looking at the old humanity anymore; He's looking at Christ. Now, God looks at *you* the same way. You are a new creation (2 Corinthians 5:17). Time to re-adjust your head.

Died with Christ? The old humanity crucified? A new creation? This was not reformation, this was revolution.

I remember my opinion of Paul back when I was a twelve-year-old, all properly pewed and gutting through another Mass. The Mass had two readings: the first and the second. The first reading was a lay person at a plain lectern, droning through an excerpt from one of Paul's letters. The second reading was more than a reading. For the record, I will call it: A Grand Holy Event in which the Priest Slowly and with Great Pomp Ascended an Elevated, Marble Platform and Read (Intoned, rather) From One of the Four Gospels.

The Four Gospels. Ah—these were the red letters of Christ.

To me and to most Christians, the red letters of Christ trumped all other Scripture. "Matthew, Mark, Luke, and John"—this was the A team. These were the four names I'd eventually see carved into the sandstone above the front doors of my high school. Where was Paul's name? It was absent. No sandstone for Paul.

As for the priest, he was the one with fancy robes that could only be called *vestments*. The priest was the trained man of God who lived in the special building with the cross on it, and never sinned. Why *wouldn't* this man get to read the rare words of Christ? The lay guy, on the other hand—usually one of our teachers, and a mere mortal—got assigned Paul. This teacher wore a shirt and tie and brown loafers—the exact opposite of vestments.

"A reading of the letter of Paul to the Thessalonians." This brings back memories for me—of how weird it sounded. I clearly remember turning to my friend Ken Malinowski one Sunday (we were still kids) and saying to him quietly enough so my mother couldn't hear: "Who the heck are the Thessalonians, and who the heck cares?"

It was nice that Paul loved God, but too bad his words were in black. Too bad they were in black, when red was the color of God. Too bad Paul was on the B team. He wanted to be one of the twelve disciples, but he wasn't. He wanted to have met Jesus while Jesus still wore sandals, but he didn't. He wanted to have a throne in the earthly kingdom, but there were only twelve thrones—and, uh, all the thrones are taken—but thanks for applying, Paul. We will keep your résumé on hand for 18 months, and then we will burn it.

Because Paul so clearly missed the Jesus train, he deserved only to have his letters read by an eighth-grade science teacher with brown pants from the Sears men's department. It was clear that Father Passoli would never stoop to reading "a letter of Paul to the Pomeranians"—or whoever.

In April of 1979, when I was 19 years old, I had what the Christian world would call a salvation experience. While watching the final installment of the *Jesus of Nazareth* mini-series at Easter with my dad, the sight of Jesus dragging His cross to Calvary leveled my soul. I hurried to my room at the first commercial, trying to outrun my tears. I dropped to my knees at the side of my bed and begged God to tell me who this Jesus was and why He had to suffer so terribly. I kept saying over and over: "I have to know You. I have to know You. I have to know You."

My first Bible was an NASB (*New American Standard Bible*). By then, I was no longer a good Catholic boy because I was actually reading this Bible for myself and discovering how many of our Catholic sacraments were merely Catholic compulsions. *Nobody is praying to Mary in the Bible. Where are the confessionals? Shouldn't Peter be saying the rosary?*

Soon I started noticing how different Paul was. But by then I was reading popular Christian writers on the side: Hal Lindsay, Fulton Sheen, and others. With the "help" of these and other institutional geniuses, I adopted the traditional view of Paul's place in God's grand scheme.

In a nutshell, here's the story:

Peter was the man. Yes, he was dorky as a donkey, but he was loveable. He was Jesus' right-hand man. And at least he was faithful enough to climb out of his boat one day and start walking on the water toward Jesus. Although the wind and waves finally got the better of him, so that he sank up to his mustache in the Sea of Galilee, nevertheless, among Jesus' disciples, his was the first name mentioned. It was always: "Peter, James, and John." He wasn't the first pope (like the Catholics said), but he was clearly a dear one to Christ. It was to Peter and to no one else that Jesus Christ said: "You are Peter, and on this rock will I be building My ecclesia, and the gates of the unseen shall not be prevailing against it" (Matthew 16:18, *Concordant Literal New Testament*).

Not only that, but Peter was to receive from Christ the keys to the kingdom:

> I will be giving you the keys of the kingdom of the heavens, and whatsoever you should be binding on the Earth shall be bound in the heavens, and whatsoever you should be loosing on the Earth, shall be loosed in the heavens.
> —Matthew 16:19, CLNT

Peter got these keys and used them fifty days after Jesus emerged from His tomb. During the Jewish feast of Pentecost, the disciples sat in the upper room, depressed ever since Jesus had returned to heaven. Suddenly, there appeared little flames of fire over their heads, accompanied by a violent blast of wind. This was the spirit of God descending into the hearts and minds (and legs, it turns out) of these men, who ran into the street proclaiming the resurrection of Jesus. They spoke an odd, miraculous language that even Israelite expatriates (out-of-town Jews visiting Jerusalem for the feast) understood. Peter ran faster than all of them (Jesus had given him the keys, after all), becoming the spokesperson of this new move of God. Acts, chapter 2, recounts all this.

If the Jewish leaders decided to accept Peter's testimony in Acts and repent of the slaughter of their own Messiah, then: 1) Messiah would return in glory, 2) the kingdom would come, 3) Jerusalem would become the new world headquarters, 4) David and the patriarchs would rise from the dead and walk into town, 5) Jesus Christ Himself would sanctify the temple, 6) Peter and his friends—the other eleven—would assume thrones and administer the kingdom, 7) the curse on the Earth would be lifted, 8) lions would no longer eat lambs, and 9) God would bind Satan for 1,000 years.

If Israel had accepted the testimony of Peter, all this would have happened. Say, on Thursday.

The first half of the book of Acts recounts this drama. In those days, suspense was in the streets, and the hustle was on to broadcast the message.

It was a big world, however, and the Internet had not been invented. The Jews were scattered everywhere the wind blew. The other nations, too, had to be told. It was only fair that Egypt and the Isles be apprised of the impending Israelite takeover.

However, there was no satellite television, so the best one could do was mount a rooftop and shout. Peter did precisely this at Pentecost. But he was only one man, with a single set of lungs.

This was where Paul came in—or so I once thought.

Several institutional Bible teachers convinced me that God

called Paul to take the same message Peter announced at Pentecost, in Jerusalem, to the rest of the nations. I pictured Peter as a runner in a relay race. He's running hard, but he's tired (the Israelites are stubborn as ever), and he despairs of finishing. He looks to pass on the baton. He would give it to his friends—the other disciples—but they lack international experience. When all seems lost, a new man arrives, Roman born, called to Christ in the oddest way possible. Fresh from an undeniable conversion, here he comes to Jerusalem, thoroughly trained in Old Testament truth, jumpy as a cat, nerves strung like a harp string, and apparently crazy enough to sail or walk anywhere in the world for the sake of Christ.

Peter entrusts him with the message, and now this man—Paul, "the apostle to the nations"—takes Peter's Israelite-supremacy message to non-Israelites. Peter sits down, catches a second wind, and then resumes his work among the sons of Jacob.

I could not have been more wrong.

The reasons I was wrong are vitally important—to you.

Not only did Paul not teach the same things as Peter, but Paul eventually taught the Gentiles truths so inconsistent with Peter's message that the Jerusalem Jews (the same believers in Jesus Christ who had repented at Pentecost) ultimately tried to kill him.

If the international evangelist, Paul, gave non-Israelites the same message Peter taught in Palestine, then why was Paul summoned to Jerusalem fourteen years *after* his conversion to explain his teaching to Peter (Galatians 2:1-2)? And if Peter—who had walked with Messiah Himself—knew everything God wanted humankind to know, why was Paul given a vision of the third heaven and shown things no mortal (including Peter) had ever seen (2 Corinthians 12:2-4)?

Even more puzzling: With all this preaching in the book of Acts, why didn't the kingdom come in the book of Acts? *And why has it still not come today?*

Oh—and why the heck is it so hard to live like Jesus—to be meek, merciful, and pure?

The answers to these questions will curl your spiritual toes.

3.
IN THE BEGINNING

IN THE BEGINNING

I'm going to start reading the Bible to you; I hope you have nothing pressing at the moment. Thanks for indulging me.

"In the beginning, God created the heavens and the Earth" (Genesis 1:1, *King James Version*).

There. That's all I'm going to read because, for now, that's all you need to know. At the forefront of God's revelation to humanity, He felt compelled to tell us He created two spheres of operation: the heavens and the Earth. (God created them both perfectly, too, for "Flawless are His deeds; His work is perfect" Deuteronomy 32:4.) We take God's creation for granted. We shouldn't. These first ten words in Genesis chapter one embody a gigantic truth, comprising one of the most epic revelations ever to emanate from God's throne. In fact, these ten words are the key to understanding the entire Bible. I do not overstate this. God spoke these ten words first because they are the key to understanding why Jesus Christ came to this planet; why Israel exists; why Jesus Christ called Paul when He already had twelve apostles; why there are two gospels (not four) in the Bible; and why, no matter how hard you try, you cannot live like Jesus.

TWO SETS OF GOOD NEWS

Most people think there are four gospels in the Bible: Matthew, Mark, Luke, and John. Not so. Matthew, Mark, Luke, and John are four accounts of the same gospel: the gospel of the Circumcision. God has given two gospels (concerning salvation from sin) to humanity, and two only (gospel, or evangel, means "good news"): one to Israel (the gospel of the Circumcision, entrusted to Peter), and one to everyone else (the gospel of the *Un*circumcision, entrusted to Paul).

Let Paul himself establish this fact. The apostle wrote to the Galatians: "I have been entrusted with the gospel of the Uncircumcision, according as Peter of the Circumcision" (Galatians 2:7). Later, I will tell you why these gospels are so oddly named. For now, the important thing to know is that God gave two gospels to humanity because, in the beginning, God created two spheres for humanity's benefit: the heavens and the Earth.

EARTH AND HEAVEN RUINED

Soon after creating the heavens and the Earth, God saw to it that both of His perfect creations became ruined. Why would God do that? Let us first establish that this is precisely what happened.

After the first ten words of Genesis, the next twelve words read like this: "As for the Earth, it came to be a chaos and vacant" (Genesis 1:2, *Concordant Version of the Old Testament*).

So much for the Earth, then. Hold that thought.

Concerning the ruin of the heavens, we must jump to Ephesians, chapter 6, and the testimony of Paul:

For it is not ours to wrestle with blood and flesh, but with the sovereignties, with the authorities, with the world-mights of this darkness, *with the spiritual forces of wickedness among the heavens.*

—Ephesians 6:12, CLNT

So much for the heavens, then. It's not essential for us to know how either the terrestrial or celestial ruin occurred. We do need to know, however, that God wanted it this way. Do not panic at that thought. (Not that you would. I would tend to panic at the opposite thought—that the universe had somehow leaped from the hands of the Potter and was running amok.) God has good reason for everything He does; I might even call His reasons "great."

God is not scrambling around the universe putting out fires. If this were so, how could He be worthy to be called, "God"? God is in perfect control of His universe—never mind how things look. Everything that happens in this world (and in this universe) happens for a reason. All of it is designed for our ultimate good. In the short run, it may not seem good, but in the long run, good is the sole purpose for everything God does.

THE CONTRAST PRINCIPLE

In order to appreciate good, however, we must be intimately acquainted with bad. This is known as the contrast principle. How could you know the joys of salvation unless you've been a sinner? The only reason resurrection will thrill you is because you have known death. How do you know you are healthy if you have never been sick? How would you know joy without an acquaintance with misery? In God's world: Darkness precedes light; sin precedes salvation; death precedes life; and bad news precedes good news. This is not madness; it is method. Would you want it any other way? God's ultimate goal is to permanently bless, but no one can appreciate that apart from a temporary curse.

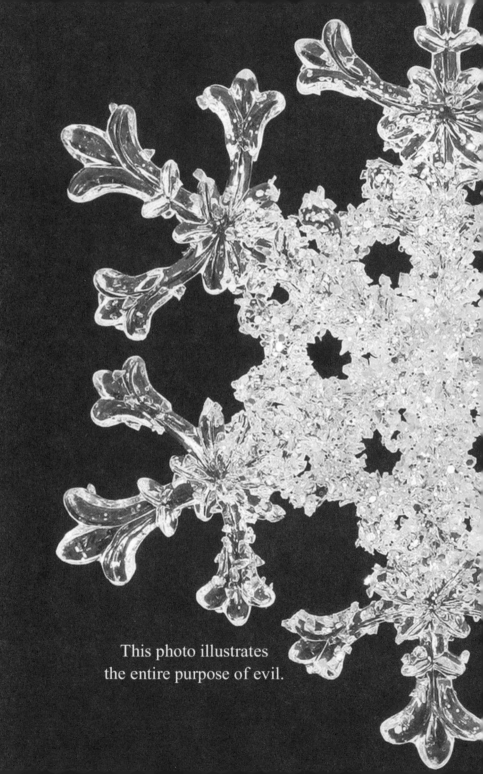

This photo illustrates
the entire purpose of evil.

When someone says to you, "I have good news and bad news, which do you want first?" Do you ever say, "Give me the good news first"? Never. You always want the bad news first, because you hope the good news will somehow eclipse the bad and make you feel better. In fact, the good news may only be good in light of the bad.

The ruination of the heavens and the Earth was (and is) bad news. At this juncture, the most important question to ask (you've probably already thought of it):

Is this a permanent situation for both the heavens and the Earth? The wonderful answer I'm thrilled to share with you is: "No!" God's intention is and always has been to reconcile both the heavens and Earth to Himself. The bad things must happen before God can bring all the good things He has planned for humanity. Along that glorious line, here is Colossians 1:20—

> Through Christ, God will reconcile *all* to Him (making peace through the blood of His cross), through Him, whether those on the Earth or those in the heavens.

That's from the *Concordant Literal New Testament*, but I also like *The Message* here:

> All the broken and dislocated pieces of the universe—people and things, animals and atoms—get properly fixed and fit together in vibrant harmonies, all because of His death, His blood that poured down from the cross.

This is the good news that follows the bad: The good that can only be appreciated in light of the bad.

The cross of Christ—His precious blood—fixes both the heavens and the Earth. Keep in mind the contrast principle, however. As glorious as the restoration of heaven and Earth will be, glory is impossible apart from ruin. In fact, future rejoicing over the restoration of these disparate spheres is impossible apart from their historical dishevelment.

WHY NOT JUST CREATE EVERYTHING PERFECT AND LEAVE IT THAT WAY?

A good question. Again, I defer to the contrast principle. Perfection is never appreciated apart from a backdrop of imperfection. So God created the heavens and the Earth (we are fine with this); then oversees the ruin (this is the hard part), but always with the future thrill of restoration in view (the promise that we believe by faith). Remember: Glory *requires* infamy; resurrection *requires* death; salvation *requires* sin.

If God made the universe perfect and left it that way, then none of us would know anything *but* perfection. Were this the case, we would yawn at it. Yes. For real. We would. Without contrast, we couldn't do anything but yawn. Yet who wants to yawn at perfection? Who wants to shrug their shoulders at living forever with God? Don't we want to praise and sing rather than *ho* and *hum* for eternity? Very well then. Eternal happiness is impossible apart from temporary misery. Impossible.

God does the misery *for* you, not *to* you.

And yet this is only part of the story. Let's return to the reason why God separated humanity into two groups: Jews and Gentiles. Let's return to why there are two gospels in the Bible: the gospel of the Circumcision and that of the Uncircumcision. Let's return to why there are two respective caretakers of these two gospels: Peter and Paul, and let's try to understand why we all have such a hard time living like God's Son. Hmm. Maybe it isn't our fault.

GOD USES PEOPLE: THIS IS GOOD FOR THEM

God is God. He could have restored and reconciled the heavens and the Earth without the sacrifice of His Son. Why was the cross of Calvary even necessary? Further—assuming the necessity of the cross—why didn't God fix things through His Son only, and skip creating humanity altogether? God is so good at everything; He could easily have gotten along quite well without any of us. Go ahead, ask the big question: *Why are we here?*

First things first. God sent His Son to show us His love. God cannot die, so He sent His visible image, Jesus Christ, to demonstrate to the universe His astonishing affection for it. Only as we watch Jesus suffering on the cross and—from there—forgiving His enemies, do we fall to our faces and adore Him. If the Son forgives His enemies while hanging out beneath a palm tree in Jerusalem, something gets lost in translation. The effect is not the same. We yawn and say, "That's nice."

The backdrop of the cross is what stuns us to worship.

Secondly, God created humanity because He wanted other creatures with whom to share His happiness. In the beginning, God was alone in the universe. In the end, He will have a myriad of beings enjoying His life and love.

That's not all. Yes, God decided long ago that He would reconcile the ruined heavens and Earth through His Son. A part of that plan was to create the human race, and then call out two select groups of people to become fellow workers with Him in the grand enterprise of reconciling the heavens and the Earth. That's astounding, I know. Yet it's true. Election is a Biblical teaching. Contrary to popular belief, however, God does not elect a few in order to damn the rest. God elects a few so that those few may then become His chosen agents in later reconciling the rest. Remember God's goal from Colossians 1:20—

> Through Christ, God will reconcile *all* to Him (making peace through the blood of His cross), through Him, whether those on the Earth or those in the heavens.

Again, God could have done everything by Himself. But no. He longed to share His glory with others. He wanted other beings created from His hand and heart to touch the Great Steering Wheel of His Amazing Journey, and to thrill with Him, not only in the journey, but in the glorious climax toward which the journey leads.

paul

peter

Here is the kernel, then, of everything I have said thus far, and the reason I wrote this book. I want you to know:

▶ To restore and reconcile a ruined Earth, God called the nation of Israel—also known as the bride of the Lamb—promising them a 1,000-year reign of righteousness over a restored planet: "They will be priests of God and of Christ, and they will be reigning with Him the thousand years ... and they shall be reigning on the Earth" (Revelation 20:6; 5:10). Israelites remain on Earth, because that's their realm of ministry. God first whispered this plan to Abraham, confirmed and ratified it through the Messiah Himself, explained it in detail via "the gospel of the Circumcision," and made a man named Peter its spokesperson.

▶ To restore and reconcile the ruined heavens (a secret plan of God, which Messiah Himself did not talk about while on Earth), God is calling out a rag-tag band of "losers" (also known as the body of Christ) from the rest of humanity and eventually taking them to heaven. In heaven: "He seats us together among the celestials, in Christ Jesus" (Ephesians 2:6), and we will rule at the right hand of God (2 Timothy 2:12), judge angels (1 Corinthians 6:3), and bring insubordinate heavenly realms (Ephesians 3:10; 6:12; Colossians 1:20) to the Deity's feet. God first whispered this plan to a blood-thirsty lunatic en route to Damascus to kill Christians (Saul; later re-named Paul). The body of writing explaining *this* call (not a hint of it can be found in other books of the Bible) is known as, "the gospel of the *Un*circumcision," and its spokesperson is the same human being (read, "lunatic") who first got wind of it: Paul.

RIGHTLY DIVIDING

Not many people know how to "rightly divide the Word of truth" (2 Timothy 2:15). Most people think this means distinguishing between the Old Testament and New Testament. It's much finer than that. If you ask your surgeon where you are to be operated upon, and she says, "the top"—you are going to want a much more precise answer. The New Testament itself must be rightly divided. Matthew, Mark, Luke, and John are, in fact, a continuation of the same message as the Old Testament.

When you turn from Malachi to Matthew, it's still *The Israelite Channel*: It's all Israel, all the time. Jesus Christ came to Earth as the greatest of the Old Testament prophets. Am I limiting Jesus? Not at all. While on Earth, He purposely limited Himself, saying, "I was not sent except to the lost sheep of the house of Israel" (Matthew 15:24, *New King James Version*).

Paul confirms the mission of the terrestrial (earthly) Christ, writing in Romans 15:8, "For I am saying that Christ has become the Servant of the Circumcision, for the sake of the truth of God, to confirm the patriarchal promises."

UNKNOWN GRACE

Paul's thirteen letters are a radical departure from the rest of Scripture, and I am including Matthew, Mark, Luke, and John in that group. The only place in the Bible where you will find details concerning God's remedy for restoring the heavens is in the thirteen letters of Paul. The only place in Scripture where you will find law tossed out the window is in the thirteen letters of Paul. The only books in the entire Bible dealing with the special salvation of Gentiles (non-Israelites), who sin as a vocation and have never even heard of Moses—are the thirteen letters of Paul.

Here, and here alone—in the thirteen letters of Paul—are found the deepest depths of grace ever to be shed abroad from God's heart. I know how shocking this must sound. It means that in the books of Matthew, Mark, Luke, and John (including the red letters spoken by the earthly Christ), you will *not* find the deepest depths of grace ever to be shed abroad from God's heart. Those books are deliberately incapable of unfolding these depths.

I read the entire New Testament, but
the 13 letters of Paul, in my Bible,
are shredded from use.

They are only meant to confirm, for Israel, a promise God gave their chief patriarch and forefather, Abraham.

At the end of Matthew, Mark, Luke, and John, grace was still God's greatest secret. There is some grace in these four accounts for the sons and daughters of Israel, but not the kind of grace Paul brought to the nations, namely, "the transcendent grace of God on you" (2 Corinthians 9:14).

Paul is the only writer to speak of *transcendent* grace. What does it transcend? It transcends the other, lesser graces mentioned elsewhere in God's Word.

PATHWAY TO PEACE

Paul begins most of his letters this way: "Grace to you, and peace, from God, our Father, and the Lord Jesus Christ." Notice that peace follows grace; this is the divine order. Unless you know grace, peace will elude you. Unless you realize that nothing you do can ever ruin God's favor of you, you will be constantly monitoring your flesh, while waiting for God to pull the rug out. How can you have peace when a lightning bolt is one misdeed away?

Only a message of transcendent grace brings the kind of transcendent peace we long for. But first, such grace must be comprehended. This is difficult to do if we are mixing Paul's message with other parts of the Bible. As soon as we start reveling in, say, Romans 5:1: "Therefore being justified by faith, we have peace with God, through our Lord, Jesus Christ," we turn to Hebrews 10:26-27, reading: "For if we sin willfully after we have received the knowledge of the truth, there no longer remains a sacrifice for sins, but a certain fearful expectation of judgment, and fiery Indignation"—and lose our peace. What do you do about this? Most people cry and eat lots of chocolate.

Try this instead: Realize these are two different messages to two different peoples. Romans was written to Gentiles, and Hebrews was written to Israelites. Israelites still have to work for their salvation; they must be worthy. They are still expected to do law, or at least try. Not so, Gentiles. For them, the law was done away. Romans 3:28— "For we are reckoning a human to be justified by faith apart from works of law." But it's even more radical than that. To the Gentiles—the law never came in the first place. In Romans 2:14, the apostle Paul clearly states that Gentiles "have no law." Romans 6:14 corroborates this, adding the cherry on top: "You are not under law, but under grace."

READ JAMES AND WEEP

The book of James starts this way: "James, a slave of God and of the Lord Jesus Christ, to the twelve tribes ..." Clearly, James wrote to Israelites. Read James with the misapprehension that you are supposed to *do* James, and you will become so bogged down in law- -and depressed by your inability to do it—you will think that either James or Paul is a liar. A fine sampling from James:

- **James 2:10**—"For anyone who should be keeping the whole law, yet should be tripping in one thing, has become liable for all."
- **James 2:13**—"The judging is merciless to him who does not exercise mercy."
- **James 2:14**—"What is the benefit, my brethren, if anyone should be saying he has faith, yet may have no works? That faith can not save him."
- **James 4:8**—"Draw near to God, and He will be drawing near to you."
- **James 5:9**—"Be not groaning, brethren, against one another, lest you may be judged. Lo! the Judge stands before the doors."

Actually, a single comparison between James and Paul highlights the contrast:

- **James 2:20**—"Faith apart from works is dead."
- **Romans 4:5**—"Yet to him who is *not* working, yet is believing on Him Who is justifying the irreverent, his faith is reckoned for righteousness."

Many Bible writers and commentators have made pretzels of themselves trying to explain James' square peg in light of Paul's round hole. None of it works. It's not meant to work. James and Paul are deliberately irreconcilable. James writes to Israelites, Paul to the nations. James is of law; Paul is of grace. James is of works; Paul's people *don't* work—they only believe (even their belief comes totally from God). James is of the gospel of the Circumcision, Paul of the Uncircumcision.

When Martin Luther realized the truths of justification—while reading the book of Romans, not coincidentally—his first instinct was to discount James. He went so far as to doubt James' rightful place in the Bible. At least he recognized the impossible contrast. Had Luther rightly divided the Word of truth, however, he wouldn't have mulled over which writer to toss from the Bible—James or Paul. If only he had realized the entire Bible was for him, but not all of it was to him. John Wycliffe puts it in a nutshell:

> It shall greatly help you to understand Scripture if you mark not only what is spoken or written, but of whom, and to whom, with what words, at what time, where, to what intent, with what circumstances, considering what goes before and what follows.

Paul says it more succinctly: "Rightly divide the Word of truth" (2 Timothy 2:15).

James says that faith apart from works is dead.

SAVED IN THE MIDST OF LOSER-HOOD

In the previous section, you read of how members of the body of Christ are justified by faith, not works. Not even voluntarily sinning (Hebrews 10:26) fouls the favor of a justified person. One who has died with Christ has been justified from sin (Romans 6:7). In the Circumcision gospel, irreverence is fatal. In Paul's gospel, it is the irreverent who are justified (Romans 4:5).

Members of the body of Christ, called out from among the nations, are saved in the midst of loser-hood: "For Christ, while we are still infirm, still in accord with the era, for the sake of the irreverent, died" (Romans 5:6). The perfect example of a reject-made-righteous is the gospel's spokesman himself: Paul. Therefore, Paul was called outside Israel in the midst of a sin-spree. He was to be a representative—and an example—of transcendent grace. If Paul had been reverent instead of rabid, how could he be grace's poster boy? God defines grace as: "Favor shown to those who deserve the opposite." As soon as one becomes deserving of grace, grace necessarily disappears. Grace flourishes only in the Petri dish of unworthiness.

Salvation by works has already been tried. It was called the law of Moses. The God-inspired directive then was: DO AND LIVE. If you did what God said, you got to keep breathing. If you didn't, well—you'd better have your life insurance paid up. Today, we are saved by grace. The God-inspired directive now is: LIVE AND DO.

In other words, live free in the realization that God sees His Son instead of your sins, and you will want to do things for such a gracious God. Because of grace, condemnation is out of the question (Romans 8:1). Once you realize you can fail without losing God's favor, you suddenly want to succeed. Isn't that a paradox? Isn't it phenomenal? Doesn't it pack power? Paul coined a word for it: GRACE.

Grace's greatest trophy is Saul of Tarsus.

Now you know why the Jews hated Paul's message. They could

not stand hearing that people worshipping trees on Monday could be declared "complete in Christ" (Colossians 2:10) on Tuesday. This clashed terribly with everything they knew about working hard and obeying law.

Only Paul could say, "Yet now, apart from law, a righteousness of God is manifest" (Romans 3:21, CLNT).

Boy, did the Jews ever hate *that* saying.

PAUL AS WRENCH

Let's conduct a crazy experiment. Let's lift Paul's thirteen letters from the Bible and see what happens. Lift Paul's thirteen letters from the Bible, and we have one smooth revelation to Israel concerning the restoration of Earth and God's means of accomplishing it. The letters of Paul—meant for a completely different people with a completely different call and destiny—throw a giant wrench into the spinning cog of Israel's terrestrial machinery. Unless the modern Bible reader rightly divides the Word of truth, his or her grasp of God's program grinds to a halt.

One smooth revelation .... to Israel

Granted, it would have been easier to rightly divide Scripture had Paul's letters been tacked on after the book of Revelation, with the introductory phrase: "Thank you for reading all about Israel's promises, struggles, and future terrestrial blessings. Now, stay tuned for a completely different message." But no. In His wisdom, God inserted Paul smack dab between Acts and Hebrews. Why would God do that?

God wants us to work for truth. As Proverbs 25:2 (*Concordant Version of the Old Testament*) says, "It is the glory of God to conceal a matter, and the glory of kings to investigate a matter." In the full context of the "rightly divide" passage, Paul tells Timothy to "endeavor to present yourself to God qualified, an unashamed worker, correctly cutting the Word of truth" (2 Timothy 2:15, CLNT). Yes, it takes some work. I wrote this book to help make that work easier for you.

The book of Acts teases Israelites with the coming earthly kingdom, and the book of Hebrews comforts Israelites concerning the obvious—and disturbing—postponement of said kingdom (the fabled Millennium). In-between these two books are the thirteen letters making evident why God put Israel temporarily on hold. In the thirteen letters of Paul, God does a new, secret thing among Gentiles: calling out for Himself a distinct body of people destined to rule in heaven and bring celestial realms into divine harmony, through the power and agency of His Son, Jesus Christ. Once the last person of this select group is called to his or her heavenly home, God takes up again with His earthly people, and the rest of Scripture proceeds on track.

HERE'S WHY

Now you know why the Bible has sometimes confused you more than blessed you. You have tried to make one message—"the gospel of the Circumcision"—agree with a completely different message—"the gospel of the Uncircumcision." (Part of the problem,

I know, is that both messages are in the same book.) You have tried to make the law expounded upon by James "match up with" the grace revealed through Paul. You have tried to make the earthly destiny of Israelites gel with the heavenly destiny of non-Israelites. You have tried to make the words of the earthly Christ—printed in religious red—fit up against the words of the exalted Christ, spoken in basic black to the apostle Paul.

If only Paul's words had been printed in pink or something.

Now you know the secret. None of these disparate messages are supposed to agree. They are written to two different groups of people, with two different destinies, two different missions—and two wildly different playbooks.

Now you know why you, a Gentile, cannot live like the Jewish Jesus Who trod the roads of Palestine. It's not your fault: You were not meant to live and walk like the earthly Jesus. Only Jews are meant to do that, and not even they can do it until Jesus Christ returns to write the law (the law that never came to *you*) on the tablets of their hearts (Jeremiah 31:33).

In no way does this mean you become amoral. You are operating under a new principle: Grace. In the gospel preached by Paul, grace has more power than law to effect right behavior. God's premier example of a sinner-turned-saint is, again, the bringer of the message: Paul. How did God do that? By giving His best to a man at his worst. In other words, "justifying the irreverent" (Romans 4:5).

I have just handed you a new Bible. You could close this book now and revel for the rest of your life in a Word of God that no longer seems to contradict itself. Transcendent peace is now yours; the rest is details. I hope you stick around for the details, however, because they are freighted with glory.

4.
LET'S TALK ABOUT EARTH FOR A FEW HUNDRED YEARS

LET'S TALK ABOUT EARTH FOR A FEW HUNDRED YEARS

After stating that God created the heavens and the Earth, the writer of Genesis (Moses) promptly forgets about the heavens, writing: "As for the Earth, it came to be a chaos and vacant." Then, for practically the rest of the entire Bible (except for you-know-where), we read about God's activities in and concerning the Earth.

What happened to the heavens? We have to wait until God reveals His heavenly plans to a certain irreverent lunatic. No one is better at keeping a secret than God.

SOME HELPFUL INFORMATION ABOUT EARTH

If you have surfed the Internet lately, or watched news on television, you will notice the Earth is one screwed-up place. Many people read the newspaper, watch the news, and then spiral into fits of despair. They wonder where God is. They wonder why God doesn't come down and fix everything—*now*. They even wonder—during moments of doubt—whether or not God realizes what is happening. It does seem at times as if the Deity has set this pot to boiling and fallen asleep. *Hello? Is anyone home up there? Excuse me, but all the water is about to burn clean out of this pot. Hello?*

What most people don't realize is that God is setting up an amazing contrast. Human beings can only find happiness when they come to the end of themselves and embrace God as their everything. God could simply tell people, "Come to the end of yourselves and embrace Me as your everything," but this doesn't work. It would only be theory. People must learn this lesson by long, hard experience. Then and only then is it real; then and only then is it true and lasting. The purpose, then, of these long ages (or "eons") since humanity's creation is for all people to experience a protracted period of futility and failure. It has to be long and hard, for only thus could it properly backdrop a smooth, eternal future.

In other words, God is doing this *for* us, not *to* us.

I tell you this to calm your nerves. If you think this world is meant to be Disneyland, you'll be forever frustrated at God and at your own life. Once you realize, however, that the world is supposed to be a boiling cauldron of human ineptitude, you can relax and let it ride. You can go to bed knowing that God is still God and that He is actually managing the ineptitude.

Why would God do that?

I just told you. He is setting up a contrast. God is having humankind build its measly towers, admire its rotundas, worship its marble statuary (of all the imposing men of religion and war) and, in short, exhaust its resources. When it all crashes, God will bring His government to Earth, and everyone will breathe a sigh of relief and shout with rejoicing. How wonderful it will feel to finally and forever unhand our personal agendas, which only agitated us anyway.

Such sighs and shouts of exultation would be impossible apart from the eons (or, ages) of frustration.

Again, here is Genesis 1:2, from the *Concordant Version of the Old Testament*:

"As for the Earth, it came to be a chaos and vacant ..."

Grasp this, and you will have grasped God's *modus operandi.* God created the heavens and Earth, perfectly, but then: "As for the Earth, it came to be a chaos and vacant." Behold the modus *and* the operandi: God creates something, and then intentionally breaks it to give humanity the exercise of trying to fix it apart from Him. (This is still going on, in case you haven't watched the news lately. And humanity is still failing—just so you know.)

Until you realize God has our ultimate good in mind, this seems cruel and unusual. After humanity has frustrated itself into oblivion, however, God will demonstrate His ability on the chaos. Watching Him from the sidelines, we will come to trust and rely upon Him. Our inability will then overjoy us ("Thank God we failed!") rather than frustrate us.

God's processes are hardly His goals.

Sometime before you die, walk onto a building site before the building is finished. You will be met with apparent chaos. Now throw your hands up and say, "This is a mess! You people are crazy!" Say it loud enough for the builders to hear. If you do all this, the builders will think *you* are the crazy one. And you would be. The mess isn't the building; the building proceeds from the mess. The building remains long after the mess has been bulldozed away. The mess is the means, the building the goal.

God knows Earth is ruined. He did not say, "Oh, no!" when it happened. He is not scrambling to keep pace with the chaos (as most religions—including Christianity— would have you believe). God knows the Earth is run by incompetent nincompoops because He Himself has empowered the nincompoops (don't believe me; read Romans 13:1—"There is no power except of God: The powers that be are ordained of God").

All is on schedule and proceeding according to plan (don't believe me; read Ephesians 1:11—"[God] is operating all according to the counsel of His will"). God knows that He will one day inaugurate perfect government on this Earth, and it will thrill the same hearts that broke during these eras of human misrule. It takes a long time to set up the contrast, I know. It has to take a long time, to make the experience unforgettable. The trouble will cease the minute God destines it to—and not a minute before.

God keeps us ignorant of that particular minute. Yet He, Himself, looks ahead to it and can already hear the praises and rejoicing at the ribbon-cutting ceremony. He can already hear the shouts of what a genius He is and how everyone sees now why He took so long, and—oh!—how it *had* to be the way it was. Meanwhile, He endures our incessant complaining. He is very patient and Godlike as He provides many Scripture verses we habitually ignore that assure us, now, of both His sovereign control and our blessed future:

Ephesians 1:11—"God is operating *all* in accord with the counsel of His will."

2 Corinthians 5:18—*"All* is of God."

Colossians 1:20—"Through Christ, God will reconcile *all* to Him (making peace through the blood of His cross), through Him, whether those on the Earth or those in the heavens."

Ephesians 1:9-10—"God is making known to us the secret of His will … to have an administration of the complement of the eras, to head up *all* in the Christ—both that in the heavens and that on the Earth."

1 Corinthians 15:22—"For even as, in Adam, *all* are dying, thus also, in Christ, shall *all* be vivified."

God will bring a kingdom to this Earth that will last 1,000 years. After that, He will do many things—more glorious things, and more longer-lasting things—but for now let's concentrate on this kingdom that will restore and reconcile our present home.

God knows exactly how the kingdom will come. He knows, too, Who will inaugurate it: He will use His own Son, sent from heaven. Yet here's the unlikely part: He will also use a specific group of people now squatting upon the very Earth He intends to fix. Stranger yet, most of the other people on the Earth will come to hate this specific group, otherwise known as "God's chosen race." This race, for the most part, will fail to even acknowledge its own Savior until the last possible moment. (Did I mention they killed Him at His first appearance? I should have.)

I am talking about Israel, of course. Before you wonder why all this sounds so absurd—please, keep in mind this is God's plan, not mine. I was born late in 1959, and God devised this plan long before then. I had nothing to do with this plan; I am only telling you about it. Again, I am so sorry. I would have chosen a vast army of gigantic, Jesus-embracing super-people to one day rule the Earth. For sure, I would have chosen people who actually believed in me. And I would have done it all before World War II.

But seriously. How *did* it come about that God chose one nation with which to habilitate our poor planet?

"SELPS UF GALOCAP, UDUO."

Before the flood of Noah, no nations existed. There were only loose family gatherings then, and probably lots of picnics. After the flood, a man named Nimrod drew up blueprints for a tower near Babel (the famous Tower of Babel, described in Genesis chapter 11). Nimrod dreamed of uniting the world and naming himself president and CEO of it. He got a pretty strong start. But the purpose of these long ages is to humble humans, so God crashed the Nimrodian development. He did it in a practical and—to me—entertaining way.

At the tower of Babel, God mixed up the language. At that time, there was only one language on Earth. Wouldn't that have been convenient for forming a one-world government? Watch what happens, though:

Men are working on the tower one sunny morning, when, around 11:00 o'clock, for the first time ever, a builder cannot understand the sentence of a man next to him. The man next to him wants a bucket of mud and says to his fellow builder: "Bring me a bucket of mud, pronto." But it comes out to the other builder as, "Selps uf galocap, uduo." So the other builder says, "Huh?" But the "huh" sounds to the first builder like, "Sphh?" So the first builder thinks the second builder is smarting off, and whacks him in the head with a brick.

Thus ended the illustrious Tower of Babel.

After that, the people sorted themselves according to who spoke what. Those who spoke a common language formed nations, which are only large groups of families, segregated. Nations are similar to families, but more controlled and organized, with their own flags, anthems, and cannon balls.

God got politically incorrect at that time. Before then, God had no opportunity for such a thing. After Babel, He favored one of these organized family groups (nations) and pretty much ignored the rest. God was about to visit a people called the Hebrews (descendants of Noah's son, Shem). More specifically, He was about to visit one man out of this famous folk stem.

For the first time ever, God was going to unveil His permanent solution for the ruined Earth. And to think He was going to unveil this to a man, standing outside his tent in the middle of the night, who had never even heard of the United Nations.

5.

A BRIEF HISTORY OF ISRAEL

A BRIEF HISTORY OF ISRAEL

Whenever you think Earth, think Israel. Israel—and no one else—is God's appointed vessel for restoring and blessing this third planet from the sun.

The call of Israel, oddly enough, began with a man sitting cross-legged outside his tent, perhaps smoking a pipe. In other words, the man never saw it coming.

Unless you understand the promise God made to Abraham, you will not understand why Jesus came to Israel (instead of, say, to Egypt or China); why Christ gave Peter keys; what these keys potentially opened; why the disciples ran like steeplechase competitors down the steps of the upper room; why the words Peter literally shouted from the literal rooftop that day struck joy into the hearts of all attending Israelites; and why another Israelite named Saul (the subject of this book, the radical, the man re-named Paul, the man who would also believe in Jesus Christ) would eventually be hated and nearly killed by these very same sweet, dear, holy Israelites listening to Peter. And—even more disturbing—why the kingdom got postponed for a couple of thousand years and still hasn't come.

Oh—and one more thing. Unless you understand the promise God made to Abraham, you will not understand why you have such a hard time being meek or trying to live like Jesus.

Who was Abraham? Abraham was literally the grandfather of Israel. Abraham had a son named Isaac, who had a son named Jacob, whose name God changed to Israel. It was this man—Israel—whose descendants adopted the name of their father. These are the Jews you know today.

God made this promise to Abraham, in Genesis 12:1-3—

> Now the Lord said to Abraham, "Go forth from your country, and from your relatives and from your father's house, to the land which I will show you; and I will make you a great nation, and I will bless you, and make your name great; and so you shall be a blessing; and I will bless those who bless you, and the one who curses you I will curse. *And in you all the families of the Earth shall be blessed.*"
> —*New American Standard Bible*

That last part is what Israelites dreamed about at night. Abraham's sons—the nation of Israel—would one day head up all the nations, and all the families of the Earth would eventually be blessed by them. Israel would be the chief nation of an actual political kingdom that would occupy this same oblate spheroid that has nearly been ruined by corrupt politicians (sorry for the redundancy). Jesus constantly referenced this kingdom while He was on Earth. It was this *earthly* kingdom to which Jesus gave Peter the keys.

Let's look in on Abraham, now, and join the call of Israel in progress.

The following is from Genesis, chapter 12. I have taken literary license, but the essential elements accord with Scripture.

Abraham could not sleep this night, so he came here to think and smoke. The sky is moonless, and the air lies still like a dead fish. This is Mesopotamia, long before anyone ever heard of Saddam Hussein. Somewhere at the base of the mountains behind him, a dog barks. Just then the stranger arrives.

Abraham sees nothing; he can only sense an overpowering presence. Alarmed, he leaps to his feet.

(This is how God used to come. He never showed up levitating in a white robe. He came as an ordinary person. It was never even Him—God, after all, is invisible: 2 Corinthians 4:4—but a God-appointed celestial representative who spoke God's mind perfectly and was worthy even to take His name. You never knew Who it was, for sure, until He started talking. But then, soon after, you knew. Every hair on your neck stood up, and you listened like you had never listened to anything before in your life.)

Rising, Abraham thinks to unsheathe his knife. The stranger, anticipating this, says, "You won't be needing that."

"Who are you?"

"Sarai is in your tent."

Abraham does not know how to answer this.

"Your wife, Sarai," said the stranger again, "is in your tent."

"Yes, but how do you—"

"She will be bearing you a son."

He knew then.

"My Lord—" he began.

"You are seventy-five years old, friend."

"Yes. And Sarai is barren," said Abraham.

"I know. Nevertheless, she will be bearing you a son. What I am about to tell you, you will not believe until tomorrow. Tomorrow, mid-morning, I will grant you understanding. It's not that you lack faith—you're to become the father of it. But you will not grasp it. Not tonight. It is too much for you. Yet I will tell you this: I am restoring the Earth. Do you understand that?"

"No."

"Well, perfect. I am bringing peace to the Earth. It will be a long time, yet. None of the timing, or the times, shall be told you. But now, it begins. This night, it begins with you. And this program of restoration will be consummated in a people who will come from you."

"I'm sorry. I don't understand."

"You will. The command, which you will obey, is this: 'Go forth from your country, and from your relatives, even from your father's house, and go to a land which I will show you. For I am going to make you a great nation, and I will bless you, and I will make your name great ...'" (Genesis 12:1-2).

Abraham stares, still uncomprehending.

"And so, you shall be a blessing," the visitor continued. "And I will bless those who bless you, and the one who curses you I will curse" (Genesis 12:3). The visitor paused then, but not for effect. This was the big part. With billions of angelic eyes in attendance, He needed what followed to be precisely right. He measured His cadence, more than before. One more breath, and now it was ready:

"And in you, Abraham ..." (here it came), *"all the families of the Earth shall be blessed"* (Genesis 12:3).

The Visitor vanished. Night passed. Abraham never did sleep.

By one o'clock the following afternoon, the belongings of Abraham and his household sat atop the backs of sixteen camels. Where the caravan was destined to stop, none of them knew.

Israel's grandfather squinted into the desert sun.

The restoration of Earth was on.

Abraham left Mesopotamia and moved to Haran. When his father died, he immigrated to the place that we now know as Israel. The progenitor of Israel was now in the land of Israel, before there even was a grandson named Israel. He stood in the place which now makes news every day; the place Arabs want to bomb; the geographic center of the Earth, where evil men crucified the Son of God; where tourists flock and are fleeced by the minute; and from whence shall one day arise the capital of the coming earthly kingdom.

At this distant time, however, Abraham was only visiting. God did not give him so much as an acre of this future famous real estate. He did, however, promise to give the land to him and his son later on. Nearly 30 years later, He promised this land to Abraham on a night similar to the one just described, only this time the stars shone brightly.

This time, Abraham lay in his tent brooding over God's promise that his seed would one day bless the Earth. Just one slight problem: Abraham was ninety-nine years old, and his wife Sarai was well past her childbearing years. Make that two problems: Abraham's confidence in God's promise was as shaky as Sarai's baby-making apparatus.

God appeared to Abraham in a similar manner as before, only this time rattling his tent flap. "Come outside," He said. Once again, the following is a Martin Zender paraphrase of Genesis chapter 15, but I cover the key ingredients:

Visitor: Look into the heavens, Abraham.
Abraham (gazing up): Okay.
Visitor: Now count the stars, if you are able.
Abraham: Seriously.
Visitor: If you wouldn't mind.
Abraham: One ... two ... three ... this is ridiculous.
Visitor: Thank you. So shall your descendants be.
Abraham: Ridiculous?
Visitor: As plentiful as the stars, friend. But, yes—ridiculous as well. Your people shall witness a string of unprecedented miracles. They will not be faithful, nowhere near. But God is faithful, and will do great things for you. Remember, Abraham, your people shall one day rule the Earth, and restore it to glory.

"Then Abraham believed in the Lord, and He reckoned it to him as righteousness" (Genesis 15:6).

"One ... two ... three ... this is ridiculous."
"So shall your descendants be."

God loves to be believed, especially when His promises and pronouncements seem ridiculous.

God also intimated that the road to the promise would not be exactly pothole-free. If the keynote of a peoples' history is to be miraculous deliverance, then trouble is inevitable.

"Your people will be moved to an alien country where they will be enslaved and brutalized for four hundred years," said God. (More of the contrast principle.) "But I will step in and take care of the slaveholders and bring My people out so they can worship me in the place where you now stand" (Genesis 15:12-14).

With "alien country," "enslaved," and "brutalized," God prophesied concerning Egypt and the Exodus, long before Moses became a household name.

Abraham wanted a sign that God would fulfill His promises, so God gave Abraham the sign of circumcision. With this answer, I would have been sorry to have asked. I would have said, *No, that's okay, God. I really don't need a sign anymore.*

Too late.

UNKIND CUT

In circumcision, the foreskin of the penis is pulled forward, away from the body, and cut off. "Circum" means "around," and "cision" means "to cut." Thus, circumcision is to cut around the penis. Why would God institute a ritual like that?

If Abraham is promised a son and, from that son, a multitude of sons as numerous as the visible stars will arise and rule the Earth, then there is going to be much sexual intercourse. And if there will be much sexual intercourse, then the penis of Abraham is the Almighty Opening Act. But if the penis of Abraham is the Almighty Opening Act, then the owner of that penis will surely come to revere his physical capabilities. He will look at his vast progeny, then at his penis, then at his vast progeny, then at his penis, and think, "I am the man. Future terrestrial glory comes through *me*."

To nip such pride in the bud (not a bad choice of words, considering what's coming), God instituted the rite of circumcision.

Circumcision was supposed to be a constant embarrassment to an Israelite male. (How odd and inappropriate that the males eventually began bragging about it.) God meant it for a continual reminder that reproductive strength—as well as the wisdom and power to rule—comes ultimately from Him, not flesh.

The flesh plays its part, yes, but God is the One Who energizes it.

I give you this background because the message of the kingdom—the kingdom that God promised to Abraham; the kingdom that would restore Earth; the kingdom that Christ came as a sacrifice concerning, and that Peter held the keys to—was eventually called, "The Gospel of the Circumcision" (Galatians 2:7).

The gospel of the Circumcision was a cooperative gospel in which God did His part and humans did theirs. Circumcision was only symbolic of this, yes, but it still required literal undertaking. It was a metaphor, true, but one still had to bandage one's manhood for a week afterward.

God required Israel to prepare herself for His divine presence and miracle-working. This began with flesh, namely, the flesh at the end of the male member. Later, when John the Baptist arrived, God added baptism. At the famous Pentecost that followed Christ's resurrection, Peter's message was circumcision, baptism, and repentance. All along, it was all about producing fruit worthy of repentance. These were all things an Israelite had to *do*.

God required these things of no other nation—only Israel. This is important to remember, as it will loom large later.

Circumcision became the pattern of works that an Israelite *had* to accomplish, and it upheld God's basic requirement of His favored nation: *Demonstrate by tangible means your acknowledgement of My sufficiency.* Acknowledgement then had to be followed up with good works. If an Israelite did these things, then he or she would

Circumcision was supposed to embarrass an Israelite male.

enter the kingdom God promised to Abraham. What kingdom? The kingdom that would see a literal people—Israel—governing the literal Earth for a literal 1,000 years:

"They will be priests of God and of Christ, and they will be reigning with Him the thousand years" (Revelation 20:6).

At first it seems oxymoronic to speak of *having* to physically acknowledge God's sufficiency. If God is truly sufficient, then why must one do anything? Yet this is how God presented salvation to Israel: It was a cooperative salvation, a mixture of works and grace. God's sufficiency required tokens.

God would eventually present the law of Moses as something that Israelites could and should accomplish in preparation for ruling and teaching all other nations. The ultimate purpose of that law, however, was to demonstrate to Israel (and to the rest of us watching from the sidelines) the inability of flesh and blood to please God (Romans 8:6-8). Israel was to learn this by long, hard experience. After all these years, she still has not learned it. And neither has the Christian religion, frankly. Religious folks of every stripe still try to please God via law—any law (including rules they invent for themselves and others).

Ideally, an Israelite was not to give up on law, but rather give up on his or her ability to accomplish law. The lesson of life, for all of us, is to realize human insufficiency in the face of divine ability. But again, an Israelite had to continually and with physical deeds demonstrate an acknowledgement of that insufficiency. Israelites had to trust their Messiah, acknowledge their weakness, endure persecution, and show fruit worthy of repentance.

Notice all the active verbs.

Judaism was and still is a religion of "Show Me the Money." This would be in contrast to, say, a message of pure, transcendent grace. If a message of pure, transcendent grace were to one day take the stage (remember, the message to Israel was a mixture of works and grace), then it would still concern human insufficiency. The difference would be that this insufficiency would thrive irrespective of any physical act hoping to acknowledge it. In reality, showing the money to a message of pure, transcendent grace would only insult it. Pure, transcendent grace would say: "I don't need your stinking money. In fact, the less you give me, the better I look."

To keep us mindful of Him, God brings trials. Trials for an Israelite are to remind the Israelite to keep trusting, acknowledging, enduring, and working. Trials for the future pure-and-transcendent-grace person would keep him or her from *having* to do these things.

Let's say that a message of pure, transcendent grace does arrive. Would trials cease? No. Again, all humans, no matter their nationality, continually forget their creaturehood and fail to thank God. Trials are a kindly slap to the face that say, *Hello? God gave you everything you have.*

Again, though, the trial for the pure-and-transcendent grace person accomplishes a different end than for the Israelite. The Israelite stubs his toe and rightly says: "I am sorry God. I need to keep trusting, acknowledging, enduring, and producing fruit, or I'll miss the earthly kingdom You promised to Abraham. Thanks for the reminder." A pure, transcendent grace person, on the other hand, stubs her toe and says: "Thanks for the reminder, God. When will I stop trying to be worthy of all you've done for me?"

If the rite of Circumcision represented the heart of a message that combined works and grace, and if that message became known as "The Gospel of the Circumcision," then what would be the best name for a message that keeps the grace but eliminates the works?

I would be tempted to call it: "The gospel of the *Un*circumcision" (Galatians 2:7). By calling it that, I would be recalling—for comparative purposes—the first message, but lending it a new and radical twist. If the keynote of the first message (works combined with grace) is a rite, then the keynote of the second message (grace alone, without works) is—no rite at all.

In other words, whereas Israel would say: Cut off the end of your penis to demonstrate your seriousness about God, my message might be:

> "LEAVE YOUR PENIS ALONE. REPEAT: DO NOTHING WITH
> YOUR PENIS AT THIS TIME."

Back now to our brief history of Israel.

Remember the scene in *Field of Dreams* when Ray Kinsella (Kevin Costner) drives to Boston to attempt to talk the reclusive writer Terence Mann (James Earl Jones) into joining him on a madcap adventure of faith? Kinsella knocks on Mann's door, only to be rebuffed. At Kinsella's second attempt, Mann yanks open the door and growls, "We got a learning disability here?"

Throughout Scripture, Israel has a learning disability: She continually forgets she owes everything to God.

God made Abraham wait until he was 100 years old for his promised son. Long before then, when no son arrived, his wife Sarai (renamed "Sarah" by the Deity) suggested that her husband have sex with her handmaiden, Hagar. Abraham didn't mind the idea at all, and produced Ishmael. By a series of painful revelations, the couple finally realized Ishmael was not the promised son. After Sarah and her husband abandoned their scheming, God produced the promised son via miracle: He revived Abraham's and Sarah's sex organs, and they brought forth Isaac.

Isaac eventually had a son, Jacob, and Jacob (whose name God changed to "Israel") became the father of twelve sons, who became the patriarchs of the twelve tribes of Israel, which will one day rule Earth and restore it to peace.

From Abraham onward, circumcision attended the birth of each son. Eight days after birth, dad takes the kid to the priest and the kid returns home with a little less skin. Why keep this going generation after generation after generation? God's means of producing the future, earthly kingdom must always be evident. Each time a father takes a new baby son to the priest, the father thinks,

"The kingdom is coming. That's what these children are: Future Rulers of Earth. God is restoring the Earth; He promised that to our forefather Abraham, and He accomplishes it through us, and no other people. I feel a swelling of pride coming on. (Foreskin hits wastebasket.) Oops. Wait. This is God's doing, not mine."

Soon after, the learning disability hits again, and the Israelite feels smug because his penis is unnaturally shorter than a Greek's.

Classic Israelite disability takes several forms. One of the most prominent forms is jealousy. Israelite jealousy will play a major role later when I introduce you to Paul, but watch how it worked early in her history. Israel is a proud people, and she hates it when God favors others besides herself. This holds true even among her own.

The eleven patriarchs had a younger brother, Joseph. They hated Joseph because their father, Israel, doted on him and made him a fancy coat of many colors, whereas their coats were—oh, I don't know—monochrome. Besides that, Joseph had persistent dreams that his brothers and his father would one day bow down and worship him. The brothers didn't care much for this (the father tolerated it), so they sold the boy to Egypt as a slave.

This was not Joseph's Plan A, but it was God's.

God never abandoned Joseph. Through a series of divine trials and rescues (the trials were just as divine as the rescues), Joseph finally grasped the contrast principle and eventually earned an audience with Pharaoh, king of Egypt. Pharaoh was so impressed with Joseph's wisdom and demeanor that he put him in charge of the whole country, even his own personal affairs.

Israelites are born to rule and run stuff; it's in their blood. But see what it takes. (The Joseph story is a template.) They are shown truth—then thrown into a pit. In one form or another, this is invariably what happens. Why? Israel is proud and greedy, chronically hoarding her advantages. She is, according to Scripture, "a stiff-necked people" (Jeremiah 17:23). Yes, even Joseph. In the pit, in jail, and under the thumb of other nations, Israel learns whence comes her sufficiency. When the lesson is learned, God pulls her from the pit and fulfills His promises to her, only by then with an educated, appreciative vessel.

One night, God gave Pharaoh a strange dream filled with fat and skinny cows, in that order. Pharaoh related the dream to Joseph, who interpreted it: A seven-year famine was coming that would wreck Egypt and surrounding territories, including Joseph's Canaanite homeland. Before that would be seven years of plenty. Pharaoh said to Joseph, "What should I do?" Joseph, being a business-savvy Israelite (sorry for the redundancy), knew exactly what to do. During the seven years of prophesied plenty, he hoarded food, later distributing it during the famine.

Thus, the world came to Joseph for bread—even those brothers who had sold him into slavery.

In parable form, this is a microcosm of the Millennium. In the Millennium, Jerusalem will become the world's dispensary of spiritual sustenance.

Joseph's immediate family, unaware, of course, that Joseph was the genius behind Egypt's food stores, traveled to Pharaoh for their quota of grain. Joseph eventually revealed his true identity to his father and brothers, and it was the first time in the history of the Bible—or in any other history, for that matter—when twelve grown men simultaneously peed themselves. The Israel family moved to Egypt (seventy-five people in all) at Pharaoh's insistence. It's a beautiful thing. Right?

Yes, and no. Yet it landed Israel in Egypt, so the Israelites could eventually be enslaved for four hundred years and ensure Charlton Heston a classic film role.

Isn't God fun? No, not in the short term. Never lose sight of the fact, however, that Israel was learning to rule. All throughout her history, she has been in boot camp—training for the Millennium. Everything points to that. Through trial, Israel is learning to fulfill the promise God gave to Abraham: to rule the world in righteousness.

For the rest of this book, I keep referring to the phrase: "The promise God gave to Abraham." I do that because God Himself keeps referring to it. You will soon see that the Son of God does it as well, when He comes to Earth as a man, wearing sandals. No one must forget that most of the Bible (except for a small sliver of thirteen letters) features one promise (the one made to Abraham), one people (Israel), and one giant group of second-class citizens who are either ignored or killed (the rest of the world).

Without Israel, the other nations are sunk.

Israel in Egypt was a midwife's dream; she reproduced like the loaves and fishes of a future era. Soon, the sheer mass of Israelites worried King Pharaoh. Only by then it wasn't the same Pharaoh whom Joseph knew. It was a new king who, when you asked him about Joseph, said, "Joseph, *who?*" He considered the people cheap labor, and enslaved them. He made them build pyramids and beat them if they abused their coffee breaks. Worse, he forced them to abandon their newborns, exposing them to the elements to die cruel deaths. The last thing this Pharaoh wanted was more Israelites.

Along comes beautiful baby Moses. Naturally, his mother and sister fear for his life, so they launch him in a basket down a river where the daughter of Pharaoh bathes. It's a risky plan, but they hope when the young princess sees how cute the baby is, she'll take him in.

This is exactly what happens.

Pharaoh's daughter mothered baby Moses like her own son, and Moses eventually attended the best schools in Egypt. When he was forty years old (better late than never), he wondered how things were going with his Hebrew relatives. So one day, he sashayed out to where the Sphinx was going up.

First thing he saw was an Egyptian abusing an elderly Hebrew man. Incensed, Moses avenged his underdog brother by beating the daylights out of the Egyptian, who died shortly thereafter. He thought his people would be glad about this and consider him an instrument of God's deliverance. Instead, they considered him a troublemaker. The next day, two of them were fighting and Moses tried to break it up, saying: "You men are both Israelites. Why are

"What a cute little baby in a basket."

you fighting each other?" The one who started the fight says, "Who put you in charge of us? What are you going to do, kill us like you did that Egyptian man yesterday?" (Exodus 2:11-15).

Moses knew then that the word was out, and he feared for his life. His promising Egyptian career at a close, he exiled himself to the suburbs of Midian.

Forty years later, in the wilderness of Mount Sinai, an angel appears to Moses, disguised as a burning bush that for some strange reason doesn't consume itself. Moses can't believe his eyes, so he creeps in for a closer look. Close enough now that his face glows orange, Moses hears the voice of God:

"I am the God of your fathers, the God of Abraham, Isaac, and Jacob."

What did I tell you? It's all about Abraham—still. The Voice does not say, "I am God," and leave it at that. No, but rather: "I am the God of your fathers, the God of Abraham, Isaac, and Jacob." It's still all about the promise God made to Abraham: That his descendants would restore the ruined Earth on God's behalf, for the sake of humankind. From cradle to grave, from Abraham to Moses, from the prophets in exile to the Son of God in sandals, this is what Israelites lived for. Why wouldn't they? *It's all God has revealed to them.*

Frightened nearly out of his skin, Moses turns to run from the flaming shrubbery. God stops him in his tracks, saying:

> Take off your sandals and kneel. You are in a holy place, on holy ground. Do not think I haven't seen the agony of my people in Egypt, because I have. I have heard their groans and have come to help them.
>
> —Exodus 3:5, *The Message*

I imagine the rest of it went like this:

"Excuse me," says Moses, "but ... it has been nearly four hundred years."

"Excuse me, but … is this your timing or Mine?"

"Yours, God."

"Then, please, be quiet and start packing. I'm sending you back to Egypt."

You know the rest of the story. If you don't, then rent the movie, *The Ten Commandments*, starring Charlton Heston and Yul Brynner.

Talk about contrast. Without the centuries of bondage and a stupidly stubborn Pharaoh withstanding the reasonable demands of God's ambassador ("Let My people go"), there are no walking sticks turned to snakes, no rivers of blood, no joyous-getting-the-heck-out-of-Egypt ("the Exodus"), no parting of the Red Sea, a lot fewer drowned Egyptians, and a pathetic lack of worship songs. No manna in the wilderness, no quail, and no giant rock that somehow yields water.

At the foot of Mount Sinai, Israel officially became a nation. Above tree line at 7,000 feet, Moses stood between God and the people, engraving the Deity's words on two stone tablets that became the Magna Carta of God's chosen people. Moses took the tablets down the mountain to begin forty frustrating years managing the most stiff-necked people ever to take flesh. And yet, these were—and are—God's chosen people.

Moses says to them: "You listen to me now—or try to—and things will go well for you. The Lord thy God, however, will raise up unto you a Prophet from your midst, of your brethren, like unto me; it is to Him that you shall eventually hearken" (Deuteronomy 18:15).

Moses prophesied concerning Jesus Christ. Does that coming Great Prophet depart from the message of Moses? One would think that He would. One would think that the Son of God sent from Heaven would come expounding upon a sparkling new celestial world and Word that would leave Old Man Moses' familiar refrain in the Sinai dust. Listen again, however, to Old Man Moses: "The Lord thy God will raise up unto you a Prophet from your midst, of your brethren, *like unto me.*"

How could the very Image of the Invisible God possibly be like the poor mortal who at first wanted to run from God's voice? He is like Moses in this respect: "Christ has become the Servant of the Circumcision, for the sake of the truth of God, to confirm the patriarchal promises" (Romans 15:8).

JESUS CHRIST ON EARTH: A CONTINUATION OF ABRAHAM AND MOSES

I took the previous verse from the *Concordant Literal New Testament.* Here's the same verse from *The Message*: "Jesus, staying true to God's purposes, reached out in a special way to the Jewish insiders, so that the old ancestral promises would come true for them."

What are "the patriarchal promises" and "the old ancestral promises" referred to here? None other than the promises God made to Abraham: His seed would be numerous; they would become the head of nations and not the tail; and through them all the inhabitants of the Earth would be blessed. In case you've forgotten, here's the quote:

> Go forth from your country, and from your relatives, even from your father's house, and go to a land which I will show you. For I am going to make you a great nation, and I will bless you, and I will make your name great. And so you shall be a blessing. And I will bless those who bless you, and the one who curses you I will curse. And in you, *all the families of the Earth shall be blessed.*
> —Genesis 12:1-3, *New American Standard Bible*

The prophets referenced this incessantly. Read Isaiah. Read Jeremiah. Read Ezekiel. Read Amos, Obadiah, and Joel. When you're finished with them, read Haggai, Zephaniah, and Zechariah. If you can find anyone else whose name ends with "iah," read them, too. They all talk about Israel. They all talk about the trials that will fit Israel to one day rule the world and restore the Earth on God's behalf.

Do you realize why reading the Old Testament has been such a difficult and not-too-pleasant undertaking for you? Because it's *The Israel Channel*. It's all Israel, all the time. You think you will get some relief when you get to the New Testament—speaking of Matthew, Mark, Luke, and John—but you don't. It's still *The Israel Channel*: All Israel, all the time. You think that maybe the Son of God in sandals is finally *your* prophet—until you read what He says to His disciples in Matthew 10:5-7—

> These twelve Jesus commissions, charging them, saying, "Into a road of the nations you may not pass forth, and into a city of the Samaritans you may not be entering. Yet be going rather to the lost sheep of the house of Israel. Now going, herald, saying that, 'Near is the kingdom of the heavens!'"

If you had been living among the nations then, how would Jesus' words (paraphrased here) have sounded to you?

> Whatever you do, don't go into any ethnic neighborhoods like Chinatown or Little Italy. I don't even want you stepping into the streets of these neighborhoods, let alone talking to the actual people. This gospel isn't *for* them. Got it?

When Jesus said, "kingdom of the heavens," what did He mean by it? Is the kingdom *of* the heavens—the same as heaven? How could it be, when God never told Israel anything concerning heaven? Remember, He created the heavens and the Earth in Genesis 1:1, and then promptly ignored all besides Earth. The kingdom *of* the heavens is the same kingdom God promised to Abraham, because, "Jesus, staying true to God's purposes, reached out ... to the Jewish insiders, so that the old ancestral promises would come true for them" (Romans 15:8).

This kingdom is heavenly in character (it's the kingdom *of* the heavens), but its location is on Earth. An earthbound kingdom is the only message ever given to Israelites: "Thou dost also make them a kingdom and a priesthood for our God, and they shall be reigning on the Earth" (Revelation 5:10); and "Blessed are the meek, for they shall inherit the Earth" (Matthew 5:5).

So what happened to *your* Messiah? If the books of Matthew, Mark, Luke, and John are humanity's—and your—one and only chance to hear truth or be lost forever, then the Herald of that Truth has an odd way of broadcasting it. The point I am making is so generally unknown that I cannot resist another Zender paraphrase of Matthew 10:5-7—

> Do not take this gospel to any other nation besides yours. I'm including Samaria in this—never mind they're your near-relatives. Listen and listen well: Do *not* take this gospel to anyone except the lost sheep of the house of Israel. And I'm including in this all non-Israelites who will be reading these gospels at Holiday Inns from Gideon Bibles in the year 2012.
>
> And here is the gospel, in case you've forgotten it, although I don't see how you could: The kingdom God promised to your forefather, Abraham, is upon us. I am a minister of the Circumcision, to confirm the promises God made to Abraham.

You still look for something that might relate to you, so you peruse Matthew, chapter 15. Ah! At last, here comes a non-Israelite woman approaching Jesus concerning her demon-possessed daughter. The following is from Matthew 15:21-28, in *The Message* and the *Concordant Literal New Testament*:

> From there Jesus took a trip to Tyre and Sidon. They had hardly arrived when a Canaanite woman came down from the hills and pleaded, "Mercy, Lord, Son of David! My

daughter is cruelly afflicted by an evil spirit."

Jesus ignored her.

The disciples came and complained, "Now she's bother-ing us. Would you please take care of her? She's driving us crazy."

Jesus refused, telling them, "I was not commissioned except for the lost sheep of the house of Israel." Then the woman re-approached Jesus, went to her knees, and begged. "Lord, help me!"

He said, "It's not right to take bread out of children's mouths and throw it to dogs. I am a minister of the Circumcision to confirm the patriarchal promises. God made no promises to you."

The woman was quick to respond: "You're right, Master, but beggar dogs do get scraps from the master's table."

Jesus finally gave in. "Oh, woman, your faith is something else. What you want is what you get." Right then, her daughter became well.

The woman got what she wanted, yes, but not without beg-ging. She implored Him first as "Lord, Son of David" but struck out there because that esteemed title belongs exclusively to Israel. She must widen the scope, dropping "Son of David" but retaining the generic "Lord," which means "master."

The result? He called her a dog. The Lord Jesus Christ, *our* Savior, called the suffering woman—who through no fault of her own got born into a non-Israelite race—a dog. And so, she must assume her place as a practical non-entity, hoping only for a scrap from the chosen people's leftovers. Only when she acknowledged her lowly station did she get what she came for.

What do you do with this? If you are like many Christians,

If this were not in the Bible, I would not believe it.

you ignore it. If you have thought of Jesus of Nazareth as a universal proclaimer of a universal gospel to all humankind, then such passages as this and the one from Matthew 10:5-7 will derail your belief system. No one likes their presuppositions threatened, not even by facts. I am showing you things that have been in the Bible for a long time now, but obscured by human philosophy and the traditions of humans.

The news is going to get good, so hang with me. The dusty Man from Galilee in Matthew, Mark, Luke, and John eventually returned to heaven, where He traded in His sandals to once again become a radiant being full of light and glory. And then, from there, several months later—

—but wait. I'm getting ahead of myself. Let us just say for now that the woman begging for scraps from Israel's table in Matthew 15 would soon hear a message that would take her lowly, second-class self and promote it so far beyond—

—oops, there I go again.

Some may suppose I am short-changing Jesus Christ, our Savior. I'm not. While on Earth, Jesus purposely short-changed Himself, ministering only to the lost sheep of the house of Israel (Matthew 15:24). I am only telling you something that—apart from the obscuring filters of human tradition—would have been obvious: the Man of Sorrows, while on Earth, limited His message to Israelites. Jesus did it for good reason. His words, printed in red, are not all He had to say. Yes, these words in red were the words that left His mouth, but He spoke again several months later through a *different* mouthpiece, whose words—

—never mind. I'm getting ahead of myself again.

Keep reading, and you will see things you have never seen. You will feel things you have never felt. Your God is about to become bigger and more loving than you dared imagine. This is not about imagination, however, but rather revelation. God has always been this big. A slight adjustment of the lens, and you will see Him. The Scriptures I will show you have graced the Inspired Pages a long time now; you have simply never seen them. No one has drawn your attention to them, or shown you how and why they differ from the words of the earthbound Christ.

Scripture remains the same; I only invite you to view it with new eyes. You have watched in horror as Moses stoned Jews in the shadow of Sinai. Later, in the books of the Bible we now call "the letters of Paul," you saw tree-worshipping fornicators bathed in the glory of God's grace. Even within the New Testament, James says, "Show me your faith by your works"; Paul, on the other hand, says, "It's faith alone; forget works." In light of all this, you have cried to yourself, or possibly aloud:

Why does the Bible contradict itself? Why is it so confusing? I hate to read the Bible because I don't understand it!

I empathize with you there; I have felt the same way. One reason my Bible looks so ratty is because I have thrown it against the wall several times in utter frustration. But then, in 1986, I saw something that seems so obvious to me now. What I saw changed my life and my perception of God. The Bible wasn't the problem: *I* was. The Bible wasn't the problem; the way I was reading the Bible was the problem. It was the way I was mixing up Scriptures.

God does not write contradictory Scriptures. The Word of God is confusing only when we mix disparate elements. If we toss every ingredient from the refrigerator and the cupboard into a cake batter, we don't get a cake—we get a catastrophe. Likewise, lump together what God told one people with things He told another people, and we no longer have revelation, but pandemonium.

When I stopped blaming God and paused long enough to consider my own prejudices, new light came. You are now benefiting from my early mistakes. I am a messenger, nothing more. I envy you that you are about to see this revelation for the first time.

When you turn the pages of your Bible from Malachi to Matthew, the programming never changes. It's like flipping through the stations during a big news story: Every head talks about the same thing. Matthew, Mark, Luke, and John pick up where Malachi left off. The story is the same, only the names have changed. It's still, *The Israel Channel*. It's all Israel, all the time. Jesus came to Nazareth, not Athens. The Jesus Who wore sandals considered non-Israelites to be dogs (Matthew 15:26). If Matthew hadn't recorded this under inspiration of Holy Spirit, I would not expect you to believe it. I, myself, would not believe it. It's too odd; it's too unlikely. It defies the commonly taught template that the Jesus of the four gospels promoted a universal salvation to the non-Judean world.

Let us now turn to John, chapter 3. Nicodemus feared what his fellow priests might think of him, so he approached Jesus in the middle of the night and said:

"Rabbi, we are aware that You are a Teacher come from God."

Notice: *We* are aware. Nicodemus referred to himself and his fellow Israelites. He desperately wished to know how he and his fellow Israelites might enter into the kingdom God promised Abraham; he sought specifics. Jesus answered:

"If anyone should not be born again, he cannot perceive the kingdom of God."

Nicodemus said, "How can a man enter his mother's womb a second time?"

Jesus must have rolled His eyes, at least inwardly. Mustering patience, our Lord responded:

"You should not be marveling that I said to you, '*Ye* [plural in the Greek] must be born again.'"

"How can these things be?" said Nicodemus.

Jesus answered: "You are a teacher of Israel, and these things you do not know?" (John 3:10).

Nicodemus must have flinched with shame. Jesus spoke no new thing to the startled clergyman. Nicodemus should have known about the new birth, for the prophet Isaiah wrote of it in the same Scriptures that were sitting, at that moment, on a shelf in Nicodemus' office. Isaiah 66:7-9—

> Before she travailed, she brought forth; before her pain came, she gave birth to a boy. Who has heard such a thing?

Who has seen such things? *Can a land be born in one day?* Can a nation be brought forth all at once? As soon as Zion travailed, she also brought forth her sons. Shall I bring to the point of birth, and not give delivery? says the Lord. Or shall I who gives delivery shut the womb?

And then Jesus said:

Verily, verily, I am saying to you, of that which we have perceived are we speaking. And to that which we have seen are we testifying. And our testimony you [plural in the Greek] are not getting. If I told you of the terrestrial [earthly] and you are not believing, how shall you be believing if I should be telling you of the celestial [heavenly]?
—John 3:11-12, *Concordant Literal New Testament*

While on Earth, the Son of God ministered only to Israelites, confirming the patriarchal promises God gave Abraham. If any Gentiles got blessed at all, they did so by assuming their rightful role as dogs under Israel's table.

What, again, was the chief promise God made to Abraham? "I will bless those who bless you, and the one who curses you I will curse. *And in you shall all the families of the Earth be blessed*" (Genesis 12:3).

What harmony now emerges when we read: "If I have told you earthly things and you do not believe, how will you believe *if I tell you heavenly things?*" (John 3:12, *New King James Version*).

Jesus' words to Nicodemus fit perfectly the role of a Man Who came to Earth as "the Servant of the Circumcision, to confirm the patriarchal promises" (Romans 15:8). The patriarchal promises concerned Earth.

But now this: "If I have told you earthly things and you do not believe, how will you believe *if I tell you heavenly things?*"

Oh. My. God.

Jesus Christ—on Earth—held something back concerning heaven.

In the early days of what would come to be known as the Pentecostal era, a disciple named Stephen raked the religious hierarchy over the coals. Some priests hauled him before the Sanhedrin to render an account of himself as a follower of that heretic, Jesus of Nazareth, who purported during His lifetime to be the Messiah of Israel. That poor, deluded Nazarene was finally killed by these very people, but later there were rumors that He had risen from the dead and was inspiring, via the Holy Spirit, this agitating outbreak of kingdom fever.

Testifying for his life, Stephen reviewed for a captivated priesthood its own history. He finally got to the part about how Israel complained to Moses (recorded by Luke in Acts chapter 7), and said: "They craved the old Egyptian ways, whining to Aaron, 'Make us gods we can see and follow. This Moses who got us out here miles from nowhere—who knows what's happened to him!'"

Stephen continued:

> That was the time when they made a calf-idol, brought sacrifices to it, and congratulated each other on the wonderful religious program they had put together. God wasn't at all pleased; but He let them do it their way, worship every new god that came down the pike—and live with the consequences, consequences described by the prophet Amos: Did you bring me offerings of animals and grains those forty wilderness years, O Israel?
>
> Hardly. You were too busy building shrines to war gods, to sex goddesses, worshipping them with all your might. That's why I put you in exile in Babylon. And all this time our ancestors had a tent shrine for true worship, made to the exact specifications God provided Moses. They had it with them as they followed Joshua, when God cleared the land of pagans, and still had it right down to the time of David. David asked God for a permanent place for worship. But Solomon built it.

Yet that doesn't mean that Most High God lives in a building made by carpenters and masons. The prophet Isaiah put it well when he wrote: Heaven is my throne room; I rest my feet on Earth. So what kind of house will you build me? says God. Where I can get away and relax? It's already built, and I built it.

—Acts 7:39-50, *The Message*

The Sanhedrin listened with strained patience up until this point. But then came this:

And you continue, so bullheaded! Calluses on your hearts, flaps on your ears! Deliberately ignoring the Holy Spirit; *you're just like your ancestors.* Was there ever a prophet who didn't get the same treatment? Your ancestors killed anyone who dared talk about the coming of the Just One. And you've kept up the family tradition—traitors and murderers, all of you. You had God's law handed to you by angels— gift-wrapped! —and you squandered it!

—Acts 7:51-53, *The Message*

Watch what happened next:

Now hearing these things, they were harrowed in their hearts, and gnashed their teeth at him. ... Now, crying with a loud voice, they pressed their ears and rush on him with one accord. And casting him out, outside of the city, they pelted him with stones.

—Acts 7:54; 57-58, CLNT

So much for Pentecost—and the kingdom. The early excitement of Acts, chapter 2, flickered to nearly nothing by chapter 7. It's only chapter 7 in a twenty-eight chapter book, and yet the kingdom God promised to Abraham and his seed was apparently sunk. The requirement for the kingdom was national repentance— a nation reborn in accord with prophetic utterance. What we have here, instead, was an incensed priesthood honoring its grim tradition of murdering God's messengers. Thus, the prospect of global Israel supremacy lay quivering beneath a pile of bloodstained rocks, exhaling the last of its life.

Yet, there is one curious footnote to this pathetic passage. The writer seems pressed to mention an odd little detail that ought to have passed beneath the radar, yet didn't. It concerns, strangely enough, the coats of the men stoning Stephen. Here it is, in verse 58 of Acts, chapter 7: "And the witnesses put off their garments at the feet of a young man called Saul."

No one, in their wildest imaginations, could have guessed what was about to happen.

6.
DAMASCUS ROAD

DAMASCUS ROAD

S torms brew in heaven, as they do on Earth. God waits and waits and waits to unfurl His greatest depths. The celestial beings attending Him must feel it coming. Even we mortals here on Earth sense approaching storms. The air feels different—there is a peculiar smell. The sky grows dark—the wind increases. Birds find trees—dogs sniff the atmosphere. No one knows for sure what's coming. So, too, in heaven. Even celestial beings sense when something—something large and unthinkable—is afoot.

Long before the ruin of our present Earth, sin wracked heaven. Why? In the beginning, God created an Adversary, Satan, to oppose Him.

■ **Isaiah 54:16**—God intended Satan to be a destroyer: "And I Myself created the Ruiner to harm" (*Concordant Version of the Old Testament*).

■ **John 8:44**—"[Satan] was a murderer from the beginning" (*King James Version*).

God is the original Shakespeare, providing the necessary an-
tagonists against whom the coming heroes will eventually shine
and conquer.

God said to Job:

> Where were you when I laid the foundation of the Earth?
> Tell Me, if you have understanding …Who laid its corner-
> stone, when the morning stars sang together, and all the
> sons of God [angels] shouted for joy?
> —Job 38:4-7, NASB

What prompted the celestial celebration described here?
Realization that here, at last, was the God-designated stage for a
future, decisive battle between good and evil forces. Apparently,
it was clear to the attending host what God intended for this rock
in space He was just then creating. Here, on the third planet from
the sun at the edge of the Milky Way galaxy—and nowhere else—
God's own Son would come to settle for all time the superiority of
good over evil. Not only this, but the ultimate showdown would
demonstrate to a universal audience the love of God. How? God
would commit His Son to hanging naked from a Roman stake
and, from there, forgiving His killers.

No heart—celestial or terrestrial—had ever felt such love in
the face of such evil. The sky itself could barely watch when it happened, darkening itself at midday. Do you not believe that heaven
convulsed then? Even a Roman soldier collapsed at the foot of that
cross and cried out: "Surely this was God's Son!"

"The Lamb was slain from the disruption of the Earth" (Revelation 13:8).

In the glint of God's eye, His Son died before Bethlehem
actually existed. Eons before Bethlehem, God held in His bosom
the answer to sin and death. Yet, before there can be an answer to
sin and death, there must *be* sin and death. With God, the cure
pre-dates the disease. In fact, He created the disease ("I create
evil"—Isaiah 45:7) as a backdrop for the display of the cure. That

The sky itself could barely watch when it happened.

is, His cure is a display of His love, grace, and power, which have always been with Him.

For a race dependent on contrast for revelation, tyranny *must* precede even a foreknown liberty. Thus, Adam precedes Christ, bondage precedes exodus, and law precedes grace. It must be so, and our God is patient to make it so. God does it *for* us, not *to* us, yet even He must endure the prerequisite evil.

Isaiah 1:11—God takes no pleasure in sacrifices: "I do not delight in the blood of bulls, or of lambs, or goats" (NKJV).

God tolerated the blood of bulls, lambs, and goats, designating these as Sunday-school pictures for the coming reality. The coming reality will unburden Him. In the early picture was the lesson: Without the shedding of blood, there is no forgiveness of sin. As instructive as this is, it lacks a deeper aspect: *The Sufferer gladly suffers for the sake of His beloved.* No goat ever figured out how to do that. In Christ's deportment on the cross, we at last see the love of God. Everything before Calvary is but a shadow of this divine utterance: "Father, forgive them ..." (Luke 23:34).

At last, the time arrived for His terrestrial birth. In the patience of God, it only took eons. Yet the day did come, and the celestial world—long sensing the coming storm—responded as expected.

When reading the following passage, one senses the sentiment behind the angelic praise-fest: "Finally!"

> In the same region there were some shepherds staying out in the fields and keeping watch over their flock by night. And an angel of the Lord suddenly stood before them, and the glory of the Lord shone around them; and they were terribly frightened. But the angel said to them, "Do not be afraid; for behold, I bring you good news of great joy which will be for all the people; for today in the city of David there has been born for you a Savior, who is Christ the Lord.
>
> "This will be a sign for you: you will find a baby wrapped in

cloths and lying in a manger." And suddenly there appeared with the angel a multitude of the heavenly host praising God and saying, "Glory to God in the highest, and on Earth peace among humans with whom He is pleased."

—Luke 2:8-14, NASB

In all probability, these angels at Bethlehem knew nothing of the coming cross. They expected an eventual showdown, but nothing so grotesque as a gibbeting. The cross cast a shadow across His entire earthly life, but the shadow remained hidden in the counsels of God. The angels at Bethlehem knew of a rocky prominence nearby, curiously shaped like a skull, but none could have dreamed what would occur there thirty-three years hence. It was all they could do, I think, to keep track of the incarnation, and the lyrics of their song.

Imagine being in attendance the night that the Son of God acquiesced to taking flesh. I am not speaking of Bethlehem now, but of the moment at God's throne when the Son of God's love nodded His assent to becoming a cluster of reproductive cells clinging in blood to the wall of a young girl's uterus. Could the morbid curiosity of even the noblest celestial mind have refused such a moment? The universe had never witnessed such a conscious lowering of Self, or greater sacrifice. I imagine a nightmarish countdown, and then an angel saying later: "It was awful, really. One moment He was there, and then He wasn't."

They waited nine months, monitoring the fetus, practicing their songs. Mary's water broke, and they lined up at the door. She pushed a final time through tears and clamped teeth, and the happy, celestial brigade leaped to Earth like millions of paratroopers jumping from an airplane.

Stephen was dead. Saul returned the murderers' coats, congratulating them on a job well done. He would have cast a stone himself, but he was too young. Never mind that; he would make a name for himself another way.

The young Pharisee loved the God of his fathers. In fact, no one loved God more. Because he was embarrassed of it, Saul never confessed his deep envy of the fathers, of Abraham, Moses, Isaac, and Jacob. He envied their calling. He envied how God had summoned these men for unique purposes. Saul would have sold his soul if only the Voice at the burning bush beyond Midian had addressed *him*. Sometimes, he lay awake at night, mentally assuming the place of Joseph, when the young man arose from prison to become Pharaoh's second-in-command. Joseph eventually saved Egypt, as well as his beloved homeland.

If only Saul could be called to something like that. (When the kingdom did come, he would surely be a leader in it.) Saul could not *wait* to rule the Earth.

What of Jacob, wrestling with the angel at Pennial, then granted a vision of heaven? Was Jacob as worthy as Saul? In no way. Yet Saul had never beheld a celestial messenger, let alone gazed into glory. If only an angel would visit him; it would confirm his divine favor. This lack incessantly nagged the Pharisee. Abraham received multiple visits; Moses saw the back of God; Jacob wrestled with the heavenly emissary; and God gave Joseph dreams fit for royalty. Even Daniel, in Babylon, received visions for the future of the world.

God failed Saul here, but for the most part Saul kept his agitation private. To publicize it would betray weakness. To Saul, projecting any insufficiency belied his lofty station. But really, why *was* greatness eluding him—him, of all people? No one kept the law as perfectly as he—not even the esteemed Caiaphas.

Since Genesis 1:1, God had ignored the heavens. Not a single heavenly magistrate dared question Him concerning this. "In the beginning, God created the heavens and the Earth," they often repeated amongst themselves, "as for the Earth, it came to be a chaos and vacant." The tacit implication was that God had unattended business. The Son had sacrificed Himself and died for the sins of Israel, becoming the perfect sacrifice for that disobedient nation in accord with the Abrahamic promises, which, they knew, concerned the restitution of Earth. Yet, were not the heavens in worse straits?

> For it is not ours to wrestle with blood and flesh, but with the sovereignties, with the authorities, with the world-mights of this darkness, *with the spiritual forces of wickedness among the celestials.*
>
> —Ephesians 6:12, CLNT

There was another consideration—or so one would think. It's tempting for us moderns—sitting here with the gift of hindsight—to imagine in that distant day a celestial questioning of the scope of Christ's death. At first glance, it would seem that Christ's blood (spilled on the cross) did not reach beyond Palestine. Would not such an astounding death as Calvary's overspill the boundaries of Judea? This question never arose. Why would it? The eventual fulfilling of the Abrahamic covenant seemed sufficient blessing for dogs (Gentiles). What more could the other nations want?

After all, the reign of fabled blessing—the coming Millennium—would forever end the Gentiles' days of begging scraps from Israel's table. Wouldn't it? Well, not exactly. Upon reconsideration, it was begrudgingly conceded, among the angels (celestials), that even in the promised earthly kingdom the nations would still be considered second-class citizens. Their blessing would exceed their present distress, yes, but not without some song and dance for the sake of their superiors. Zechariah had prophesied concerning that time:

> This is what the Lord of Armies says: In those days ten people from every language found among the nations will take hold of the clothes of a Jew. They will say, "Let us go with you because we have heard that God is with you."
>
> —Zechariah 8:23, NASB

But at least the scraps will be bigger. Right?
God smiled at this celestial bantering, biding His time.

If God refused to show Saul something, than Saul would show God something—something He would never forget. Saul would become a champion defender of His name and honor. Furthermore, he would accomplish this without a single vision, a single dream, a single angel, or a single heavenly apparition. Some men, apparently, required such miracles to fuel their aspirations. Saul outstripped all others; he needed nothing but his own conviction.

For the task at hand, his personal depth of resolve more than sufficed him. What further fire besides the justness of his own cause could raise his fervor a degree higher? Saul was not weak, like Jacob. Unlike Moses, Saul relished his gifts. Abraham at one time doubted God's promise; Saul doubted nothing. If this Jesus the Nazarene was a blasphemer—and surely he was—then so were his stupid followers.

The priesthood was weak. They stoned Stephen, but that un-educated man—though eloquent—was merely the foot soldier of a swelling rebellion. *Why was Peter still alive? And where was John? Was the priesthood so foolish as to suppose that the movement had not gone underground?* The leaders rested in their corpulence, conversing. Talk accomplished nothing. If the Sanhedrin would not act, Saul would. If this new wave of so-called Jesus People feared the elites who stoned Stephen—they had not seen anything.

Jesus Christ accomplished the unthinkable, dying for the sins of the world. Then He returned to heaven to sit at God's right hand. Jesus knew what He had accomplished; *God* certainly knew. The entirety of the Plan had been signed and sealed. Now, all that remained was the delivery.

Was Pentecost, by any stretch of imagination, the delivery of the entire Plan of God?

No. It was only an installment.

"God no one has ever seen. The only-begotten God, Who is in the bosom of the Father, He unfolds Him" (John 1:18).

I love this word "unfolds" from the *Concordant Literal New Testament*. "Unfolds" is the literal translation of the Greek *exegeomai*, whose literal elements are *ex*, meaning "out," and *egeomai*, meaning "lead." To unfold, then, is to "lead out."

Think of a road map, folded accordion-style. All the rivers and roads, all the lakes and rest stops, all the state parks, time zones, and county boundaries—all are secreted within. The full landscape lives inside the folds; the mapmakers have accomplished grand feats, folded them multiple times, and returned home. Future viewers need only discover their work. And so, bit-by-bit, the map yields its treasure. A little at a time, fold-by-fold, one horizon gives way to another.

Thus also with God. From Adam to Abraham, we begin to see Him. From Abraham to Moses, we see a little more, only then realizing how little we grasped in Adam. From Moses to the prophets, an even grander perspective arrives. Fold-by-fold, until at last the Son arrives. The fortunate ones who witnessed the days of His earthly sojourn never heard richer details concerning the kingdom of God and the future of Earth. The Messiah outdid Moses; remember, Moses looked ahead to Him. The Messiah of Israel unfolds God, for the sake of that generation, and for ours.

Did Jesus Christ, on Earth, unfold the entirety of God's plan? Or was there still an ocean yet to uncover?

"If I have told you earthly things and you do not believe, how will you believe *if I tell you heavenly things?*" (John 3:12, *New King James Version*).

Abraham Lincoln, the man most written about in history, keeps getting ink. How can that be, 145 years since the man's death? New authors continually discover new aspects of the famous man's life. If this is true of Lincoln, a mere human, what can be said of God's Son, Who came to die, not only for us earthlings but for the sake of a yet-untended universal distress?

We know about Pentecost. But will we assume that Peter announced the be-all and end-all of Jesus Christ's sacrifice—fifty *days* after He escaped the tomb?

"Repent and be baptized, each of you in the name of Jesus Christ for the pardon of your sins, and you shall be obtaining the gratuity of the Holy Spirit. For to you is the promise and to your children ..." (Acts 2:38).

Where is the mention of heavenly things concerning which the Savior, on Earth, withheld the telling?

Saul liked breaking into homes in the middle of the night, carrying the torch himself. The shock factor fascinated him. This particular night, he learned of a family that had purportedly entertained Peter.

Doors were easy to break down then, although he had others do that for him. The first few times he raided a home, the crying children bothered him. By exercise of his intense mental prowess, Saul trained himself to think of them not as children, but as enemies of God. Older children were kicked or heaved against walls. When the raids became routine, younger children got the same treatment. Overly emotional children grabbing for parents got tied to furniture. Only twice was it necessary to snap a neck.

(Saul would never forget the second of these, no, not even fifty years later, in a prison in Rome—it had been a baby girl. He had not meant to kill her, only to quiet her. She would not stop crying; it had been an accident. He had not meant to do it. The stress of his work and the nature of the crying got to him. *Why had God found it necessary to make that baby cry so much?*)

He beat people in a special room off the court, adjacent to the robing area. "He beat them" is a figure of speech; he left the actual work to others. He was too heavily dressed to sweat. Others with suppler arms attended to that. Which is not to say the methodical reduction of human wills occurred apart from his direction.

Saul assigned himself the task of staring into each face as a subordinate obtained confessions. The closer, the better. The disparity between bondage and freedom fascinated him; the closer he was to it, the more intoxicating it became. So exotic was the gulf between pain and privilege, to him, that the mere sight sent chills down his back. To be so near to the writhing face, and yet so far away—he could not say enough about it.

"You, sir, can get anyone to say anything," was a frequent comment from the priests.

"That is so true," Saul would say, a hint of smirk at his upturned lip. "And so the world is rid of yet another heretic."

God brooded in rapturous joy, as did His Son. They could do this only because they knew the future. They knew what was coming for *all* humanity. God knew that even the murderous priesthood of Israel would eventually praise Him. Even Roman magistrates would eventually fall before God for what He was about to do.

God watched Saul return home to his family. God sees to the end; He looks *through* things. We, on the other hand, stare *at* things. We bury loved ones and stare at the tombstones. God looks *through* the tombstones into our future, divinely altered bodies moving twice the speed of light. Peter spoke splendidly atop a stone roof at Pentecost in downtown Jerusalem, but as far as the score written upon God's mind, Peter's performance was Mozart at age five. Fast approaching—finally—was a time when a curtain would be drawn back to a Symphony unimagined.

"In the beginning, God created the heavens and the Earth. *As for the Earth* ..." For hundreds of years, God appeared to ignore the heavenly rebellion of which Paul wrote in Ephesians, chapter 6. God kept near His bosom, away from view, the long-planned gathering of all creation unto Him.

> For all things originate with Him and come from Him; all
> things live through Him, and all things center in and tend
> to consummate and to end in Him.
> —Romans 11:36, *Amplified Bible*

Thus far, God had called one nation, Israel, and given to them
His counsels for terrestrial realms. They were His earthly people,
and to them came the rites of circumcision, baptism, and the law.
They were His peculiar people, and He was their God. To them
alone came the divine legislature, and through them alone would
come the rest of Earth's only hope of knowing God.

What of the other nations? For all practical purposes, God
ignored them. This phenomenon is pathetically yet graphically
described for us in Ephesians 2:11-12—

> Wherefore, remember that once you, the nations in flesh—
> who are termed "Uncircumcision" by those termed "Cir-
> cumcision," in flesh, made by hands—that you were, in that
> era, apart from Christ. Being alienated from the citizenship
> of Israel, and guests of the promise covenants, having no
> expectation, and without God in the world.
> —*Concordant Literal New Testament*

- ■ Apart from Christ
- ■ Alienated from the citizenship of Israel
- ■ Guests of the promise covenants
- ■ Having no expectation
- ■ Without God in the world

In other words: People without hope.

Even before the first human stood upon Earth, it was in God's
heart to call out from humanity a select group of beings—the dregs
of the Earth—to be seated with Him in heavenly realms, at His
right Hand. The Son of His Love (Colossians 1:13, CLNT) would
be His first Son—but there would be others. The Son would take
flesh so that He could inhabit the lowest realms of this terrestrial

sphere, suffering the most shameful death imaginable. Yet He would be only the first of the low-goers.

The divine principle is: The lowest become the highest; the last shall be first. The more last you are, the more first you shall be.

God creates diseases to reveal cures. God's cure was love and grace—the disease, Adam. God made the race, and then supervised its ruin with the goal of rebuilding it stronger *because* of the sin.

Consider Adam in Eden. Not one song of praise escaped that primal man's lips: Adam knew no contrast. Only subsequent to the "tragedy" of sin come the sweetest songs of praise.

God will save the entire race.

"As in Adam *all* are dying, thus also in Christ shall *all* be vivified" (1 Corinthians 15:22).

"Vivification" means being given life beyond the reach of death. Lazarus was not vivified; he was only resurrected. He walked out of his own tomb, but then was eventually carried in again and still has not re-emerged.

"As in Adam all are dying, thus also in Christ shall all be vivified."

Yet God kept this plan a secret for many eons. No one could appreciate it without a backdrop. If that backdrop takes thousands of years to paint, and if He needs several shades of black paint to backdrop the coming glory, who are we to question Him?

The program for Israel and Earth continued for centuries. The failure of the people required a Savior—a Messiah. Thus, He came—and they rejected Him. He gave them another "chance" at Pentecost, to believe in the testimony of the twelve that the kingdom was indeed at hand. They rejected this also. They rejected the earthly kingdom in accord with larger divine wisdom: Their rejection became the occasion for the unveiling of the Symphony, the music not yet heard.

> And He is the Head of the body, the ecclesia, Who is Sovereign, firstborn from among the dead, that in all He may be becoming first, for in Him the entire complement

The more last you are, the more first you shall be.

delights to dwell, and through Him to reconcile all to Him
(making peace through the blood of His cross), through
Him, whether those on the Earth or those in the heavens.
—Colossians 1:18-20, CLNT

The ultimate plan, long known to Divinity, was now at the
eve of revelation.

"If I have told you earthly things and you do not believe, how
will you believe *if I tell you heavenly things?*" (John 3:12).

Now, He would tell. But first, God had to choose the perfect
vessel. Logically (or perhaps ironically), the perfect vessel for a message of transcendent grace would have to be—by standards of polite
society—a complete ruin: in our vernacular, "a prick." By spiritual
standards (and for spiritual purposes), it would be most helpful
for us if he were to actually hate God from the core of his being.

Ravaging Jerusalem was fine, but it was not enough for Saul.
His work mattered. He had actually done something. Saul con-
ferred with the priests, who had received reports from Saul's spies
among the people.

Commenting upon these reports, the priests said, "You have
made a difference, Saul. The people fear now. Life is easier for
us. The rebellion appears to be crushed here; you are to be commended."

Saul grimaced. "Many have run."

"What do you mean?" (They knew what he meant, but wished
to avoid upsetting him.)

"They have escaped beyond Israel, many of them. You don't
think I know? They've taken the name of Jesus abroad."

Considering the caliber of the man standing before them, the
priests' next question was as obvious as it was rhetorical:

"So what will you do? Chase them to where they have run?"

Saul unconsciously fondled his knife in its sheath. "Do we
know specifics?"

One of the priests said, "Many have gone to Damascus. We don't know why."

"Who cares why?" Saul said. "What's involved?"

"There's no precedent. I assume you'll go to Caiaphas for some kind of writ."

Saul nodded. "Then everything would be legal … even if it weren't."

"That would help matters."

Saul's wife eyed him suspiciously.

"Where the hell are you going now?"

"Damascus."

"That's nine days, one way."

"Thank you for the geography lesson. I will do it in six."

"Our taxes are due at the end of the month."

Saul withdrew a silver shekel and slapped it on the table. Without another word, he left. Before dawn the next morning, he was headed west with six men, two soldiers, and a slave.

The wind was oddly strong into their faces.

On day five of their journey, at precisely 11:59 a.m. (Damascus time), eleven cubits off the north side of the road at the well of Dara, eleven furlongs from the caravansary at Al Qunaytirah—all plans for Damascus got permanently curtailed.

7.

ONWARD IN ACTS

ONWARD IN ACTS

Years later, standing upon the steps of a Roman citadel in the city of Jerusalem, Saul addressed a large, agitated convocation of his own people—a mob, actually—who were quite prepared to stone him. Saul temporarily mesmerized them with an account of what had occurred that memorable day near Al Qunaytirah:

My dear brothers and fathers, listen carefully to what I have to say before you jump to conclusions about me.

When they heard him speaking Hebrew, they grew even quieter. No one wanted to miss a word of this.

He continued, I am a good Jew, born in Tarsus in the province of Cilicia, but educated here in Jerusalem under the exacting eye of Rabbi Gamaliel, thoroughly instructed in our religious traditions. And I've always been passionately on God's side, just as you are right now. I went after anyone connected with this "Way," went at them hammer and tongs, ready to kill for God. I rounded up men and women right and left and had them thrown in prison. You can ask the Chief Priest or anyone in the high council to verify this; they all knew me well.

Then I went off to our brothers in Damascus, armed with official documents authorizing me to hunt down the followers of Jesus there, arrest them, and bring them back to Jerusalem for sentencing. As I arrived on the outskirts of Damascus about noon, a blinding light blazed out of the skies and I fell to the ground, dazed.

I heard a voice: "Saul, Saul, why are you out to get me?"

Who are you, Master? I asked.

He said, "I am Jesus the Nazarene, the One you're hunting down."

My companions saw the bright light, but they didn't hear our conversation.

Then I said, What do I do now, Master?

He said, "Get to your feet and enter Damascus. There you'll be told everything that's been set out for you to do."

And so we entered Damascus, but nothing like the entrance I had planned—I was blind as a bat and my companions had to lead me in by the hand. And that's when I met Ananias, a man with a sterling reputation in observing our laws—the Jewish community in Damascus is unanimous on that score. He came and put his arm on my shoulder.

"Look up," he said. I looked, and found myself looking right into his eyes—I could see again!

Then he said, "The God of our ancestors has handpicked you to be briefed on His plan of action. You've actually seen the Righteous Innocent and heard Him speak. You are to be a key witness to everyone you meet of what you've seen and heard. So what are you waiting for? Get up and get yourself baptized, scrubbed clean of those sins and personally acquainted with God."

Well, it happened just as Ananias said. After I was back in Jerusalem and praying one day in the Temple, lost in the presence of God, I saw Him, saw God's Righteous Innocent, and heard Him say to me, "Hurry up! Get out of here as quickly as you can. None of the Jews here in Jerusalem are going to accept what you say about Me."

At first I objected: Who has better credentials? They all know how obsessed I was with hunting out those who believed in You, beating them up in the meeting places and throwing them in jail. And when Your witness Stephen was murdered, I was right there, holding the coats of the murderers and cheering them on. And now they see me totally converted. What better qualification could I have?

But He said, "Don't argue. Go. I'm sending you on a long journey to outsider non-Jews."
—Acts 22:1-21, *The Message*

Watch carefully what happened next:

The people in the crowd had listened attentively up to this point, but now they broke loose, shouting out, "Kill him! He's an insect! Stomp on him!" They shook their fists. They filled the air with curses.
—Acts 22:22-23, *The Message*

This crowd of believing Israelites listened patiently to Paul—until he relayed to them these fateful words given him by the vivified Christ: "I am sending you on a long journey to outsider non-Jews." Then these Jewish believers wished to stomp Paul like a rogue spider. Had not the Romans intervened, they surely would have.

Did I just say, "believing Israelites"? I did. The Jews who were then ready to literally kill the apostle Paul were believers in the Lord Jesus Christ.

Could it be? Watch. We find a positive identity of those gathered to hear Paul this day in the previous chapter, Acts 21. Paul was in town for meetings with Peter, James, and the others. Paul greeted the Jerusalem elders of "The Way" (for thus was the new Jesus Movement designated), relaying to them the acts God worked among the nations, through Paul's dispensation. The elders liked some of what they heard, but other parts bothered them.

Luke writes in Acts 21:17-21, again from *The Message*:

> In Jerusalem, our friends, glad to see us, received us with open arms. The first thing next morning, we took Paul to see James. All the church leaders were there. After a time of greeting and small talk, Paul told the story, detail by detail, of what God had done among the non-Jewish people through his ministry. They listened with delight and gave God the glory. They had a story to tell, too: "And just look at what's been happening here—thousands upon thousands of God-fearing Jews have become believers in Jesus! But there's also a problem because they are more zealous than ever in observing the laws of Moses.
>
> They've been told that you advise believing Jews who live surrounded by unbelieving outsiders to go light on Moses, telling them that they don't need to circumcise their children or keep up the old traditions. This isn't sitting at all well with them. We're worried about what will happen when they discover you're in town. There's bound to be trouble."

"Trouble"? Talk about understatement.

From this, you can begin to see that not only was Paul teaching a message radically different than what Israel had accepted from Abraham and Moses, but his newfound enemies were not ornery Christ-killers, like Caiaphas. Rather, Paul's enemies were believers in Jesus Christ—in the *Jewish* Jesus Christ. This is our first hint that Paul heralded (or was beginning to herald) an aspect of the Messiah of Israel no one had ever heard of. Could it be that the Son of God was more than a mere mute Lamb, sacrificed only for the sins of Israelites?

"If I have told you earthly things and you do not believe, how will you believe *if I tell you heavenly things?*" (John 3:12).

A similar meeting had occurred back in Acts, chapter 15, with the same theme. Listen in:

> It wasn't long before some Jews showed up from Judea insisting that everyone be circumcised: "If you're not circumcised in the Mosaic fashion, you can't be saved." Paul and Barnabas were up on their feet at once in fierce protest. The church decided to resolve the matter by sending Paul, Barnabas, and a few others to put it before the apostles and leaders in Jerusalem. After they were sent off and on their way, they told everyone they met as they traveled through Phoenicia and Samaria about the breakthrough to the non-Jewish outsiders.
>
> Everyone who heard the news cheered—it was terrific news! When they got to Jerusalem, Paul and Barnabas were graciously received by the whole church, including the apostles and leaders. They reported on their recent journey and how God had used them to open things up to the outsiders. Some Pharisees stood up to say their piece. They had become believers, but continued to hold to the hard party line of the Pharisees. "You have to circumcise the pagan converts," they said. "You must make them keep the law of Moses."
>
> —Acts 15:1-5, *The Message*

After this meeting, a letter went forth from the heads of the Jerusalem church (Peter and James, mainly), exempting believing non-Jews from the ancient rite. Although this angered the hardliners, it delighted Paul. It was a start. Not that Paul required permission from Jerusalem to teach his new revelation, but in these early days Paul understood that support of the Jerusalem church was politically expedient.

Paul had so many enemies out-of-the-gate that were it not for Peter and James and their influence among the Jerusalem law-lovers, Paul might have been stopped in his tracks—with a dagger in his back—before the new message could even be considered. As it was, Paul carried a letter from Jesus headquarters with a Peter signature that would bless and comfort the non-Jews and near-Jews among whom Paul traveled.

Here's how it eventually worked out, recorded in Acts, chapter 15. James speaks, from *The Message*:

> So here is my decision: We're not going to unnecessarily burden non-Jewish people who turn to the Master. We'll write them a letter and tell them, "Be careful to not get involved in activities connected with idols, to guard the morality of sex and marriage, to not serve food offensive to Jewish Christians—blood, for instance."

> This is basic wisdom from Moses, preached and honored for centuries now in city after city as we have met and kept the Sabbath. Everyone agreed: apostles, leaders, all the people. They picked Judas (nicknamed Bar-Sabbas) and Silas—they both carried considerable weight in the church—and sent them to Antioch with Paul and Barnabas with this letter:

> "From the apostles and leaders, your friends, to our friends in Antioch, Syria, and Cilicia: Hello! We heard that some men from our church went to you and said things that confused and upset you. Mind you, they had no authority from us; we didn't send them. We have agreed unanimously to pick representatives and send them to you with our good friends Barnabas and Paul. We picked men we knew you could trust, Judas and Silas—they've looked death in the face time and again for the sake of our Master Jesus Christ. We've sent them to confirm in a face-to-face meeting with you what we've written.

"It seemed to the Holy Spirit and to us that you should not be saddled with any crushing burden, but be responsible only for these bare necessities: Be careful not to get involved in activities connected with idols; avoid serving food offensive to Jewish Christians (blood, for instance); and guard the morality of sex and marriage. These guidelines are sufficient to keep relations congenial between us. And God be with you!"

And so off they went to Antioch. On arrival, they gathered the church and read the letter. The people were greatly relieved and pleased. Judas and Silas, good preachers both of them, strengthened their new friends with many words of courage and hope. Then it was time to go home. They were sent off by their new friends with laughter and embraces all around to report back to those who had sent them.

These days, it's difficult for us to imagine how significant this was. It was a first, baby step toward the formation of a new group of Christ-believers who would eventually (it took several years of gathering revelation) be freed from every physical rite, including the ones mentioned in this letter.

All ties to Israel would eventually be severed—and that would be only the beginning.

Israel had no idea what was coming. Even these few regulations that James warned the non-Jews against, were, as I said, eventually repealed by Paul. Not that Paul would suddenly be *for* immorality and idol worship, but God eventually revealed to Paul that the grace of Christ—apart from rules of any kind—was all believers needed for the weaknesses of flesh.

Israel was always to be a priesthood nation. A priest is one who acts as an intercessor between humans and God. Israel was a stiff-necked people who would keep her blessings to herself, thank you very much. When Paul started in and told so many of the non-Jews to believe in Jesus apart from ritual, most of Israel balked. They had begrudgingly given up circumcising Gentiles, but were loathe to see all ties with the "mother church" severed. Israel, as a priesthood nation, will always be the go-between—on Earth. (What about heaven? Ah! She has no pre-eminence there. This is significant, in light of what is coming.) They were willing to accept other nations into the fold, as long as those other nations came through them. As long as Israel was the channel of blessing, Israel could tolerate non-Jews. At this early time, I don't think even James or Peter could imagine that this new thing God was bringing to non-Jews through Paul would eventually stand alone—apart from any letter, word, or patronizing nod from any Jewish notable, including Peter.

Be impressed that Peter even accepted Paul. This was no small accomplishment. Peter would never have done this apart from a vision God gave him in Acts, chapter 10.

Peter was in Joppa one evening, and hungry. He was on his rooftop, praying. That's when the vision came. A giant sheet descended from heaven, in which frolicked all sorts of unclean animals that Peter, as a Jew, was forbidden to eat. A voice addressed Peter then, saying: "Rise, Peter! Sacrifice and eat!" (Acts 10:13). Peter recoiled in horror.

> Yet Peter said, "Far be it from me, Lord, for I never ate anything contaminating and unclean!" And again, a second time, a voice came to him [saying], "What God cleanses, do not you count contaminating!"
> —Acts 10:14-16, CLNT

God did this specifically to prepare Peter, the leader of the Way, to accept the testimony of a man he would soon meet, a former Christian-killer, named Saul, who would tell Peter of his amazing encounter with the risen Savior on the road to Damascus. The Savior told Saul that he was to be a light to non-Israelites.

Apart from this vision in Joppa, Peter never would have entertained even the thought of transcendent grace for non-Israelites.

At the same time of this vision, a God-fearing Gentile in the city of Caesarea, named Cornelius—a devout follower of the God of Israel—called for Peter. In those days, remember, a non-Jewish seeker wanting a blessing had to take his or her place as a dog beneath Israel's table. While Cornelius prayed, *he* was visited by an angel.

Cornelius was at first afraid (this seems to be standard biblical procedure whenever angels show up), but the angel told him to calm down, and then said to him (Acts 10:4-6):

> Your prayers and neighborly acts have brought you to God's attention. Here's what you are to do. Send men to Joppa to get Simon, the one everyone calls Peter. He is staying with Simon the Tanner, whose house is down by the sea.
> —*The Message*

While Cornelius' men were en route to Joppa, Peter received his vision of the sheet. When you see what happens next, you will further understand why Peter needed this vision. Not only would Peter have to accept a newcomer into the fold (Paul) with his radical new bend toward Gentiles, but Peter also needed to realize God was embarking on a new program that would eventually, for the men and women of the nations, give them a divine calling and an expectation completely separate from the priest nation of Israel.

Peter himself strained to grasp the message Paul brought to the nations. This seems incredible, but listen to what Peter later wrote, in 2 Peter 3:14-16. From the *Concordant Literal New Testament*:

> Wherefore, beloved, hoping for these things, endeavor to be found by Him in peace, unspotted and flawless. And be deeming the patience of our Lord salvation, according as our beloved brother Paul also writes to you, according to the wisdom given to him, as also in all the epistles, speaking in them concerning these things, *in which are some things hard to apprehend.*

I can almost hear this P.S.: "But I am trying to apprehend them."

That's how radically different Paul's message was from what Jesus had told Peter (and priests like Nicodemus) while He was on Earth; Peter had a difficult time grasping Paul's evangel.

"If I have told you earthly things and you do not believe, how will you believe *if I tell you heavenly things?*" (John 3:12).

Remember, for hundreds and thousands of years, there was only one religion, and one people in touch with God, and only one way to get to God—through that chosen nation, a priesthood nation. This was the way it was, and, to a Jew, the way it always would be. *They* were pre-eminent. *They* were the people. *They* owned the franchise on God. *They* held the Scriptures. *They* decided who got a scrap and who didn't. *They* had to learn how to begrudgingly accept hangers-on like Cornelius (who was known as a proselyte of Judaism), and it took visions and direct revelations to get there. Israel's task was to eventually bless all the nations of the Earth, but—by God—the Earth's inhabitants had better come through *them*; they'd better pay their dues; they'd better acknowledge their benefactors—and some degree of groveling is expected, thank you very much.

This is how an Israelite thought.

So then some of Cornelius' men came to Peter. Their plan was to get Peter to go to Caesarea to talk to their boss. Watch the timing of God. Peter was just recovering from his rooftop revelation when there was a knock at the door.

Acts 10:17-23, from *The Message*:

> As Peter, puzzled, sat there trying to figure out what it all meant, the men sent by Cornelius showed up at Simon's front door. They called in, asking if there was a Simon, also called Peter, staying there. Peter, lost in thought, didn't hear them, so the Spirit whispered to him, "Three men are knocking at the door looking for you. Get down there and go with them. Don't ask any questions. I sent them to get you."

Peter saw inside a new room, but never went in.

Peter went down and said to the men, "I think I'm the man you're looking for. What's up?" They said, "Captain Cornelius, a God-fearing man well-known for his fair play—ask any Jew in this part of the country—was commanded by a holy angel to get you and bring you to his house so he could hear what you had to say." Peter invited them in and made them feel at home.

Peter acquiesced. Without the vision, he never would have gone. But watch what he does in Acts 10:23: "The next morning he got up and went with them. Some of his friends from Joppa went along. A day later they entered Caesarea."

Why did Peter take friends from Joppa with him to the home of Cornelius? For company? No. There was only one reason: Peter was forbidden by law to enter the home of a Gentile. Peter was entering new territory here; he was walking on the moon. There would be hell to pay back in Jerusalem if it were ever known that he, Peter, entered the home of a dog without good cause. The vision was good cause; Peter needed that; he needed a direct revelation that God was cleansing dogs. Peter wasn't sure why, yet. The sheer fact was shocking enough. Now God was asking him—no, telling him—to make nice inside the house of a dog. Peter took witnesses who eventually corroborated what could only turn out to be a strange event. Little did he know how strange. Not even the vision had sufficiently prepared Peter for what was about to occur at the home of Cornelius.

Peter arrived with his Circumcision brethren at the home of Cornelius. From the *Concordant Literal New Testament*, Acts 10:28-29—

He entered, and is finding many come together. He said to them, "You are versed in the fact how illicit it is for a man who is a Jew to join or come to another tribe, and God shows me not to say that any man is contaminating or unclean. Wherefore ... being sent after ... I came. I am inquiring to ascertain, then, on what account you send after me."

Cornelius then describes to Peter the visit from the angel, ending with:

"Now we are all present in God's sight to hear all that you have been bidden by the Lord" (Acts 10:33).

Then Peter spoke. I love the power of this out of the literal version:

> Of a truth I am grasping that God is not partial, but in every nation who is fearing Him and acting righteously is acceptable to Him. Of the word He dispatches to the sons of Israel bringing the evangel of peace through Jesus Christ (He is Lord of all), you are aware, the declaration coming to be down the whole of Judea, beginning from Galilee after the baptism which John heralds: Jesus from Nazareth, as God anoints Him with Holy Spirit and power, Who passed through as a benefactor and healer of all those who are tyrannized over by the Adversary, for God was with Him.
>
> —Acts 10:34-38, CLNT

Notice two things. Although Peter is bringing the good news of the advent of Jesus Christ to Cornelius, a man of the nations, Peter still bases the good news of God's acceptance on "fearing Him" and "acting righteously." It's all Peter knows. Secondly, he still associates the good news with "the baptism which John heralded." What was the baptism John heralded? "Now in those days, coming along is John the Baptist, heralding in the wilderness of Judea, saying: 'Repent! For near is the kingdom of the heavens!'" (Matthew 3:2).

What does John say to the Pharisees who came down to the Jordan River to investigate his ministry?

> Produce fruit worthy of repentance ... every tree which is

not producing ideal fruit is hewn down and cast into the fire
… For I, indeed, am baptizing you in water for repentance,
yet He Who is coming after me is stronger than I, whose
sandals I am not competent to bear. He will be baptizing
you in Holy Spirit and fire, Whose winnowing shovel is in
His hand, and He will be scouring His threshing floor, and
will be gathering His grain into His barn, yet the chaff will
He be burning up with unextinguished fire.
                                        —Matthew 3:8; 11-12

Peter, as we already know, carried on this theme of "repent,
then we'll talk about water." He did this on the day of Pentecost
in Acts 2:38: "Repent and be baptized each of you in the name of
Jesus Christ for the pardon of your sins, and you shall be obtaining
the gratuity of the Holy Spirit."
    Up until then, it had always been: Repent, then the spirit will
come; do right things for God, and He will do right things for
you; produce fruit, or you're toast.
    Five minutes before the shocking thing in Caesarea happened,
Peter was still saying to Cornelius: "Of a truth I am grasping that
God is not partial, but in every nation he who is fearing Him and
acting righteously is acceptable to Him" (Acts 10:34).
    Then the shocking thing happened.

    While Peter is still speaking these declarations, the Holy
    Spirit falls on all those hearing the Word. And amazed were
    the believers of the Circumcision, whoever came together
    with Peter, seeing that on the nations also the gratuity of
    the Holy Spirit has been poured out.
                                        —Acts 10:44-45, CLNT

    Their richest source of amazement was not that the Holy Spirit
was poured out, for that had happened before, not too long ago
on the famous day of Pentecost. Peter had begun his address that
day with: "Men, Jews, and all who are dwelling in Jerusalem!"
Question: If Peter's ensuing message at Pentecost was only for Jews,

then why did he add "and all who are dwelling in Jerusalem"? The audience is further defined for us in Acts 2:8-10, when each listener miraculously hears Peter's words in his or her native tongue.

> Now they were all amazed, and marveled, saying, "Lo! Are not all these who are speaking, Galileans? And how are we hearing, each in our own vernacular in which we were born? Parthians and Medes and Elamites and those dwelling in Mesopotamia, Judea, as well as Cappadocia, Pontus, and the province of Asia, Phrygia, Pamphylia, Egypt, and the parts of Libya about Cyrene, and the repatriated Romans, *both Jews and proselytes.*
>
> —CLNT

Jews were Jews, and proselytes were non-Jewish "hangers-on" to the Jewish message—dogs under the table. The blessing of Pentecost was for them as well, but no matter who got blessed then, they had to do one thing first:

"Repent and be baptized each of you in the name of Jesus Christ for the pardon of your sins, and you shall be obtaining the gratuity of the Holy Spirit" (Acts 2:38).

And it had to happen through the priestly mediation of Israel.

But now, this. For the first time since the coming of Christ, the Holy Spirit was poured out upon a non-Israelite, prior to baptism by an Israelite.

Needless to say, this stunned the Circumcision. Peter, flabbergasted, still couldn't operate apart from baptism. He needed the rite. He was raised in rites. Peter could not imagine that anything, even this, could occur without getting ceremoniously wet. If by some oddball occurrence he could not precede the spirit with baptism, he would sure as heck go out of his way to accomplish it afterward. "Then Peter answered, 'There cannot be anyone to forbid water, so that these are not to be baptized ...'" (Acts 10:47).

God's point had already been made, however. A baby-step had been made into the stunned Israelite mindset (and ours as well) that God was doing a new thing. There was coming a time in the not-too-distant future when any good and worthy thing a human did would occur after God's acceptance of him or her, not before it. This was unheard-of. We need to appreciate that. It was completely unheard-of and undreamed-of that God would accept into His bosom unrepentant, hardened, self-worshipping devil people.

The first example of this was Saul of Tarsus.

At the calling of Saul, no one yet knew that this Pharisee had just become the first member of an entirely new organization that not even Peter would belong to—*the body of Christ.* No one yet knew that God was beginning the formation of a people whom He would take to heaven to be the agents by whom He would reconcile that celestial world to Himself.

Neither did anyone know (not even Saul at the moment) that the keynote of the calling of this new body of people—from Saul onward until the last member of the body of Christ is called— would be grace. The world had seen a measure of God's grace throughout history, but nothing like the transcendent grace that God would reveal through the deranged Pharisee.

In "Rooted and Grounded in Love: Ephesians," A. E. Knoch writes:

> Love delights in secret surprises. Love's gifts gather grace as they are undeserved and unexpected. The precious quality of grace greatly enhances the riches of God's love. From love's hiding place in the inmost recesses of His affections, He has brought forth a surprise such as He only could have planned, so wondrous is the wisdom it reveals, so fathomless the affection it unfolds.

> Among the many secrets of Holy Writ, we have chosen to meditate upon the one which most closely concerns us in this eon (that secret administration which God concealed from previous eons in Himself, but which is now made known in this epistle). In Ephesians, the very heavens are

apprised of the variety of God's wisdom, and the whole universe will yet learn the transcendent wealth which is found in His favor. The object of such love is love responsive. The secret that reveals the activities of His heart should kindle a kindred flame in ours, and lead to the adoration which is His due.

Why did God choose Saul to bring this message to light? The answer should be obvious by now: Saul was His sworn enemy. True, Saul did not realize at the time that he was God's sworn enemy. By persecuting the followers of God's Son, though, that's what Saul became. As such, there was no more perfect vessel for God's display of transcendent grace.

HITLER-STYLE GRACE, ONLY MORE

Remember God's definition of grace: "Favor bestowed on those who deserve the opposite." If anyone deserves grace, then grace can no longer be called grace. When people chide me for teaching that because of the cross God will eventually—through rehabilitative judgments—shed His grace upon the entire race (Colossians 1:20; 1 Corinthians 15:22-23), the first figure of history to be shoved before me is Adolph Hitler. It happens every time.

"Do you mean to tell me," they say, "that Christ died for Hitler? Do you mean to tell me that He intends to reconcile the man who oversaw the killing of six million Jews?"

People launching this objection simply cannot believe that Hitler could ever fall beneath the cross in adoration. None of them were ever stubborn to the truth, I guess (never mind Romans 3:10, "There is none righteous, no not one"). Apparently, they all emerged from the womb sinless, praising Jesus. The famous verse, Romans 11:32, "God locks *all* up together in stubbornness," does have its notable exceptions, it seems. Theirs is the only case on record (beware; I am about to become completely facetious) in which anyone ever deserved grace. (Deserving grace is an oxymoron: I hope you see that.)

Objectors repeat by rote: "I am what I am by the grace of God," but their Hitler problem belies this pat religious sentiment. (It's only a pat religious sentiment when one doesn't really believe it.) What the objectors mean to say—and what they really believe—is: "I am what I am because I am good, and Hitler was a jackass."

(That last sentence would make a great Christian bumper sticker. But don't worry—you'll never see it.)

How could salvation be of grace—in these objectors' minds— when they have convinced themselves that Hitler blew it? If Hitler blew it, then *they* must have aced it. If they aced it (aced the salvation challenge, that is), then salvation is by acing it, rather than by grace. (I have searched my Scriptural concordance, and cannot find the phrase, "By acing it are you saved," anywhere.)

I'm not saying these people don't talk grace. They do. They sing it, too. They talk and sing grace, but can't play it. If they could play it, they would have to ask themselves, *Why me and not Hitler?* This golden question can only be asked by one awakened to and finally cognizant of one's deadly similarity to the Nazi dictator: "All have sinned and are wanting of the glory of God" (Romans 3:23).

In the wake of such an awakening (whenever it comes), the former Hitler-haters (i.e., grace-doubters) would arrive at the same Scriptural conclusion I've come to: *The God of all circumstances breaks everyone at different times.* By the grace of God, some of us realize the grace of God now; Hitler realizes it later.

"As in Adam all are dying; thus also in Christ shall all be vivified, *yet every one in his own order*" (1 Corinthians 15:22-23).

"We rely on the living God, Who is the Savior of *all* humans, *especially* of those who believe" (1 Timothy 4:10).

THE FOREMOST SINNER

I really make a nuisance of myself when I say to the objectors: "Why are you bringing up Hitler in the first place, when the worst sinner in history was Saul of Tarsus?" Generally, they dislike this line of questioning.

Paul—formerly Saul—is the one who called himself the foremost sinner. In his first letter to Timothy, he said:

> Faithful is the saying, and worthy of all welcome, that Christ Jesus came into the world to save sinners, foremost of whom am I. But therefore was I shown mercy, that In me, the foremost [sinner], Jesus Christ should be displaying *all* His patience, for a pattern of those who are about to be believing on Him.
>
> —1 Timothy 1:15-16, CLNT

Hitler persecuted the Jews; he did not persecute God. Saul was the enemy of God Himself, and His Son, Jesus Christ. No matter how many Jews Hitler killed, Saul's attempt to annihilate God trumps it. At his spiritual smiting on the road to Damascus, Saul cried out, "Who art Thou, Lord?" The answer came: "I am Jesus, the Nazarene, Whom you are persecuting" (Acts 22:8-9).

That was a *nice* way to put it.

If God displayed *all* His patience in the case of Saul, then not even Hitler elicited more of God's patience. Please re-read the preceding sentence. It took every bit of God's patience not only to tolerate, but to shower with grace this freak of nature—Saul. This is a simple point of logic.

God exhausted all His patience with Saul; therefore, Saul of Tarsus was the worst sinner ever to walk the planet. Saul was worse than Adam, worse than Judas, worse than Stalin, worse than Hitler, and worse than Charles Manson. None of these people required *all* of God's patience.

So what did God do to the one man on Earth deserving the direst doom? "Yet the grace of our Lord overwhelms, with faith and love in Christ Jesus" (1 Timothy 1:14).

Perfect. If God cracked the hardest nut—against Saul's will— then what can stop God from overwhelming everyone else when the time is right? According to the testimony of Romans 5:18-19, nothing will stop Him:

> Consequently, then, as it was through one offense for all humankind for condemnation, thus also it is through one just award for all humankind for life's justifying. For even as, through the disobedience of the one human, the many were constituted sinners, thus also, through the obedience of the One, the many shall be constituted just.

Some will say, "Yes, well, Paul was an exception to the rule. We still have to be worthy nowadays. We have to make a wise decision for Christ."

Paul may have been an exception to the rule *then*, but no one has been called any differently *since* then.

Saul was not on his way to a prayer meeting. Saul was not on his way to a revival. Saul no more chose Jesus Christ on the road to Damascus than a man shoved beneath Niagara Falls chooses to get wet. Saul said, "The grace of God overwhelmed me." Then he said: "But therefore was I shown mercy, that in me, the foremost

If Hitler blew it, then they must have aced it.

[sinner], Jesus Christ should be displaying *all* His patience, for a pattern of those who are about to be believing on Him" (1 Timothy 1:16).

Paul, then, became the pattern of those about to be believing, not the exception. Not everyone gets struck to the ground and literally blinded by Christ, but the essence of salvation is the same: overwhelming, unavoidable, unrejectable. When God decides to do it, He does it—and does it independently of human effort or acquiescence. Acquiescence follows, rather than precedes, God's call. God did not ask Saul, "Would you like to have your life turned around today?"

Damascus Road was not an altar call.

BENEVOLENT INVADER

People have told me: "God is a gentleman." I say, "Really? Show me the verse." Rather, God is a Benevolent Invader of peoples' lives. If God does not act upon us, we do not act. His is a despotic grace. It overwhelms first, asks questions later. Belief is not the quarter that kicks out the gumball of salvation: Belief is the reaction to one's realization of God's historical act.

Christ saves us, then gives us belief. That is the divine order. Belief is the caboose to the engine that delivers from sin. The engine is the cross. In Romans 5:8, Paul says, "While we are still sinners, Christ died for our sakes."

Belief is an act of righteousness that no sinner can muster. And yet Christ died for our sakes while we were still sinners. Therefore, it is sinners who are saved, not believers. Belief, while important, merely assents to a foregone fact. Otherwise, salvation comes via belief, rather than Christ.

This cannot be.

We are not saved because we believe; we believe because we are saved.

Faith in faith is deadly doctrine. Better to see faith as a gift, which it is (Romans 12:3; Philippians 1:29), than a self-wrought token bartered for heaven.

Back to Saul. Every person apprehended by Jesus Christ since Saul has followed in the pattern of being overwhelmed by God, not invited by Him. They might not feel the full fury of the invasion, as did Saul, but it's no less there.

It's no less a knocking off of our socks.

God waited until Saul had ventured outside Israel to pinch him by the scruff and bring him to eye level. This outside-the-city-limits call is significant—and suggestive of the new move of God that would soon grace tree-worshippers with not only grander doses of God's favor than anyone had ever known, but a destiny undreamed-of by Israelites. Eventually, this provoked Israel to such jealousy and fury that her first instinct was to kill the messenger.

Paul needed the sessions with Jesus Christ in Arabia. He needed them before all hell broke loose.

Directly following Paul's conversion, the spirit of God led him into the desert. Whenever men of God need to get away and let go of earthly treasure for a spell, God takes them to deserts. I love this. There's something pure and clean and simple, so undistracting, about a desert region. Besides the summits of mountains, deserts may be the grandest earthly places in which to embrace the truly important.

Paul wrote later to the Galatians:

> Now, when it delights God, Who severs me from my mother's womb and calls me through His grace, to unveil His Son in me that I may be evangelizing Him among the nations, I did not immediately submit it to flesh and blood, neither came I up to Jerusalem to those who were apostles before me, but I came away into Arabia, and I return again to Damascus.
>
> —Galatians 1:15-17, CLNT

What exactly happened in Arabia? Oh, nothing much. Just personal meetings with the Lord Jesus Christ.

Much later, when Paul defended himself to King Agrippa in Caesarea on his way to Rome for trial, he related to the king his conversion, saying:

> I hear a voice that was saying to me in the Hebrew vernacular, "Saul! Saul! Why are you persecuting Me? Hard is it for you to be kicking against the goads!" Now I say, "Who art Thou, Lord?" Now the Lord said, "I am Jesus, Whom you are persecuting.
>
> "But rise and stand on your feet, for I was seen by you for this, to fix upon you before for a deputy and a witness *both of what you have perceived and that in which I will be seen by you*, extricating you from the people and from the nations, to whom I am commissioning you, to open their eyes, to turn them about from darkness to light and from the authority of Satan to God."
>
> — Acts 26:14-18, CLNT

Paul saw Jesus Christ on that road, yes. However, this was only the first installment of several visits to come. Note that Paul was to be a witness both of what he had perceived (on the day Christ blinded him), "and that in which I will be seen by you (further revelations to Paul)" (Acts 26:16).

Paul's ministry went "from glory to glory" (2 Corinthians 3:18). Paul saw—then he saw more. And then he saw even more. For Paul, it was progressive. God unfolded the secrets to Paul a little at a time. After Paul, there have been no new revelations. In Colossians 1:25, Paul says one of the boldest things a human being can possibly say. Either this man is the biggest egotist ever to walk Earth, or he wrote the truth. I endorse the latter view.

I am now rejoicing in my sufferings for you, and am filling

> up in my flesh, in His stead, the deficiencies of the afflictions of Christ, for His body, which is the ecclesia of which I became a dispenser, in accord with the administration of God, which is granted to me for you, *to complete the Word of God*—the secret that has been concealed from the eons ...
> —Colossians 1:24-25, CLNT

This crazy ex-Pharisee completed the Word of God.

What was begun by Moses thousands of years before when he wrote the first five books of the Bible was completed by Paul when he put the last bit of ink to parchment in his second letter to Timothy. The scroll got rolled; someone took it from the prison, delivered it to Timothy—and that was it. God had revealed Himself to humanity. Every final thing God wanted to say to us in this grim and dusty life—including His final secret of the reconciliation of the universe through the body of Christ—God said through Paul.

How the angels in heaven must have rejoiced at the birth of this man. How they must have watched him through childhood, witnessed his coming manhood, cringed to see his developing enmity against the very Deity he would one day die for, rejoiced again at his calling, and then executed celestial somersaults when he penned the last of God's instructions for us mortals this side of immortality.

Paul's letters are the latest, greatest revelations to human beings from the Creator of the universe.

Imagine sitting in the desert next to a campfire at night, your butt on the hard desert floor, legs folded, conversing with the Creator *of* that desert floor, a Creator whose face—incredibly enough—reflects orange from the fire, just like yours. He tells you secrets hidden from the foundation of the world—and then pours you a cup of coffee.

Honestly.

Then imagine you are a young Gentile man—a proselyte of

Judaism—sauntering toward an outdoor Damascus market to buy onions and pomegranates for your mother. Approaching the same market is the man recently returned from desert episodes in Arabia with the risen Savior of Israel. This man looks like every other man—maybe a little worse—and yet his being is infused with new revelations unknown to any other human.

Someone nudges you and says, "Look! That's him!"

You have always had spiritual thoughts and questions. You have always looked to the stars and wondered, "Why?" So you approach him (God has given you a spirit of boldness) and introduce yourself. The man is here for olives. Yet it's at the onion table where you start talking. Three hours later, you are finishing coffee with him at the Al-Kassour Café on Oukaibeh Street. An hour after that, you are helping your mother unload her groceries.

"What took so long, Hijaz?"

"I met a man at the market. He told me things about God that I have never heard before."

"We worship the God of Israel. What can be new?"

"Mother! In our generation, only a few miles from here, the Son of God took flesh. Think of it. We are a nine-day walk away. We could have actually spoken with Him. What were we doing the day He was crucified? Do you remember? The prophesied Messiah was being crucified, and what were we doing?"

"Was that the day it got dark?"

"Yes! We were playing cards. Do you remember?"

"Of course. With the Roummahehs."

"Yes. We were playing cards—while they were killing God's Son. Certainly, *that* was new."

"Who is this man you speak of?"

"Saul is his name. He is from Tarsus originally, but after that he was of the religious order in Jerusalem that—"

"Pshah! Not the one who came here to take us away. To kill us. *That* Saul?"

"I know what you're thinking, but it is not that way."

"What does he tell you? Does he say it with a knife to your

throat?"

"Mother, please. The risen Christ—"

"I asked you a question, Hijaz! I said—what does he tell you?"

"He tells me things we have never heard before, not even from the Jews. He says we do not need to be baptized. He says God is blessing us now apart from Israel. There's to be no more circumcision—no more rites. None at all."

"Hijaz!"

"And we are not just forgiven our sins. Listen: God is *justifying* us. He is giving us His own righteousness through the shedding of His blood. Our sins are not even to count against us any more."

"Stop! Show me *any* of these things in the sacred writings of the Jews."

"Some of these things are there, Mother … but some are not."

"Oh! I see. He makes things up out of his head, then. And you believe him, Hijaz?"

"These are new things. They are secrets that have been hidden in God."

"Secrets that the Messiah Himself did not speak. Is that what you are telling me?"

"It was not the time. But He speaks again. We are still to be holy, like Israel, but God is taking us further. He is blessing us with *spiritual* blessings—blessings that shall not be upon this Earth."

"You are drunk then. It must be, for you speak as a crazy person. What do you mean, 'He speaks again?' Who would dare add to the Writings? Are the Writings of the prophets and the fathers not good enough for this Saul?"

"But he, too, will write things …"

"Blasphemy!"

"It's not blasphemy. I know how this must sound."

"And tell me, Hijaz, if you can: Where does he hear these evil things?"

"They are not evil. He hears them from the resurrected Christ Himself. This is what I meant when I said, 'He speaks again.' Jesus Christ appeared to Saul personally; He came to him as a light brighter than the sun."

"Oh! Now I see. Of course. Not found in the Jewish Writings, but of course. Jesus *Christ* comes to him. Personally. I should have known that. And He speaks with Him. Yes. And does He meet with Him regularly, Hijaz? For coffee perhaps?"

"In fact, he does. He speaks with him in the desert."

"Perfect! In the desert. How much did you pay for these onions, my dear son?"

"I know how this must sound."

"*How much did you pay for these onions, Hijaz?*"

"Six and a quarter."

"Good, now chop them for the soup. You are mad, and I will hear no more of this."

Hijaz wrote later, in his diary:

> *Mother is incredulous and cannot even entertain the idea. I can only imagine, then, what the Jews themselves must think, or will think. I meet with Saul again tomorrow, at the Al-Kassour Café. I am praying for him. Of one thing I am certain: This man speaks truth. I have never been more sure of anything. I suppose it can only be the witness of the Holy Spirit inside me. Another man in the community, a respected man, Ananias, has befriended him. I told this to Mother, but she would not hear it.*
>
> *Saul's life cannot be anything but hard now. I cannot imagine how he will suffer. He knows it, too. Saul said Jesus Himself told him that he would suffer for the message he will bring to bless us, to bless we who were without God in the world, but who will now be blessed above all. Praise the name of God! And to think I was one of the first to hear. Dear Holy God, please protect Your messenger Saul. I pray for him by the day, and sometimes by the minute.*

After Peter's vision of the sheet and the unclean animals, and his encounter with Cornelius in Caesarea, one would think Peter would now be revved up to gather some of the other apostles and head out to the nations to preach the gospel of the kingdom. Yet nowhere in the remainder of Acts does this occur.

When Peter returned to Jerusalem, the leadership had already heard about his encounter with Cornelius—at the home of Cornelius.

> Now the apostles and the brethren who are of Judea hear that the nations also receive the Word of God. Now when Peter went up into Jerusalem, those of the Circumcision doubted him, saying that, "You entered to men having uncircumcision, and you ate with them!"
> —Acts 11:2-3, CLNT

Remember, these are not apostate Jews; they are believers in Jesus Christ, just as much as Peter is a believer in Jesus Christ. They know they are destined to eventually herald repentance and baptism to all the nations. But this isn't supposed to happen until the 1,000-year kingdom—the Millennium. Judgment begins in the House of God, they know. And they are the House of God. God must call them out and refine them before they are fit to proselytize the world.

Giving a handful of dogs a taste of the good news was one thing. But eating with them?

"You ate with them!"

It was a good thing Peter had taken witnesses. The next verses of Acts chapter 11 detail Peter's defense to the brethren. Only Peter could have gotten the following result: "Now, on hearing these things, they are quiet, and glorify God, saying, 'Consequently, to the nations also God gives repentance unto life!'" (Acts 11:18).

Watch what happens next. "Those indeed, then, who are dispersed from the affliction, which is occurring over Stephen, passed through as far as Phoenicia and Cyprus and Antioch, speaking the word *to no one except Jews only*" (Acts 11:19).

The brethren also spoke to Hellenists (verse 20), who were displaced Jews assuming Greek customs. But there was not a full-fledged follow-up on the part of Israel to Peter's revelation. Rather, as I said earlier, the way was then paved for Saul to begin a completely new tack among the heathen, with the blessing of Peter and the other leaders.

Peter and the other leaders could not have dreamed how far and how deep the gospel to the heathen would go.

Paul liked Peter, and vice-versa. Whenever Paul was in town, the two would hang out. Within the circles of those professing Jesus Christ, Peter and Paul were celebrities, often mentioned in the same breath. Paul later wrote adamantly to a group of believers in Galatia: "Paul, an apostle not from men, neither through a man, but through Jesus Christ and God, the Father" (Galatians 1:1).

Peter could easily have taken offense at that, but he knew how true it was. How could it have potentially offended the biggest name in the Jerusalem church? You can see it more clearly out of *The Message*: "My authority for writing to you does not come from any popular vote of the people, nor does it come through the appointment of some human higher-up" (Galatians 1:1).

"Nor does it come through the appointment of some human higher-up." This was a nice way for Paul to say: "I know Peter is my friend. I know you have seen me hanging out with him. I know we have many things in common. But you need to know one very important thing concerning the particular gospel I herald to Gentiles: *I did not get it from Peter.*"

In case anyone missed this in the first part of his letter, Paul reiterates it a few paragraphs later: "For I am making known to you, brethren, as to the evangel which is being brought by me, that it is not in accord with humans. For neither did I accept it from a human, nor was I taught it, but it came through a revelation of Jesus Christ" (Galatians 1:11-12).

This corroborates the fantastic fact I submitted earlier—the gospel Paul taught to non-Israelites came via a direct revelation from the glorified Christ. Otherwise, we would have seen Paul traveling immediately to Jerusalem to sit at the feet of Peter to take a "Jesus 101" course. Yet here's how it actually happened:

> When it delights God, Who severs me from my mother's womb and calls me through His grace, to unveil His Son in me that I may be evangelizing Him among the nations, I did not immediately submit it to flesh and blood, neither came I up to Jerusalem to those who were apostles before me, but I came away into Arabia, and I return again to Damascus.
> —Galatians 1:15-17, CLNT

Thus, it was Paul who had to teach the new Jesus course ("Jesus 202") to Peter. Check out the first two verses of Galatians, chapter 2:

> Thereupon, after the lapse of fourteen years, I again went up to Jerusalem with Barnabas, taking Titus also along with me. Now I went up in accord with a revelation, and submitted to them the evangel which I am heralding among the nations, yet privately to those of repute, lest somehow I should be racing or ran for naught.
> —CLNT

These are the verses which finally convinced me that Paul preached a different evangel (gospel) than Peter, the man to whom Jesus gave the keys to the terrestrial kingdom: *Paul had to go to Jerusalem to explain his gospel to Peter.*

Let's not overlook Titus. "I again went up to Jerusalem with Barnabas, taking Titus also along with me." Who was Titus? Titus was an uncircumcised Greek—a non-Israelite with an intact penis. To employ even baser terms, Titus was a guinea pig, a test case. If circumcision was essential for a man to be right with God—as it always had been up until that point—then Titus would have to submit to it. If it were not essential, then Titus would (and did) become a walking testimony to a new truth. "But not even Titus, who is with me, being a Greek, is compelled to be circumcised"

(Galatians 2:3).

In this distant day, we can scarcely grasp the significance of this; how important it was—how radical it was. If I were Titus, however, I'm not sure I would have embraced with joy my new mission and purpose in life:

"Titus, you're a believer in Jesus Christ, correct?"

"Yes, sir."

"Accepted completely into the family of God?"

"As far as I know, sir."

"Then, please, sir—so I may verify with my own eyes the fantastic thing told me concerning you—would you kindly lift your toga?"

8.
"MY GOSPEL"

"MY GOSPEL"

Our Lord was either the biggest deceiver in the history of the planet, or Jesus Christ was precisely Who He said He was. Israel's priests killed Him because He claimed to be God's Son. The boldest statements of Christ left no middle ground as to His identity and mission. Other religions, such as Islam, make Jesus Christ merely a great prophet. If this is so, then He was not a great prophet, but rather a lying prophet. What prophet claims the right to be worshipped as Deity? Prophethood was not His testimony. Jesus' testimony was that He was the very Son of God—and that He pre-existed Abraham (John 8:58).

Not much wiggle room there.

Thus also with Paul. Either this man had an ego the size of the Acropolis and was the worst deceiver since his Master, or God *had* brought to Earth a completely new gospel and handed it exclusively to Paul.

Here, from the *Concordant Literal New Testament*, are a few of Paul's most audacious statements:

■ **Romans 2:16**—

"God will be judging the hidden things of humanity, according to *my evangel*, through Jesus Christ."

■ **Romans 16:25**—

"Now to Him Who is able to establish you in accord with *my evangel* ..."

■ **Ephesians 3:6-7**—

"In spirit the nations are to be joint enjoyers of an allotment, and a joint body, and joint partakers of the promise in Christ Jesus, through *the evangel of which I became the dispenser.*"

■ **Ephesians 3:8-10**—

"*To me*, less than the least of all saints, was granted this grace: to bring the evangel of the untraceable riches of Christ to the nations, and to enlighten all as to what is the administration of the secret, which has been concealed from the eons in God ... that now may be made known."

■ **Colossians 1:22-23**—

"And you, being once estranged and enemies in comprehension, by wicked acts, yet now He reconciles by His body of flesh, through His death, to present you holy and flawless and unimpeachable in His sight, since surely you are persisting in the faith, grounded and settled and are not being removed from the expectation of the evangel which you hear is being heralded in the entire creation which is under heaven *of which I, Paul, became the dispenser.*"

DIVINE SWITCH-UPS

The book of Acts graduates from flesh to spirit. Appropriately, it is a series of acts and counter-acts. Something bad happens to Israel—at the same time something good happens for the nations. Therefore, at the stoning of Stephen, the writer of Acts

ACTS CHAPTER 1

Israel

Nations

ACTS CHAPTER 28

Nations

Israel

Acts is a series of acts and counter-acts.

(Luke) mentions that the murderers laid their coats at the feet of a Pharisee named Saul. God closes a door (the stoning of Stephen), while opening a window (the introduction of Saul)—and both in the same context; thank you, God.

In the first few chapters of Acts, Israel was flying high at the door of the kingdom, while the nations were nowhere. But by Acts chapter 12, Israel's fortunes had deteriorated: Stephen was stoned, the disciples scattered, James killed, and Peter eventually exiled to Babylon. In chapter 9, however, God called Saul, and by chapter 13, the nations were rejoicing in unprecedented grace. No one yet knew that God had something up His sleeve for the Gentile nations (a secret concealed in God until Paul, Ephesians 3:9), which required Israel to be blinded, become apostate, and to have the fulfillment of her calling stalled for a couple of thousand years. By the end of the book of Acts, then, Paul was in Rome writing Ephesians, and Israel was set aside (Acts 28:25-28) until the complement of the nations may be entering (Romans 11:25).

NEW SPIRITUAL HEADQUARTERS

In conjunction with this gradual declension of Israel and ascension of the nations, Antioch replaces Jerusalem—in Acts 11:25—as the spiritual headquarters of the world. What a major switch-up. Where did Peter preach at Pentecost in Acts chapter 2? Jerusalem. How long had Jerusalem been God's headquarters? For a long time—up until Paul.

The Greek elements of the name "Antioch" are INSTEAD-UPHOLD. God's truth is now upheld here, among heathen, instead of in Jerusalem, where Israelite apostasy reigns.

A fascinating thing happens, in Antioch, in Acts, chapter 13, which serves as a microcosm of the whole of God's purpose in these apparently chaotic times.

THE ADVENTURES OF SERGIUS AND DR. KNOW-IT-ALL

Acts 13:1-3, from *The Message*:

> The congregation in Antioch was blessed with a number of prophet-preachers and teachers: Barnabas, Simon, nicknamed Niger, Lucius the Cyrenian, Manaen, an advisor to the ruler Herod, and Saul. One day as they were worshipping God—they were also fasting as they waited for guidance—the Holy Spirit spoke: "Take Barnabas and Saul and commission them for the work I have called them to do." So they commissioned them. In that circle of intensity and obedience, of fasting and praying, they laid hands on their heads and sent them off.

You heard the testimony from *The Message*, above. "So they commissioned them. In that circle of intensity and obedience, of fasting and praying, they laid hands on their heads and sent them off."

I love the words, "intensity and obedience"; that's precisely what was about to happen.

As I have been telling you, the body of Christ is a distinct entity, apart from those Israelites God called to be part of the earthly kingdom. In Scripture, there's no such thing as "the bride of Christ." Israel is continually referred to as a bride. But the nations? Never. God did not marry the nations, but He surely did marry Israel. He divorced her as well, but He will take her back. Israel is compared to the New Jerusalem, and she is called "the bride of the lambkin" (Revelation 21:9). Sounds like the closest relationship one could possibly have with Christ—to be His bride. It isn't. The closest relationship is to be a member of His body. God revealed this secret through Paul—that there was such a thing as the "body of Christ."

The nations are not to become the bride, for Christ already has one of those. They will become His very body—the Groom

Himself.

Paul was the first member. It had to start sometime, with someone. When we think of God we think "infinite," forgetting that He works step-by-step through the process of time. Until Christ apprehended Saul on the road to Damascus, there was no such thing as a member of the body of Christ. Paul was the first one. For awhile, he was the only one.

When the spirit separated Paul and Barnabas for the work of this singular and unique commission, a man of the nations—a heathen government official—was about to become the second purely Gentile member of the body of Christ.

Acts 13:4-7, from *The Message*:

> Sent off on their new assignment by the Holy Spirit, Barnabas and Saul went down to Seleucia and caught a ship for Cyprus. The first thing they did when they put in at Salamis was preach God's Word in the Jewish meeting places. They had John along to help out as needed. They traveled the length of the island, and at Paphos came upon a Jewish wizard who had worked himself into the confidence of the governor, Sergius Paulus, an intelligent man not easily taken in by charlatans. The wizard's name was Bar-Jesus. He was as crooked as a corkscrew.

Allow me to formally introduce our leading players in this drama about to unfold upon the island of Cyprus.

Paul: First member of the body of Christ.
Sergius Paulus: Governor of Paphos; man of the nations; intact penis; tree worshiper; intelligent man, not easily taken by charlatans.
Bar-Jesus: Jewish wizard; Sergius Paulus suck-up; crooked as a corkscrew.
Barnabas: Along for the ride.

Again, something was about to happen that would define our

era. A picture is worth a thousand words. Watch:

> The governor invited Barnabas and Saul in, wanting to hear God's Word firsthand from them. But Dr. Know-It-All (that's the wizard's name in plain English) stirred up a ruckus, trying to divert the governor from becoming a believer. But Saul (or Paul), full of the Holy Spirit and looking him straight in the eye, said ...
> —Acts 13:7-9, *The Message*

We'll be getting to what Paul said in a moment.

First, I want you to notice that here—right here before your eyes—is the magical moment when Saul becomes Paul: "But Saul (or Paul), full of the Holy Spirit ..."

The *Concordant Literal New Testament* says: "Now Saul, who is also Paul ..."

I call Acts chapter 13 the beginning of Paul, the apostle, and the start of his official ministry. Not only has God just changed his name from Saul to Paul (Saul is Hebrew; Paul is Greek), but this name change coincides with Paul's new commission to non-Israelites. For the first time, Paul encountered Jewish antagonism toward new truth in the presence of a Gentile—get used to it, Paul; it's going to be your lot in life for the next half-century.

God set up this encounter in Antioch as a parable for our instruction. Paul teaches on it directly, later, in Romans, chapter 11, which I will be getting to soon.

The governor wants to hear truth. In parable, this man represents the nations who are naturally curious to hear what God could possibly have for them, seeing as they have been "alienated from the citizenship of Israel, and guests of the promise covenants, having no expectation, and without God in the world" (Ephesians 2:12), since Genesis, chapter 12.

What is the perpetual crime of Israel? Incessantly damming up the river of God's favor and blessing. As we have already seen, Israel is willing—albeit begrudgingly—to see a few dogs blessed, as long as the dogs come through them. God forbid the dogs should be blessed directly. May God forbid even further that they should be graced and granted to skip any and all works of law—required for Circumcision believers—and be blessed in the act of idol-worship.

In Antioch, the role of the grace-damming Jew falls, in parable, to Bar-Jesus.

"But Dr. Know-It-All stirred up a ruckus, trying to divert the governor from becoming a believer" (Acts 13:8). The Concordant version has: "Now Elymas, the 'Magician' (for thus is his name construed), withstood them, seeking to pervert the proconsul from the faith." The Concordant version is literal, yes, but you can't beat Dr. Know-It-All stirring up a ruckus.

Watch what Paul does and says to Dr. Know-It-All. Here's the parable, a microcosm of our present era. I'm quoting from *The Message*:

> But Saul (or Paul), full of the Holy Spirit and looking him straight in the eye, said, "You bag of wind, you parody of a devil—why, you stay up nights inventing schemes to cheat people out of God. But now you've come up against God Himself, and your game is up. You're about to go blind—no sunlight for you for a good long stretch." He was plunged immediately into a shadowy mist and stumbled around, begging people to take his hand and show him the way.
> —Acts 13: 9-11

Oh, how I love that. What must the governor be thinking? How will the governor, Sergius Paulus, react to this stranger—this Paul, whose name was Saul five minutes ago—landing on this island with a new message of grace and acceptance from God, and blinding his personal Jewish Know-It-All? Will he have Paul's head on a platter? We don't have to guess. Verse 12 of Acts, chapter 13 says: "When the governor saw what happened, he became a believer, full of enthusiasm over what they were saying about the Master."

Here, God presents His program in a vignette on the island of Cyprus: God blinds a Jew (via Paul) to make way for a man of

Before the big meeting, Barnabas doubts their chances.

the nations. If the Jews are going to withstand God's plan, then God will blind them to make way for the nations. In the book of Acts, the 1,000-year kingdom proclaimed by Abraham, by Moses, by John the Baptist, by Jesus Christ Himself, and then by Peter at Pentecost, is slowly—albeit temporarily—dissolving into the shadows. But not for naught. Far from it. For as the kingdom-hope of Israel dissolves, the light to the nations—Paul—takes up the slack, and then some.

"You are about to go blind—no sunshine for you for a good long stretch."

Paul explains the parable in Romans 11:7-8:

> What then? What Israel is seeking for, this she did not encounter, yet the chosen encountered it. Now the rest were calloused, even as it is written, God gives them a spirit of stupor, eyes not to be observing, and ears not to be hearing, till this very day.
>
> —CLNT

What we saw in a span of five minutes on the island of Cyprus, today encompasses an entire era. To make way for this new evangel, this gospel of grace, it was first necessary for God Himself to blind His chosen nation to their own calling. In a manner of speaking, He had to "make space" for the nations. By temporarily clearing Israel from the table, He allows for the coming grace. Think about it. Had Israel accepted her Messiah in the book of Acts, chapter 2, where would we be? (Where would Sergius Paulus have been if Paul had not silenced his magician?) Where would we be if Israel had accepted Him in Acts, chapter 7, instead of stoning Stephen? We weep at the stoning of Stephen, and yet at the same time are forced to rejoice at what Israel's failure has produced. We must rejoice, for: "If their offense is the world's riches and their discomfiture the nations' riches, how much rather that which fills them!" (Acts 11:12).

Israel will one day be filled (Romans 11:26-27), but for now she is blinded, and nothing can stop it. God Himself did this. God does not adjust to circumstances. God did not witness the stubbornness of Israel, slap His forehead, and then devise a Plan B that would bless the nations with an unheard-of gospel of grace and peace. Read: "God *gives* them a spirit of stupor."

God blinded Israel as surely as Paul blinded the Jewish magician. The magician did not blind himself; Israel does not self-stupefy. Some people would like to believe that, so they could blame her. It's so easy to feel self-righteous. Paul anticipates this, so he also tells the Romans in this same context, chapter 11, verses 25-26:

> For I am not willing for you to be ignorant of this secret, brethren, lest you may be passing for prudent among yourselves, that callousness, in part, on Israel has come, until the complement of the nations may be entering. And thus all Israel shall be saved, according as it is written.
>
> —CLNT

The Message is good here:

> I want to lay all this out on the table as clearly as I can, friends. This is complicated. It would be easy to misinterpret what's going on and arrogantly assume that you're royalty and they're just rabble, out on their ears for good. But that's not it at all. This hardness on the part of insider Israel toward God is temporary. Its effect is to open things up to all the outsiders so that we end up with a full house. Before it's all over, there will be a complete Israel.
>
> —Romans 11:25-26

What would *you* think? For centuries, Israel has been God's pet and you, a Gentile, have been nothing. You have heard of the goings-on in Jerusalem, and some people say that the kingdom is about to arrive—the 1,000 years of peace when Jesus Christ will rule on Earth with a reborn Israel, giving obedient dogs some choice handouts.

But as you watch the goings-on in Israel, something strange happens. Things were off to a fabulous start in Acts, chapter 2, when the disciples ran from the upper room in a holy froth and the leader of the band—Peter—spoke eloquently in fifty-two languages simultaneously. On this day, thousands came to the faith of Jesus Christ and were baptized. Even people of the nations were baptized, but blessed only in relation to their subservience to Israel.

Then come some disturbing trends. The Sanhedrin call Peter, James, and John into the temple, to explain themselves. They do, and get beaten. This is a bad sign. These men—Peter, James, and John—are to be the leaders of the kingdom, and Israel is supposed to be reborn as a nation. This ancient prophesy now looks doubtful.

Next, Stephen is stoned; James (the Lord's brother) is killed by the sword; the faithful are dispersed by a terrible persecution (perpetrated by none other than our good man, Saul), and, well, it doesn't look much like the 1,000 years of peace to you.

Then you hear from this rogue teacher that you are to be blessed with heavenly blessings (not earthly ones, like Israel), and that God accepts you as you are—apart from rites and ceremonies like baptism and circumcision. You don't have to go to the temple; you don't have to pay alms; you don't have to humble yourself; you don't even have to call Peter to come to your house, so that he can hurry and baptize you after the spirit falls. Rather, you are justified by faith alone (it can happen in the privacy of your own home), and now you have peace with God because of what Jesus Christ did on the cross, not because of what you might or might not do for Him.

And then you discover (though much later) that not only are you hopping-skipping-and-jumping over Israel in the matter of undeserved blessing, but you are to be taken to heaven and seated among celestial beings, far above the place where Israel is supposed to manage a kingdom with Jesus Christ as Chief Priest.

What else would you think but that poor Israel was done for;

you have taken her place, and God surely thinks more highly of you than those disobedient Jews.

Paul combats precisely this attitude in Romans, chapter 11. For a person of the nations—a Gentile—it would be so easy to misinterpret the new development. In fact, it was easy for everyone to misinterpret it (Jews and Gentiles alike) because no one except Paul realized that a new era—a pause in God's plan for Israel—had come. So, Paul said in Romans 11:25: "I am not willing for you to be ignorant of this secret, brethren."

HIDDEN BY GOD

Paul wrote an utter secret ("I am not willing for you to be ignorant of this secret"), hidden in the counsels of God from the foundation of the world. No one could have dreamed that the kingdom God promised to Israel (ruling the Earth) would be rejected by Israel and temporarily set aside, let alone that her rejection would make way for unfathomable draughts of grace to be unleashed upon—of all people—non-Israelites.

> By revelation the secret is made known to me ... in spirit the nations are to be joint enjoyers of an allotment, and a joint body, and joint partakers of the promise in Christ Jesus, through the evangel of which I became the dispenser, in accord with the gratuity of the grace of God, which is granted to me in accord with His powerful operation.
> —Ephesians 3:3-7, CLNT

The hardness on Israel is temporary. God's purpose was to inaugurate an era of grace unforeseen by anyone. It was a secret revealed only to Paul. Not even Peter knew about it; Paul had to tell him. Paul had to tell everyone.

We are still living in this era. It's called, "the era of the nations," or "the time of the Gentiles." Where would we be if this hadn't

You are hopping-skipping-and-jumping over Israel.

happened? Before you go cursing Israel for her stupidity, think of that. If Israel had not been stupid, you would not be a member of the body of Christ. Had Israel not been divinely hardened, you would never have known the grace of God. You would still be apart from Christ, alienated from the citizenship of Israel, and guests of the promise covenants, having no expectation, and without God in the world (Ephesians 2:11-12).

Apart from this era of Israel's blindness, you are a nobody; you may not have even been born. Well? If Israel had accepted her Messiah in Acts, chapter 2, then the kingdom would have come; lions would have lain down with lambs, and by this time everyone would be luxuriating on a New Earth. Why would God have needed *you?* But God does need you. He longs for you, and He made gracious provision for you by giving Israel a spirit of stupor. So don't curse Israel. Rather, thank God for her.

"SPIRITUAL ISRAEL": A BAD MISTAKE

Thinking God has finished with Israel is a bad mistake. In spite of Paul's clear testimony here in Romans 11 that the callousness upon Israel is temporary, some insist it is permanent. What about the hundreds of Old Testament prophesies concerning the literal people and her literal kingdom? Forget those prophesies. Israel was too stubborn, so God threw up His hands and gave up on her, they say.

Ah—but God's promises stubbornly remain. The only way the God-is-permanently-finished-with-Israel crowd can save face (and keep from the tacit implication that God lies) is to say that, yes, God will fulfill His promises to Israel, but not literally. He will fulfill them "spiritually" (I believe they mean, "metaphorically") in an entirely different people, namely, Gentiles. Thus, the nations become "spiritual Israel," and God somehow still gets credit for literally fulfilling His promises to the literal descendants of Abraham.

Such thinking is not only convoluted—but erroneous. How

much more God-honoring and straight-forward to believe Paul's plain testimony in Romans, chapter 11; namely, that God temporarily set aside Israel to make way for a new administration ("the administration of the grace of God"—Ephesians 3:2), and will re-engage His covenant people once this secret administration concludes.

I do not wish to disparage the God-is-permanently-finished-with-Israel crowd, but Paul himself calls them ignorant: "For I am not willing for you to be ignorant of this secret."

I am not averse, then, to calling them ignorant.

Anyone either ignorant of or denying the secret of Israel's temporary blindness (the blindness that made way for a new, unprophesied administration) commits the very crime Paul warned against. Paul says, "Don't misinterpret what's going on and arrogantly assume that you're royalty and they're just rabble, out on their ears for good" (Romans 11:25-26). This, Paul defines as, "passing for prudent among yourselves."

ANOTHER FASHIONABLE MISTAKE

Another fashionable mistake, also based on an ignorance of Paul's secret administration, is "Preterism." Preterism states that because John the Baptist and Jesus Christ said the kingdom was "at hand" and "near," and Jesus prophesied concerning the end times, and then said, "By no means *may* this generation be passing by till all these things *should* be occurring" (Matthew 24:34), then the kingdom must have necessarily come. Preterists believe that the fall of Jerusalem in A.D. 70, by the armies of Titus, constituted all the prophesied judgments of Israel and the world, described in the book of Revelation. In other words, the book of Revelation is historical. Nothing in it is future. It all happened already, they say.

According to Preterists, the 1,000-year kingdom has come and gone; the Earth has already been covered with the knowledge of the glory of God as the waters cover the sea; and lions have lain down with lambs. (Sure wish I could've seen that. Lions usually eat lambs, and I am tired of it.)

But still, there is more.

They believe Satan was already bound for 1,000 years (which Revelation says will happen), between A.D. 70 and A.D. 1070, during which time Jesus Christ assumed the Chief Priest role in a kingdom headquartered in Jerusalem.

Not only this, but, if these modern Preterists were correct, then we are now on the New Earth, prophesied in Revelation, chapter 21, and indeed have been on it since A.D. 1070. On the New Earth, "death will be no more, nor mourning, nor clamor, nor misery; they will be no more, for the former things passed away" (Revelation 21:4). Also, there will be no more sea (Revelation 21:1).

But, no. I still hear clamor. On occasion, I feel miserable. At a recent funeral, the corpse seemed fairly dead to me. Last summer, my wife and I visited the Pacific Ocean, and the sea looked powerfully intact to us.

Suffice it to say, the earthly kingdom has not yet come. When Christ returns to Earth, God's promises to Israel will be literally fulfilled, during the Millennium.

The consequences of an ignorance of the secret of Romans, chapter 11, are both tragic and foolish. The kingdom *was* near, but was withdrawn. The Lord's generation *would* have witnessed the coming judgments and Millennial blessing, but that generation rejected the spirit's testimony (repentance was one of Jesus' prerequisites) and wandered in a spiritual wilderness from which its descendants have yet to emerge. (Near-but-withdrawn promises have befallen Israel before, as we shall soon see. Withdrawn promises are in no way revoked promises, however.)

In light of all the "near is the kingdom" passages, those people straining to believe Scripture can do one of two things: they can either believe the kingdom did come—in which case they must "spiritualize away" every literal promise and prophesy of God and look silly doing it—or else they can realize the secret Paul spoke of in Romans 11:25; that is, God temporarily blinded the Jews to make way for an un-prophesied administration of grace, and God will resume with Israel as soon as "the complement of the nations may be entering" (Romans 11:25).

THAT WAS THEN, THIS IS NOW

Many modern Christians look to the book of Acts as a formula for how to build a church. Turning to chapter 2 and the day of Pentecost, they start by championing baptism and repentance. Next, some of them try to speak in other languages. Some even go so far as to sell all their goods and have all things in common, as the early disciples did. Next thing you know, they start making pilgrimages to the Holy Land.

This Acts-as-a-modern-model brigade lives for Acts-type miracles and tries hard to manifest them. When miracles don't happen, these people are tempted to act as if they did. Many people get "talked into" miraculous cures, only to wake up the next day with the same headache.

One man I know (let's call him Fred) attempted to raise the dead at a funeral. (You can't make this stuff up, folks.) Most embarrassingly, Fred's command, "Rise! I said, *Rise!*" failed on application—in spite of Fred's italic placement and exclamation point. The corpse, it turned out, was smarter than Fred. Even the corpse realized that Acts was a bygone era and smartly refused to cooperate. Fred blamed himself, chalking up the failure to "a lack of faith." Rather, it was a lack of intelligence: Fred failed to grasp God's timing. God still sometimes works miracles, but He no longer performs miracles when humans gather en masse, and certainly not when they command Him to perform.

The Holy Spirit does not own a watch. Thus, one cannot schedule a "Holy Spirit revival" for 7 p.m. without inviting falsehood. God's spirit operates independently of human time demands.

If this is the new Earth, I want a refund.

Acts-type commands fail because the Acts administration has been superseded by a better one; Acts is out-of-synch with *God's* time demands. Some want to duplicate the Acts spirit so badly, however, that, like Fred, they will call upon flesh. Loud, cadenced preaching (with well-placed italics and exclamation points) may excite the masses, but God never spoke that way. In the upper room at the real Pentecost, none of the disciples swayed or chanted. Not a single disciple barked, screamed, or collapsed.

During the real Pentecostal era, Peter's mere shadow healed people (Acts 5:15). The disciple would walk by an encampment of sick on a sunny day, hear a commotion, and have to look behind him to see what had happened. Real Pentecostal power oozed from their pores then, practically in spite of the vessel. Such healing did not need worked up, sweated over, or shouted upon. No one needed to clench their eyes shut and groan into heaven. When so-called miracles happen today on the heels of such contortions, the manifestations are false.

Yes, Paul worked miracles early in his career, but his ministry went "from glory to glory" (2 Corinthians 3:18). Paul weaned believers from a reliance on miracles to pure faith. Therefore, in spite of his early wonder-working, Paul later left Trophimus sick in Miletus (2 Timothy 4:20), and recommended that Timothy drink wine for his stomach and "frequent infirmities" (1 Timothy 5:23). Why didn't the man whose mere handkerchiefs used to banish disease (Acts 19:12) miraculously cure the simple ailments of his dearest friends? By Paul's later career, the new administration of faith, grace, and spiritual blessings had finally come. Paul wrote in Ephesians 1:3, "Blessed be the God and Father of our Lord Jesus Christ, Who blesses us with every spiritual blessing among the celestials, in Christ."

We all want spiritual blessings. We all want to manifest the power of God. If you watch Christian television (try not to), it's likely you have the wrong idea about how God's spirit and power are manifested. You may have come to believe that the power of God has to do with feeling wonderful, clapping your hands, raising your arms in praise and victory, or being divinely delivered from a migraine headache. These things may occur in the wake of divine activity, but divine activity has higher goals in mind. As Paul wrote to the Colossians:

> Therefore we do not cease praying for you and requesting that you may be ... growing in the realization of God; being endued with all power, in accord with the might of His glory, for all endurance and patience with joy; at the same time giving thanks to the Father, Who makes you competent for a part of the allotment of the saints, in light.
> —Colossians 1:9-12, CLNT

What a statement: "Being endued with all power." It makes one think the next line will be: "So that you may walk on water." Or, "so that you may raise the dead." Or, "so that you may be so happy you'll never have another bad day."

But no. Paul wants the saints endued with all the power of God so that they can "endure with patience and joy." It takes all the power of God to cause a person to not only suffer patiently, but to suffer with inner joy, knowing this very endurance makes him or her "competent for a part of the allotment of the saints in light." Here's the astounding part, from verse 12: *At the same time giving thanks to the Father for it.* It takes a spiritual giant to not only endure trials with patience and joy, but then to thank God for them. Is this you? Then congratulations: You possess all the power of God—but you'll never qualify for Christian television.

Someone once wrote me and asked, "Why doesn't God speak to me? I pray to see Him or hear Him, but I don't. Is there something wrong with me?" I answered:

> There is nothing wrong with you. Perhaps you are focusing on the wrong parts of the Bible. If you are reading the Old Testament, or the four gospel accounts—or even the book of Acts—you might get the impression that God is in the business today of outward, obvious manifestations of His

spirit, such as an audible voice or a staff turned into a snake. God operated that way at one time (delivering Israel from Egypt, for instance), but this is not His current method. Jesus said to Thomas, "Happy are those who have not seen, and yet believe." Our Lord was introducing here a new era of spiritual manifestation: FAITH.

Nothing pleases God more than faith, and nothing encourages faith more than *not* seeing things. After all, that's what faith is: not seeing things (Hebrews 11:1). God speaks to you today through quiet manifestations of His power, such as love, joy, peace, and patience: all the gifts of the spirit. He is also speaking through His Word. Are you worried that God is either ignoring you or not loving you? Read Romans, chapters 5-8, and call me in the morning.

The Acts administration is not only anachronistic, but a recipe for failure. Why? The Acts administration, itself, failed. It began in glory and ended with James killed, Peter exiled, Jerusalem starved, and the Jews scattered. (Today's pastors and church leaders ought to be grateful their models aren't "working," otherwise they would all be killed, exiled, starved, and scattered.) The so-called Acts administration was meant to fail. Why? It was another demonstration of Israel's stubbornness.

Apparently, stubbornness dies hard.

9.
"PAUL" MEANS "PAUSE"

"PAUL" MEANS "PAUSE"

"Paul" is derived from the Greek root *pau*, which means, "a pause." Paul's new name is perfect, then. At the calling of Paul, God begins to press the "pause button" on Israel. That button is fully engaged in Romans 11:8—"Now God gives them a spirit of stupor, eyes not to be observing, and ears not to be hearing, till this very day." Precisely what happened to poor Dr. Know-It-All.

Before we get too sad for the good doctor, we must rejoice in the fortunes of the nations in the person of Sergius Paulus, who became a believer, full of enthusiasm, over Paul's testimony concerning the Master.

Imagine a bookcase, with all the books of the Bible lined up. The ends of this bookcase are spring-loaded. Take out Paul's books of the Bible—from Romans to Philemon—and you have one smooth revelation to Israel.

Paul's letters thwart the progression and symmetry of divine revelation to Israel—*until one learns to separate them from the rest of Scripture.*

Take away Paul's letters, his thirteen books, and the book of

Acts snaps up against the book of Hebrews, and the Bible is all Jewish again. Acts shows us the kingdom proclaimed through the mouth of Peter, but the door closed to Israel in chapter 28. Then the book of Hebrews comes on the scene, telling the faithful Israelites to wait patiently for the promise. Hebrews sets forth for the Israelites their heroes of faith (especially in chapter 11), who died, "having not received the promises." Paul wrote Romans chapters 9-11 to explain to the nations what had happened with the Jews. Hebrews was written to the Jews, to explain to the Jews what had happened with the Jews. Pity them, really: They had seen their kingdom at the door, and then—wham!—the rug got pulled out. Read the book of Hebrews, and you will see what I mean.

One smooth revelation .... to Israel

So then comes the book of James, telling dispersed Israelites how to behave, and the books of Peter, written to Israel, encouraging them to persevere in their suffering, and the books of John, which set forth Jesus Christ as an Entreater between the Father and His children. Like the book of Hebrews, it's all entreaty—all of it—to a people in waiting. Jude is a prelude to apocalyptic judgment, with the central theme being the coming of the Lord in judgment upon the irreverent. Then, of course, we have the book of Revelation, which at last brings the long-awaited earthly, Millennial kingdom to political reality, albeit not apart from the severest of trials.

Paul fits none of this: none of it. Theologians have fought for centuries, arguing about how to reconcile Paul and James. Paul says we are saved by faith, without works (Ephesians 2:8-9); James says faith is dead, without works (James 2:20). Many are the linguistic acrobatics attempting to harmonize these disparate accounts. It's useless. All efforts are moot. The accounts cannot be harmonized. They are purposely distinct. Paul's gospel is that of the Uncircumcision, and James' of the Circumcision. Paul is a round hole; James is a square peg. Anyone attempting to harmonize them will look silly and soon require aspirin.

The presence of the body of Christ in the world is what keeps the rest of the books of the Bible (Hebrews through Revelation) from continuing on their course. Again, Paul is the Big Pause. What undoes it? The snatching away of the body of Christ (commonly referred to as the "rapture"; I will have more to say on this shortly), which completes God's secret administration among the nations. Paul says it quite clearly in Romans 11:25: "Callousness, in part, on Israel has come, until the complement of the nations may be entering."

The only thing keeping Israel from a re-assumption of her call, and its eventual fulfillment, is—us.

The snatching away of the body of Christ will occur when God removes His finger from this 2,000-year-old pause, also known as, "the gospel of the grace of God" (Acts 20:24), and resumes with Israel.

One common objection I hear: "God would never have the kingdom come so close, and then pull the rug out. God does not play time games."

He doesn't?

IT HAPPENED TO ISRAEL BEFORE

Back in the days of Moses, Israel was at the door of the Promised Land. Remember that? They camped at the border of Canaan, looking lusciously at what they would soon enter into. They sent spies into the land—Joshua and Caleb—who returned to testify: "The native inhabitants are enormous and smell bad, but God will conquer them on our behalf."

The result? Israel balked. Because of unbelief, the Israelites refused to go in. What did God do? He caused them to wander in the wilderness for forty years.

The Promised Land (which foreshadowed the kingdom) had been near in the desert. Israel was at the door—ten kilometers and an afternoon's walk away—and yet they wandered in the wilderness for forty years, until the unbelieving cowards died and a new generation assumed the mantle.

Do you think it's a coincidence that the time-frame in the book of Acts—from chapter 1 when Israel was at the door of the kingdom, to chapter 28 when Paul slammed the door in their faces (verse 28)—was approximately forty years?

God doesn't play time games, you say?

A TRICKY THING GOD DOES WITH TIME

In Luke chapter 4, starting with verse 17, Jesus entered into the synagogue and rose to read:

> And the scroll of the prophet Isaiah was handed to Him, and, opening the scroll, He found the place where it was written,
> "The spirit of the Lord is on Me,
> On account of which He anoints Me to bring the Evangel to the poor.
> He has commissioned Me to heal the crushed heart,
> To herald to captives a pardon,
> And to the blind the receiving of sight;
> To dispatch the oppressed with a pardon,
> To herald an acceptable year of the Lord ..."
> And furling the scroll, giving it back to the deputy, He is seated.
> —CLNT

Why did Jesus stop in the middle of a sentence? First of all, yes, He did stop in the middle of a sentence. He paused, and then handed the scroll back to the deputy and sat down. He was reading from Isaiah 61, verses 1 and 2. Why not just continue on with the sentence, with the entirety of verse 2? And yet He did not. Jesus stopped in the middle of a sentence, for crying out loud.

Why didn't He go on? He couldn't go on. The very next statement refers to the end of this present "era of the nations," and the great judgments of the book of Revelation that will usher Israel, at last, into the Millennial kingdom. Had our Lord continued to read Isaiah 61, verses 1 and 2 (He read verse 1 completely, but passed the scroll and sat down in the middle of verse 2), the next line would have been: "and the day of vengeance of our God."

This part of the prophecy was not yet to be fulfilled—not in that day.

After He sat down, Jesus said to the assemblage: "This day is the Scripture fulfilled in your ears." This was true, as far as what He had read. He did bring the evangel to the poor; He did heal the crushed heart; He did herald to captives a pardon; He did herald an acceptable year of the Lord. But He could not have said, "This day is this Scripture fulfilled," had He continued reading. For only He knew how distant was the fulfillment of the next line: "and the day of vengeance of our God."

Here's what I want you to see. In the *King James Version*, and in most other versions, there's only a comma between the two lines. This is where Jesus sat down. He sat down between the phrases:

"To herald an acceptable year of the Lord ..."
and
"And the day of vengeance of our God."

Our Lord quit reading and sat down at a comma, for heaven's sake.

The second clause of this sentence has yet to occur. At present, more than 2,000 years have transpired, for which this simple comma does duty. Like this:

> To herald an acceptable year of the Lord **(insert 2,000 years)** and the day of vengeance of our God.

What an amazing comma, then. What an amazing place for our Lord to roll up the scroll and stop reading. What a God-given prescience Jesus had of an un-prophesied secret era to come.

Now you understand the significance of our Lord's answer to the disciples when, upon the Mount of Olives, they asked Him just seconds before He rose from their midst to assume His celestial glories and prepare for the calling of Saul: "Are you at this time restoring the kingdom to Israel?" (Acts 1:6).

Who can blame them for asking? The object of their fondest hopes and dreams was to enter into that blessed 1,000-year experience. What was His answer?

Yet He said to them: "It is not for you to know times or eras which the Father placed in His own jurisdiction" (Acts 1:7).

I like *The Message* here: "You don't get to know the time. Timing is the Father's business" (Acts 1:7).

And so it is. Back to John 3:12. Remember this? (Not that I will ever let you forget it.) "If I have told you earthly things and you do not believe, how will you believe *if I tell you heavenly things?*" (John 3:12).

The heavenly things belonged, not to Israel, but to the nations. As He read Isaiah, Jesus Christ knew that Israel would reject Him. Jesus knew an unprecedented, secret era sat on the cusp of time. The disciples longed to know about the times, but how could He tell them? How could Jesus tell them their beloved kingdom would be indefinitely postponed while God ("Timing is the Father's business" Acts 1:7) did a new thing, which they could not have imagined in their wildest dreams? Jesus kept them ignorant of it. Why?

CIRCUMCISION

The Kingdom on Earth proclaimed by Christ, and rejected

Matthew
Mark
Luke
John

The earthly Kingdom re-proclaimed by 12 disciples, and rejected

Acts

The earthly Kingdom temporarily on hold

The present, parenthetic pause, i.e., Paul

GOD CALLS OUT BODY OF CHRIST

Secret time period revealed through Paul—Rom. 11:25

Romans	*1 Thessalonians*
1 Corinthians	*2 Thessalonians*
2 Corinthians	*1 Timothy*
Galatians	*2 Timothy*
Ephesians	*Titus*
Philippians	*Philemon*
Colossians	

WRITINGS

The earthly Kingdom reaffirmed

Hebrews
James
1 and 2 Peter
1, 2, and 3 John
Jude

The earthly Kingdom realized

Revelation

God needed an enthusiastic testimony on the day of Pentecost. Israel had to go through the experience and the motions of once more rejecting Him. It had to happen, not only as a testimony against them but as a means of humbling them in the future, so they could eventually fulfill their calling and their place as a vessel of blessing rather than jealousy.

If Jesus had told them of the coming national failure that would make way for non-Israelites to hop-skip-and-jump them into unheard-of glory, I doubt they would have run from the upper room shouting that the days of refreshing spoken of through the prophet Joel were on the cusp.

They *were* on the cusp, but then suddenly they weren't. In the destiny of Israel, there was a divine pause coming, which no one then anticipated.

His name was Paul.

10.
A RACEWIDE GOSPEL

A RACEWIDE GOSPEL

The cross of Jesus Christ was never presented to Israel as good news. In fact, it was something Israel had to repent of for salvation:

> Let all the house of Israel know certainly, then, that God makes Him Lord as well as Christ—this Jesus Whom you crucify! Now, hearing this, their heart was pricked with compunction. Besides, they said to Peter and the rest of the apostles, "What should we be doing, men, brethren?" Now Peter is averring to them, "Repent and be baptized each of you in the name of Jesus Christ for the pardon of your sins, and you shall be obtaining the gratuity of the Holy Spirit."
> —Acts 2:36-38, CLNT

Repent of what? Repent of crucifying the Messiah. Here's how it worked in Israel at Pentecost, and how it still works:

"Christ has been crucified!"

"Oh, no!"

In the body of Christ, it's exactly opposite. Paul writes in Galatians 6:14—"Now may it not be mine to be boasting, except in the cross of our Lord Jesus Christ, through which the world has been crucified to me, and I to the world."

Can you imagine an Israelite today—or in any day—boasting in the cross of Christ? Whenever the cross gets mentioned, an Israelite looks the other way.

I would not diminish the death of Christ, not even for Israel. Christ was still the fulfillment of the Passover lamb (Exodus 12:21-27), which had to die. (While enslaved in Egypt, each Israelite family had to kill a Passover lamb to protect the household from death.) To Israel, the death and resurrection of Christ proved He was the fulfillment of the Old Testament type. It proved that meekness and humility, even unto death, out-muscles physical prowess. Israel supposed that swords and clubs would pry them into the kingdom. God gave Circumcision and the Passover lamb to drive such thinking from their minds.

Israel needed the death of Christ, but not the cross. It was the manner of Christ's death—and its implications for humanity—that consumed Paul and prompted his pen.

DEPTH OF THE CROSS AND THE NEW CREATION

The cross of Christ reached far deeper into humanity's need than merely giving one sad nation a new heart. Each year, the Passover lamb was not tortured; its throat was slit—that was it. Not so Christ on the cross. Jesus Christ's six hours of torture touched an aspect of humanity's condition that the mercifully killed Passover lamb could not reach. The Passover lamb leaves Israel intact—the cross wipes out everything and everyone in its path. The cross of Christ says:

> The whole race is finished. Watch the depth of suffering; see the six hours on the Roman stake. We're pulling humanity out by the roots here; that's how deep this goes. Forget Abraham and David; we're going back to Adam now.

It's that bad. When this Man rises from the grave, a new
creation will have come into the lives of those believing it.
Eventually, all shall come to believe it. (As Paul makes clear
in 1 Timothy 4:10—"We rely on the living God, Who is
the Savior of *all* humans, *especially* of those who believe.")

Peter never taught this; he was not a new creation. The new
creation eliminates fleshly distinctions, and Peter has to be an
Israelite in the kingdom—he has to be. Jesus told him he would
sit on one of twelve thrones judging the twelve tribes of Israel
(Matthew 19:28).

Yet what does Paul say? "For whoever are baptized into Christ,
put on Christ, in Whom there is not Jew nor yet Greek" (Galatians
3:27).

Peter never taught this; he couldn't. He has to be a Jew in the
kingdom. Peter was not, and is not, in the body of Christ.

Paul alone discusses how one man, Adam, affects all humanity. Not coincidentally, Paul alone boasts in the cross. Only Christ
on the cross—not the Lamb sacrificed for Israel—undoes the
condemnation of Adam.

No other writer discusses Adam. They speak of Abraham,
Isaac, Jacob, David, Daniel. Paul alone traces our entire spiritual
history to the inaugural human. Only through Paul's message does
the entire race become new. The Hebrew Scriptures demanded a
new birth for Israel. Paul's teachings are to the new birth what a
well is to a tea saucer.

Now I know why Paul always seemed like Mr. Absolute to me.
Why I always sensed he went deeper. Because he did go deeper. I
failed to see specifically then that Paul was the only writer returning us to Adam, relating Adam's failure to the manner of Christ's
death, and removing the old humanity by the roots.

When I was a kid, one of my chores was to pull dandelions.
My dad always said: "Get 'em by the root."

The gospel of the Circumcision does not get humanity by
the root. Rather, it remakes humanity. It takes the raw material

Paul alone discusses how one man affects all humanity.

of the present creation and fashions it anew. This is what being "born again" means. "Born again" puts God's spirit into Israelite flesh, so that Israel can at last enact God's commandments. Being born again merely spruces up the old humanity; it reforms it. No wonder the other writers always struck me as reformers; they *were* reformers. Modern so-called men of God always wanted me born again. I never embraced that. I needed more. My root was wrong. Fix me today, and I am back in a month to re-confess my sins, as the Catholic church did to me. They never extracted my sin by the root. Their fix was a Band-Aid; ten "Our Fathers" and ten "Hail Marys," and I was back next month—back on the wheel like a gerbil. The root never left me. (Protestant churches aren't much different. Protestants say you must confess your sins each day or you'll be "out of fellowship" with God, and then poor, helpless God can't bless you.)

Thus also, Israel. With Israel, flesh is still recognized. In Israel, Jew and Greek remain. As I said, these must remain, because there are twelve thrones in the kingdom, representing the twelve tribes of Israel. What about Paul's throne? There are not thirteen thrones. I wondered about this. Poor Paul. He was the most awesome, energetic apostle of them all. Where was his throne? Now I know: Paul does not have a throne on Earth; his future is not tied to Earth. Only Paul announced the truth: "There is neither Jew nor Greek." This was beyond radical. Peter never did quite understand. *Not be a Jew? How could it be?* Yet Paul, in the book of Philippians, despises his nationality and throws it away. Either this is dangerous and stupid—or else it sits at the core of the most liberating message ever to visit humanity:

> For the love of Christ is constraining us, judging this, that, if One died for the sake of all, consequently all died. And He died for the sake of all that those who are living should by no means still be living to themselves, but to the One dying and being roused for their sakes.

> So that we, from now on, are acquainted with no one accord-
> ing to flesh. Yet even if we have known Christ according to
> flesh, nevertheless now we know Him so no longer. So that,
> if anyone is in Christ, there is a new creation: the primitive
> passed by. Lo! There has come new.
> —2 Corinthians 5:14-17, CLNT

New creation takes the old humanity, shoves it into the grave
with Christ, and considers it dead. New creation also takes the
earthly Jesus (including His words in red) and puts Him behind
us, replacing Jesus with the glorified Christ. We no longer know
Christ according to flesh. Only then can it be said: "There is a
new creation."

"If one died for the sake of all, consequently all died."

Such sweeping death eliminates all physical advantage. This
message is the death knell to Israel; therefore this message never
came from Peter's lips. With Israel, it's all about physical advantage. Yes, the flesh must be fixed; Israel will be given a new heart,
enabling her present flesh to be remolded into Messiah's image.
But this is not Paul's message. Paul's message is: *We have started
from scratch.* "I am no longer living," he says, "but living in me is
Christ" (Galatians 2:20).

I am no longer living? No one had ever heard such a thing. Israel
merely reforms the flesh. The cross eradicates it. This was the cross'
deepest aspect, hidden from Peter at Pentecost and from Israel as
a whole. Thus, the nations—in spirit—outreach Israel. Israel still
wrestles with her sins, while the nations see sin so far removed that
in one moment they are worshipping idols, and in the next, they
are praising Christ for divine completion:

> And you are complete in Him, Who is the Head of every
> sovereignty and authority, in Whom you were circumcised
> also with a circumcision not made by hands, in the stripping
> off of the body of flesh in the circumcision of Christ. Being
> entombed together with Him in baptism, in Whom you
> were roused together also through faith in the operation of

God, Who rouses Him from among the dead, you also being
dead to the offenses and the uncircumcision of your flesh;

He vivifies us together jointly with Him, dealing graciously
with all our offenses, erasing the handwriting of the decrees
against us, which was hostile to us, and has taken it away
out of the midst, nailing it to the cross, stripping off the
sovereignties and authorities, with boldness He makes a
show of them, triumphing over them in it.
                                   —Colossians 2:10-15, CLNT

How could completion happen so fast? For a Jew, this would
take years of training and devotion and festivals … years of bringing your lamb to Jerusalem, baptizing yourself, weeping upon your
prayer mat. But for a human of the nations, the flesh problem
disappears in a single declaration by Paul:

So that we, from now on, are acquainted with no one according to flesh. Yet even if we have known Christ according to
flesh, nevertheless now we know Him so no longer. So that,
if anyone is in Christ, there is a new creation: the primitive
passed by. Lo! There has come new.
                                   —2 Corinthians 5:16-17, CLNT

Corpses cannot be reformed. "If One died for the sake of all,
consequently all died" (2 Corinthians 5:14). Thus, the beneficiaries
of Paul's gospel are freed from ever again having to worry about or
fix flesh. Their identity is now tied to Christ's. His circumcision is
their circumcision; His death is theirs; His entombment is their
entombment; and because He rose from the dead, they are now to
reckon themselves as being raised with Him (see my book, *How to
Be Free From Sin While Smoking a Cigarette*).

Paul had never known Christ according to flesh. We have no
record that the Pharisee, Saul, ever gazed into the eyes of the terrestrial Jesus. A good thing. It was easier for Saul, then, to grasp
the greater depth of the cross, accomplished by the glorified One,

sitting at the right hand of God.

Yet still, Paul had baggage. All the Jews did. This concept of "I died with Christ" does not find an easy home in one who, for his entire life, dedicated himself to the eradication of flesh. How can flesh be gone in a day? In one flash of inspiration? In one revelation?

Jews were burdened with baggage. The nations never had baggage. Thus, the nations could more readily receive and believe a message of pure grace; they had never heard anything different. In a sense, then, the depth and hopelessness of sin is good preparation for slosh-bucket application of God's unmerited favor. You are so far gone that you realize nothing can fix or reform you. Your only hope is a new creation, a clean sweep of the old. Thank God this is accomplished by Another, completely without you, because in your deepest heart you know your inadequacy for the task.

Therefore, Jesus could more easily speak with tax-collectors and prostitutes and publicans. They knew their need. But still, they were Israelites. Still, they had baggage. Still, they looked for a Messiah Who could help them be worthy.

Worthy? Contrast worthiness with the following, from Paul's letter to the Romans:

> We then were entombed together with Him through baptism into death, that, even as Christ was roused from among the dead through the glory of the Father, thus we also should be walking in newness of life.
>
> For if we have become planted together in the likeness of His death, nevertheless we shall be of the resurrection also, knowing this, that our old humanity was crucified together with Him, that the body of sin may be nullified, for us by no means to be still slaving for sin, for one who dies has been justified from sin.
>
> —Romans 6:4-7, CLNT

Sin always was the problem. An Israelite had to at least try to stop sinning. For sin, God gave the law. Law, however, was merely the prettying-up of the dandelion. God had to first show humanity the futility of beautifying the outside. Yet for centuries He tarried with the outside. He set forth a program (the law) to pretty-up from without. Even when the new covenant was announced, as I have said, it gave the same body (the Israel body) a new heart. Sin was still fought against, but fought against with a higher, inner power.

With Paul, on the other hand, sin was no longer fought against. Sin was done away. The old humanity—the one that sinned—has been considered crucified with Christ. The deepest aspect of Christ's suffering is the death of the old humanity. This truth is still completely unknown to Israel, as well as to most modern-day Christians. We, not Israel, are "planted together in the likeness of His death." Everything that happened to Christ, happened to us. The result is astounding: "For one who dies has been justified from sin" (Romans 6:7).

Justification from sin goes so much deeper than forgiveness, which was the only thing available to Israelites, through law. For-giveness says: "You did wrong, but we will overlook the penalty." Justification says: "You did not even do wrong. In fact, you are right."

How can this be? Only one way: God must be looking at a new creation. He cannot justify the old creation, ever. God must do something with humanity that will enable Him to look upon it with new eyes. So He did: He killed the old humanity—the whole of it—along with His Son. In God's mind, when His Son died, the old humanity died. Thus, when God now sees us, He sees His Son.

This truth remains unknown to Israel—and will remain un-known, even in the 1,000-year kingdom. In the kingdom, it will "merely" be that Israel's flesh has been reformed from an outside-in miracle. They still won't have identity with Christ. Israel will remain the bride, not the body. One thinks the bride is close to Christ, until one hears of a people called the body of Christ.

For most people, it's too hard to believe. Most people are too proud to consider themselves dead with Christ. They want to prop themselves up. Oh, for the joy of the revelation that, with us, it is not about propping up flesh, but about the historical destruction of flesh at Calvary, a destruction that allows God to now look at us and say: "You are perfect!"

How few people realize that the cross must reconcile the entire universe to God, else it is a failure. We all know of the turmoil on Earth, but few know of the turmoil in heaven. Not only humans, but evil celestial beings—angels—need the saving work of Calvary. Not only beings above Earth and upon Earth, but under Earth as well:

> Wherefore, also, God highly exalts Him, and graces Him with the name that is above every name, that in the name of Jesus every knee should be bowing, celestial and terrestrial and subterranean, and every tongue should be acclaiming that Jesus Christ is Lord, for the glory of God, the Father.
> —Philippians 2:9-11, CLNT

To Israel, Jesus was the fulfillment of the Old Testament Passover lamb. No wonder they failed to grasp the whips, the spit, the nakedness, the crown of thorns, the six hours of torture. Jesus was far more than a sacrificial lamb. The cross was so deep and so encompassing that the first revelation concerning it—Pentecost—could only fall pitiably short of explaining it. The full revelation of what the cross meant for the race, for the celestials, and for sin itself, would be given to the most unworthy person on the planet—for only then could it be seen how truly unworthy flesh was. Never could Peter have written Romans 5:20—"Where sin increases, grace superexceeds."

With the law of Moses, sin invited wrath. In this new message, sin invites more blessing. Few today even dare to believe this: The modern church still mixes law and grace. Why? Christians confuse the lamb with the cross. They think they are a bunch of Israelites. They invent absurd terms such as, "the Christian Sabbath." They like propping themselves up, prettying their dandelions, condemning others. If everyone is in the same boat, then where is their advantage?

If one died for the sake of all and consequently all died, then "There is no one righteous, no not one" (Romans 3:10), and the Christians can no longer prove their worthiness to God. How Israel loves proving herself to God. Take this away, and they are just like everyone else. The worst and most dreadful thing one can say both to a Jew and to a Christian: "You are just like everyone else." Tell them this, and they will persecute you. If they can get away with stoning you, they will. Yet the gospel of Paul levels everyone; it puts everyone in the same boat.

So much for works, then. In less time than it takes a person to say, "I accept what Christ says: I am finished. God now considers me as righteous as His Son. My sins cannot condemn me anymore"; he or she is justified before God and walks away whistling.

No wonder Jews and Christians froth at this. They hate any happiness not purchased via the sweat and tears that accompany hard-won righteousness—the kind of righteousness *they* compete for.

DANGER OF MIXING GOSPELS

At the heart of this Christian confusion is the failure to distinguish the gospel of Paul from that of the Circumcision. Mixing the two messages is what condemns the modern, "evangelical" message. This brigade does exactly what Paul said not to do in Galatians, chapter 1. There, Paul said:

> I am marveling that thus, swiftly, you are transferred from that which calls you in the grace of Christ, to a different evangel, which is not another, except it be that some who are disturbing you want also to distort the evangel of Christ.
> —Galatians 1:6-7, CLNT

The modern Christian message is a distortion of the evangel of Christ. It is, "a different evangel, which is not another."

Paul knew there was a contemporaneous, legitimate evangel that differed from his: the evangel of the Circumcision. Yet he also knew there was a different evangel, "which is not another." This different evangel was not the gospel of Peter (for Peter's was a legitimate evangel), thus, it was not *another* evangel. The different evangel was a pseudo-evangel, an "evangel" that distorted the true evangel of Christ. This pseudo-evangel took pure grace and watered it down with law so that grace was no longer pure grace. It elevated law, and demoted grace. Thus, it was a non-message, a condemning message, a message of confusion. Concerning it, Paul said: "But if we also, or a messenger out of heaven, should be bringing an evangel to you beside that which we bring to you, let him be anathema!" (Galatians 1:8).

Paul pronounced a curse on the message that mixed law and grace, the very message that reigns today in the modern Christian church. This mixed message confuses and disturbs, breeding fear, false guilt, and shame. Many people hearing this mixed message wonder if they are really saved. Those hoping for truth in the realm of Christianity see some light in the writings of Paul, but then they read James and despair comes. Something in Romans thrills them, such as: "There is no more condemnation in Christ Jesus" (Romans 8:1), but then here comes Peter. Or here comes James. Or Jude. Or Hebrews. Or here come even the red letters of Christ.

What these folks fail to realize (no one has ever told them) is that the red letters of Christ, while inspired, are not the final words of Christ.

"If I have told you earthly things and you do not believe, how will you believe *if I tell you heavenly things?*" (John 3:12).

What follows when people mix the two gospels, then, is the guilt and condemnation of religion; it's a pseudo-grace in Israelite garb that attempts to couple "total grace" with a do-this-or-else mentality. How few people read the address on Scriptural envelopes; how few distinguish between what is theirs and what belongs to Israel.

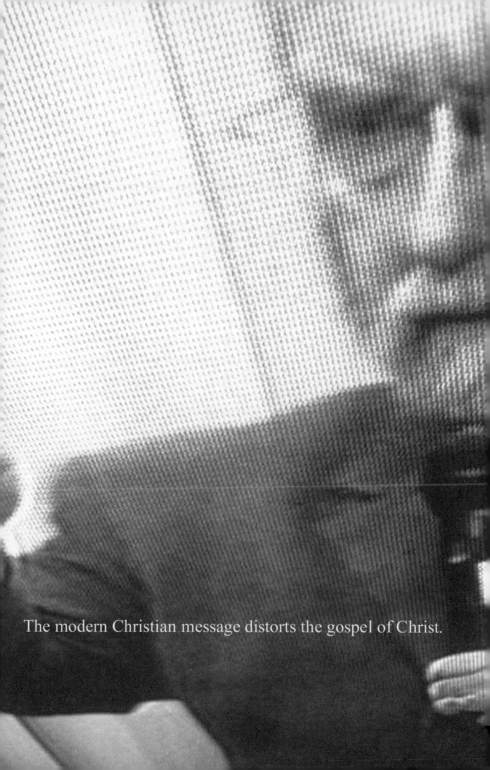

The modern Christian message distorts the gospel of Christ.

They open other peoples' mail and try to pay other peoples' bills.

On the one hand, the Christian religion will *say* you are a new creation in Christ, and all your sins are justified. On the other hand (the hand they slap you with), they will say you'd better confess your sins and at least attempt to reform yourself before Christ returns and finds you slacking. Otherwise, *how do you know if you're even saved?*

Again, the source of this confusion is the inability to distinguish between the gospel of the Circumcision, and that of the Uncircumcision. Failure to distinguish between the Lamb of Israel (Who requests a little sorrowful repentance) and the Man Who died on the cross (Who took the old creation with Him and now sees us as a new creation— no repentance necessary).

The remedy? Stop going to the place where you hear the mixed message (see my book, *How to Quit Church Without Quitting God*).

Only one who has seen himself or herself crucified and entombed with Christ can believe new creation truth. Only one who has completely given up on himself or herself can believe what God says concerning flesh.

We can either confess our sins day in and day out, or we can believe that sin no longer condemns us. This "no more condemnation" message is the deep fix situating us in the lowest, most blessed place possible: looking up at Calvary's stunning accomplishment.

Embrace the gospel of Paul: It is the only gospel for everyone.

11.
A HEAVENLY DESTINY

A HEAVENLY DESTINY

If you had been on Earth with Peter in the days when Jesus ate figs and slept by the campfire next to you, and you'd said to Peter, "Hey, dude. Won't it be awesome when we get to heaven?" Peter would have looked at you as if you'd lost your mind.

Peter never wanted to go to heaven. In fact, no one back then had ever heard of going to heaven. Christianity is so infatuated with this idea of "going to heaven" that they forget to consider what God's Word says about it.

Remember God's promise to Abraham way back in Genesis, chapter 12? I'm not going to let you forget:

> Go forth from your country … go to a land which I will show you. For I am going to make you a great nation, and I will bless you, and I will make your name great. And so you shall be a blessing. And I will bless those who bless you, and the one who curses you I will curse. And in you, *all the families of the Earth shall be blessed.*

All the families of the *Earth*.

Do you remember one of the most famous lines from the Sermon on the Mount?

"Blessed are the meek, for they will inherit the Earth" (Matthew 5:5).

They will inherit what? The Earth. Entirely consistent with the call of Abraham. If Israel is to shepherd and bless the nations of Earth, why would they want to go to heaven?

Revelation 5:10 plainly describes the future of an Israelite: "Thou dost also make them a kingdom and a priesthood for our God, and they shall be reigning on the Earth."

Are you noticing a common theme? Now back to Peter.

The disciples asked our Lord some honest questions. Normal men with normal ambitions, they'd left everything to follow Jesus, and therefore put much stock in their future. They all wanted to ask Jesus: "Excuse me, but, what's in this for me?"

A legitimate question. Naturally, Peter was the only one bold enough to articulate it.

Let's set the scene. A young man approached Jesus asking Him what he had to do to find true life. Jesus said, "Obey the commandments," and so on and so forth. The man said, "Been there, done that. But I want to be perfect. What's next?" Jesus answered, "Sell all your possessions and follow me." This was the last thing the young man wanted to hear, so he walked away. A rich man, he could not bear the thought of unhanding all his stuff. Jesus and the disciples watched the man go, and that's when Jesus said:

> Verily, I am saying to you that the rich squeamishly will be entering into the kingdom of the heavens. Yet again, I am saying to you that it is easier for a camel to be entering through the eye of a needle than for a rich man to be entering into the kingdom of God.
> —Matthew 19:23-24, CLNT

What is "the kingdom of God"? Better to ask: "What did that

phrase mean to an Israelite?" These days, everyone assumes it means heaven. The phrase, "kingdom of the heavens" appears multiple times in the book of Matthew, and most people think (I understand why they do) that the "kingdom of the heavens" is identical to "heaven." You already know it would have been impossible for an Israelite to grasp anything of the celestial realm. All an Israelite knew was the call of Abraham, which would be shepherding and blessing nations on Earth.

As I said earlier, the kingdom of the heavens is a kingdom that is heavenly in character (it is *of* heaven), but its location is on Earth. We will confirm this shortly with Peter's question and our Lord's answer. Remember, this line of questioning concerns the kingdom of the heavens.

When the Lord said how difficult it was for a rich man to enter it, the disciples were staggered. They asked Him:

> Then who has any chance at all? Jesus looked hard at them and said, "No chance at all if you think you can pull it off yourself. Every chance in the world if you trust God to do it." Then Peter chimed in, "We left everything and followed You. What do we get out of it?"
>
> —Matthew 19:25-27, *The Message*

Peter has a way of getting right to the point. The Concordant version has: "Lo! We leave all and follow Thee. What, consequently, will it be to us?" Our Lord answered:

> Verily I am saying to you, that you who follow Me, in the renascence whenever the Son of Mankind should be seated on the throne of His glory, you also shall sit on twelve thrones, judging the twelve tribes of Israel.
>
> —Matthew 19:28, CLNT

Twelve thrones; twelve tribes of Israel. Where does Israel belong? Where is her realm of ministry? Nowhere except on Earth. Israel's realm always was on Earth, where she will judge not only redeemed Israelites from all twelve tribes, but individuals from all earthbound nations.

Israel will judge Earth people. In contrast, what kind of beings does the body of Christ judge? Hang onto your seat, and I will tell you: "Do you not know that we will judge angels?" (1 Corinthians 6:3).

Until Paul wrote the book of Ephesians (around A.D. 61), no one had ever heard of "going to heaven." This was another one of the secrets hidden in God—revealed only to Paul—that a select group of human beings would have their bodies changed even more radically than the resurrected bodies of Israelites, suiting them for a realm never before visited by humans, namely, the realm above the stars.

1 Corinthians 15:35-42, from the *Concordant Literal New Testament*:

> Now someone will be protesting, "How are the dead being roused? Now with what body are they coming?" Imprudent one! What you are sowing is not being vivified if it should not be dying. And, what you are sowing, you are not sowing the body which shall come to be, but a naked kernel, perchance of wheat or some of the rest. Yet God is giving it a body according as He wills, and to each of the seeds its own body.
>
> Not all flesh is the same flesh, but there is one, indeed, of humans, yet another flesh of beasts, yet another flesh of flyers, yet another of fishes. There are bodies celestial as well as bodies terrestrial. But a different glory, indeed, is that of the celestial, yet a different that of the terrestrial, another glory of the sun, and another glory of the moon, and another glory of the stars, for star is excelling star in glory. *Thus also is the resurrection of the dead.*

Watch the correlation here: "There are bodies celestial as well as bodies terrestrial. *Thus also is the resurrection of the dead.*"

Following His resurrection, our Lord appeared to His disciples, as recorded in Luke chapter 24. The disciples who had walked to Emmaus with the risen Lord returned to Jerusalem to tell the eleven disciples the amazing news. As they were speaking, "Jesus Himself stood in their midst and is saying to them, 'Peace to you!'"(Luke 24:36).

He came out of nowhere. At first, they thought they were beholding a spirit (Luke 24:38-43). Yet Jesus said:

> Why are you disturbed? Perceive My hands and My feet, that it is I Myself. Handle Me and perceive, for a spirit has not flesh and bones according as you behold Me having. And saying this, He exhibits to them His hands and feet. Now, at their still disbelieving from joy, and marveling, He said to them, "Have you any food in this place?" Now they hand Him part of a broiled fish, and, taking it, He ate before them.
>
> —CLNT

This was not unlike a circus act. Indeed, Jesus was performing for His disciples. "He exhibits to them His hands and feet." Our Lord had a body, but it was a body suited to Earth. Mind you, it was still a fantastic body. Considering that the text tells us He all of a sudden "stood in their midst," one assumes this amazing new body of Jesus' had no trouble passing through walls—without need of a door. Why else would the disciples have been frightened out of their wits? Why else would they have assumed He was a spirit? Yet He was not a spirit; He was a body. "There are bodies celestial, as well as bodies terrestrial" (1 Corinthians 15:40).

The body the disciples handled that day was a glorious body. As glorious as it was, it still had hands and feet. It was a glorious, *spiritual* body. It was not a *spirit*, but a spiritual *body*. A spiritual body is a body energized by the force of spirit. A spiritual body does not preclude that body from being flesh, or taking up space, or having hands and feet, and an alimentary system allowing it to process broiled fish.

The body of our Lord, which Saul saw on the road to Damascus, however, was another body entirely. "There are bodies celestial, as well as bodies terrestrial" (1 Corinthians 15:40). Unlike when Jesus was on Earth, Christ's celestial body was not Jewish.

Our Lord Jesus Christ's celestial body shone brighter than the noonday sun, so bright, in fact, the glory of it knocked Saul to the ground.

We do not see this occurring with the disciples in Luke, chapter 24. Rather, we see a man eating a fish and eleven men saying, "Hmm."

> There are bodies celestial, as well as bodies terrestrial. But a different glory, indeed, is that of the celestial, yet a different that of the terrestrial, another glory of the sun, and another glory of the moon, and another glory of the stars, for star is excelling star in glory.
> —1 Corinthians 15:40-41, CLNT

Differing only in the measure of glory, the body that entered the upper room was no less a spiritual body than the one which leveled Saul. "Now we all, with uncovered face, mirroring the Lord's glory, *are being transformed into the same image*, from glory to glory, even as from the Lord, the spirit" (2 Corinthians 3:18).

> For our realm is inherent in the heavens, out of which we are awaiting a Savior also, the Lord, Jesus Christ, Who will transfigure the body of our humiliation, to conform it to the body of His glory, in accord with the operation which enables Him even to subject all to Himself.
> —Philippians 3:20-21, CLNT

Consider the glory of this. Members of the body of Christ, are destined—not to assume bodies like Jesus', when He ate a fish in the upper room, but—to receive bodies like that of the glorified Christ. After Christ assumed His new celestial dignities, He revealed Himself to the first member of the body of Christ … to the first member of a body of people whose realm is inherent, not on Earth, but in the heavens. "For our realm is inherent in the heavens" (Philippians 3:20).

Why? Because that's where we're going. Finally, after thousands of years, God has chosen to reveal His means of reconciling the heavens to Himself.

I started this book with Genesis 1:1—"In the beginning, God created the heavens and the Earth. As for the Earth …" and from that point on, it was all about Earth. Beginning in Genesis, chapter 12, it was all about the calling of a man, Abraham, whose descendants would shepherd and teach the nations of the Earth. Yet, as you will recall, we learned that the purpose of the cross of Christ Jesus was not only to reconcile the Earth to Himself, but also the heavens.

> And He is the Head of the body, the ecclesia [ones who are called-out], Who is Sovereign, Firstborn from among the dead, that in all He may be becoming first, for in Him the entire complement delights to dwell, and through Him to reconcile all to Him (making peace through the blood of His cross), through Him, whether those on the Earth or those in the heavens.
> —Colossians 1:18-20, CLNT

Who knew the heavens were antagonistic to God? Yet Paul himself writes in Ephesians 6:12: "It is not ours to wrestle with blood and flesh, but with the sovereignties, with the authorities, with the world-mights of this darkness, with the spiritual forces of wickedness among the celestials."

Among the celestials! Our realm, that is, where we naturally belong, is inherent in the heavens (Philippians 3:20).

Israel's task: to wrestle with blood and flesh. Israel's task is, and always was, to manage and teach and disciple the nations on Earth. To fit them for this task, God will transform their bodies into spiritual (albeit still physical) bodies such as the one our Lord assumed on Earth, in Luke, chapter 24.

Yet for those who will judge angels ... for believers who were chosen in Him for a task unheard-of—to reconcile the evil forces of wickedness in celestial realms—we are given different bodies suited to our task.

"For there are bodies celestial, as well as bodies terrestrial" (1 Corinthians 15:40).

"If I have told you earthly things and you do not believe, how will you believe *if I tell you heavenly things?*" (John 3:12).

To emphasize the point, our Lord appeared to the first member of this amazing, blessed, and rare company of people—not as a being eating a fish, but as light brighter than the noonday sun.

What else would you expect, though, for a truth so new, a truth so unknown, and a truth so nearly impossible for an Israelite to believe? What could be more consistent with a message of total grace than a man like Paul delivering a secret from heaven that no one had yet heard of?

Paul told the Corinthians:

> Lo! A secret to you am I telling! We all, indeed, shall not be put to repose, yet we all shall be changed, in an instant, in the twinkle of an eye, at the last trump. For He will be trumpeting, and the dead will be roused incorruptible, and we shall be changed.
>
> —1 Corinthians 15:51-52, CLNT

To the Thessalonians, Paul wrote:

> For we are saying to you by the Word of the Lord, that we, the living, who are surviving to the presence of the Lord, should by no means outstrip those who are put to repose, for the Lord Himself will be descending from heaven with a shout of command, with the voice of the Chief Messenger, and with the trumpet of God, and the dead in Christ shall be rising first.

Thereupon we, the living who are surviving, shall at the same time be snatched away together with them in clouds, to meet the Lord in the air. And thus shall we always be together with the Lord. So that, console one another with these words.

—1 Thessalonians 4:15-18, CLNT

"Lo! A secret to you am I telling!" The resurrection of the dead was not a secret. Daniel had prophesied years before (Daniel 12:1-3) that there would be a resurrection of the dead of the worthy ones in Israel. Centuries before Paul, God had given Daniel the amazing truth that human bodies, long decayed, would walk from the grave. During our Lord's sojourn on Earth, we saw this happen when He raised Lazarus and others. Scripture tells us that over 500 walked from the tombs following Jesus' resurrection.

Amazing. Yes. But then came Paul.

If these truths from 1 Corinthians and 1 Thessalonians were a secret, then they cannot be teaching the same truth Daniel taught—and they aren't. This secret resurrection taught by Paul will occur *before* the saints of Israel are raised. Again, if this resurrection Paul refers to is the same resurrection Israel looked forward to, then it could not be called a secret.

What we are considering here is a different resurrection of a different people with a different gospel—believers who shall rise from the dead with different bodies to go to a different realm where they will have a different task than Israel's.

I realize how spiritually fashionable it is among many "believers" today to disbelieve these plain passages of Scripture (1 Corinthians 15:51-52; 1 Thessalonians 4:15-18). Once again, it's due to a wholesale ignorance of the difference between the gospel of the Circumcision and that of the Uncircumcision: Ignorance of the presence of a different body of teaching to a different body of people (non-Jews), with a different destiny, for which they will require different bodies.

The Christian religion states that all who believe in Jesus Christ will fly away to heaven at "the rapture." This will amount to about several hundred million people, they say.

Imagine the chaos. Should a Christian be piloting a jetliner during the rapture, his or her sudden absence will bode poorly for all unchurched passengers. With any luck, the co-pilot will be a backslidden Christian who will assume the pilot's vacated seat and land the plane safely. No passengers will thank God, however, for they will all be atheists.

No need to imagine any of this, for Christian movie producers have already enacted such traumatic scenes in the film, *Left Behind*. See the shock. Feel the pain. Watch the puzzled faces at Rand McNally as mapmakers begin asking one another, "Hey! What happened to Colorado Springs?"

This is why I don't believe in the "rapture." But I do believe in the "snatching away."

IT MEANS WHAT IT SAYS

I believe the passages our apostle Paul wrote. I believe Jesus Christ will descend from heaven, for that's what 1 Thessalonians, chapter 4, clearly says He will do. I believe the dead in Christ will be rising first. I believe those who are alive at that time will be snatched away. This is the Scriptural term: "snatched away." These people will be snatched away, then, not "raptured."

These people will rise (which means "to go up") to meet the Lord in the air (which is what we breathe), in clouds (which are "masses of visible vapor").

The passage is plain enough. What is to keep mature believers from believing it?

Three things. Because of what the Christian religion has done with this passage (made a world-wide disaster of it), many serious-minded saints simply cannot swallow a literal rendering. Secondly, along this same line, some saints equate "literal" with

It means what it says.

"unspiritual." Thus, these serious-minded people constantly seek secret, allegorical meanings to plain, literal passages.

For instance, even though clouds are often found in the air, and the same Greek word, *nephele*, is used by Jesus in Luke 12:54 to describe what produces a rainstorm, these allegory-minded people take the clouds of 1 Thessalonians to be clouds of saints.

Only once in the New Testament is *nephele* used figuratively. In Hebrews 12:1, we read of a cloud of witnesses. But a rule of thumb for Scriptural interpretation (for those who care for rules) is: literal if possible. As the saints of 1 Thessalonians are rising to meet the Lord in the air, a literal rendering of *nephele* (clouds) is not only possible, but probable.

Now tell me. How is this not spiritual?

Though physical, the cloud that led Israel in the wilderness was as spiritual as could be. It was spiritual (though not in molecular structure) in that God employed it for His purposes. This cloud served as a divine guidepost. The clouds of 1 Thessalonians? These clouds hide heavenly doings from the gaze of earthlings. It's spiritual as can be.

As for rising in the air to meet the Lord, the dead rising first, and the saints always being together with the Lord, I have not been initiated into the "secret, allegorical meanings" of these phrases. Neither have I any idea how one could be disappointed in the literal rendering, or be desirous of a more spiritual chain of events.

A REAL DOOR-OPENER

Thirdly, many believers fail to distinguish the body of Christ from the bride of the Lambkin. That is, they do not appreciate the different destinies of Israel's saints and proselytes (Israelite "wannabes")—who embrace the evangel of the Circumcision—and the mix of Jews and Greeks who embrace Paul's evangel of the Uncircumcision (see Galatians 2:7). Without this key, many doors simply will not open. One of them is the door to the glory of 1 Thessalonians, chapter 4.

Not all living people who believe in Jesus when He descends from heaven will be snatched from Earth's Tribulation to meet Him in the air. (If the number of people who embrace Paul's evangel today is any indication of how many will embrace it on *that* day, then the number will be small and the event quiet; the vast majority of believers today are Circumcision believers, as I explain in chapter 14. So forget, if you can, the pilotless jetliner scenario mentioned earlier. Forget *Left Behind*.)

Scripture clearly states (in Revelation, chapter 7) that there will be 144,000 out of Israel, sealed on their foreheads, whom God will preserve through (not out of) the Day of Indignation, otherwise referred to as "the Tribulation." Concurrently, some saints will have attained martyrdom ("A vast throng ... out of all nations, tribes, peoples, and languages" Revelation 7:9), precluding any possibility of them being snatched from harm's way.

Now, if one assumes the saints of Revelation, chapter 7, to be the same saints of 1 Thessalonians, chapter 4, one *must* "spiritualize away" the clear teaching of 1 Thessalonians, to make it fit the clear teaching of Revelation.

May the reader of these lines now realize these two passages are not meant to fit, but are rather describing the different destinies of two distinct, discrete peoples, or groups of believers. Israel shall become "a kingdom and a priesthood for God," and "they shall be reigning on the Earth" (Revelation 5:10). They are the "bride company," the "kingdom saints," the "Overcomers," whatever you want to call them. Those of Christ's body, however, shall be "displaying the transcendent riches of His grace among the celestials" (Ephesians 2:6-7). A different realm altogether.

Everything should now make sense. The saints of Christ's body are snatched away in the air and transferred to the realm of their ministry. ("For our realm is inherent in the heavens" Philippians 3:20.) It's practical.

Kingdom saints (Circumcision-gospel believers) who live through the Day of Indignation (the Tribulation) remain on Earth, for Earth becomes their place of business for the kingdom era.

Doesn't this make sense? Isn't it practical?

Yes. And it's also spiritual as all get-out.

12.
THE HIGHEST PURPOSE OF GOD

THE HIGHEST PURPOSE OF GOD

For more than seven millennia, generations of humans, like shadows, have appeared and disappeared. Whence came these countless millions of human beings, and whither do they go?

This problem has preoccupied the world's thought since the dawn of history. The problem of Final Destiny is for humankind the question of questions. Nothing else equals it in practical importance.

It vitally affects humanity's existence in this life and in the next. It concerns every individual and touches every problem of enduring interest.

All that this world can give does not satisfy heart or mind ... without some reasonable assurance as to whether or not the hereafter will be one of infinite weal or woe.

So long as this point remains uncertain, everything is precarious, peace is impossible. Life is a vapor that appears for a while and vanishes away. But there is a beyond. What is that beyond to be?

From *The Ages in the Scriptures* by Vladimir Gelesnoff

Only one human in the history of the world holds the answer to humanity's most pressing question: *What is the final destiny of humanity?*

God gave the answer to this question, and the authority to record it, to the apostle Paul. Only Paul answers this crucial question, concerning everyone and everything ever created.

The question of humanity's final destiny, which has vexed philosophers for centuries, has already been answered. Few on this planet, however, have grasped the answer.

A.E. Knoch sums it up in *Unsearchable Riches*, Vol. 32 (Jan. 1941): 42:

> The secret of Christ [that is, to eventually bring everything ever created under the headship of Christ] is the capstone of divine revelation. Until this secret was made known, Scripture was incomplete. Before this, Scripture was confined mostly to one nation and one race upon the Earth. The rest of the universe seemed to be outside the range of Christ's sacrifice.
>
> The Circumcision evangel, though it occupies the bulk of Scripture, deals with only a small segment of creation. But Paul embraces *all* within the scope of his unfolding. Paul is the one who rounds out, or completes, the Word of God.

There's only one reason all creation will eventually live for eternity with God: Jesus Christ, on the cross, abolished death. Christ dealt the death-blow to death, for everyone, for all time. Paul is the only Bible writer to unveil this most victorious result of the cross. In 1 Corinthians 15:26, Paul wrote: "The last enemy being abolished is death."

The outworking of this victory does not happen all at once, but in increments:

"For even as in Adam all are dying, thus also in Christ shall all be vivified. *Yet each in his own class*" (1 Corinthians 15:22).

When death is abolished, nothing remains but life. When all are vivified in Christ, none remain dead.

Again, we do not yet see the full results of His victory, for graves are yet among us. Nevertheless, the victory is assured. Jesus Christ will wipe away every tear. Thus the battle is won, while victory appears gradually over coming horizons. As Paul wrote in 1 Timothy 2:5-7—

> For there is one God, and one Mediator of God and hu-mankind, a Man, Christ Jesus, Who is giving Himself a correspondent Ransom for all, *the testimony in its own eras*, for which I was appointed a herald and an apostle (I am telling the truth, I am not lying), a teacher of the nations in knowledge and truth.

This lifetime is not the end of the grace road. Far from it; this life is only the beginning.

PURPOSES OF GOD FULFILLED IN THE BODY OF CHRIST

In Colossians 1:25, Paul said he completes the Word of God. Why? The message God gave to Paul (and the group of people who benefit from and enact the message) *will complete the universe.*

I know how unimaginably grand this must sound. Yet no other meaning can be gleaned from the following passage:

> He chooses us in Him before the disruption of the world, we to be holy and flawless in His sight, in love designating us beforehand for the place of a son for Him through Christ Jesus; in accord with the delight of His will, for the laud

of the glory of His grace, which graces us in the Beloved:

In Whom we are having the deliverance through His blood, the forgiveness of offenses in accord with the riches of His grace, which He lavishes on us; in all wisdom and prudence making known to us the secret of His will (in accord with His delight, which He purposed in Him) *to have an administration of the complement of the eras, to head up all in the Christ—both that in the heavens and that on the Earth*—in Him in Whom our lot was cast also;

Being designated beforehand according to the purpose of the One Who is operating all in accord with the counsel of His will, that we should be for the laud of His glory, who are pre-expectant in the Christ.
—Ephesians 1:4-12, CLNT

That's a mouthful. Let's analyze it.

God will use us to reconcile the universe to Himself. We were chosen for this amazing call before we were born. I do not intend here to probe the truth of predestination, but if you do not see it in this verse, you may not ever see it—not in this life, anyway.

God designated us beforehand—not only to believe in Him, but—to have the place of a son. As sons and daughters, we are qualified to accomplish this astounding work on God's behalf.

Having a Father is deeper truth than having a God.

The word "God" means "placer." The term speaks of One Who works all things after the counsel of His own will (Ephesians 1:11). Indeed, He is our God (our Placer, the Arranger of our lives and our days), but He is also our Father, the One with Whom we enjoy a relationship. As God, we worship and honor Him. As Father, we lay our heads on His breast and entrust our all to Him.

Our calling—to accomplish this great purpose—is for the delight of His will, and for the laud of His glory. Although we feel joy, God is the premier beneficiary of all His actions.

Whenever we start feeling unworthy of this call, we are tempted to crawl into our Father's lap and cry, "Father, why me?

Why have you chosen me above all others? I am so unworthy!" Let's rethink this. It delights God to call us; He derives far more pleasure from it than we do. The deepest source of His pleasure is to astound unworthy people. Were we worthy of His favor, it would pop His grace bubble. Instead, it thrills Him to carry such sinners as us to heaven's summit. Therefore, we should stop all the, "Oh, I'm unworthy" talk, and let God have His day. For, truly, only one thing warms God's heart more than seating us at His right hand: placing His Son there—fresh from Calvary—first.

We are His sons and daughters, and so He "makes known to us the secret of His will." As we have already discussed, He hid many things from Israel. When Jesus told Nicodemus of Israel's new birth, He kept mum about celestial secrets. To whom, then, does God make known the deepest secret of His will? To Adam? To Abraham? To Moses? To Elijah? To Daniel? To Isaiah? To Nicodemus? To Peter? None of the above. God makes known the secret of His will to *us*, through our apostle Paul—the first human apprised of it.

The secret of God's will is cached in the purpose of the cross. It always was cached here, even at Pentecost when Peter felt but a flicker of its flame. Now, finally, the secret of the cross—a secret hidden from the eons in God—is revealed to a murderer, and then passed on, by him, to we who were without hope in the world, without expectation, and without God: "To have an administration of the complement of the eras, to head up all in the Christ—both that in the heavens and that on the Earth" (Ephesians 1:10).

This passage sparkles in the J.B. Phillips paraphrase, *The New Testament in Modern English*:

> For God has allowed us to know the secret of His plan, and it is this: He purposes in His sovereign will that all human history shall be consummated in Christ, that everything that exists in heaven or Earth shall find its perfection and fulfillment in Him.
>
> —Ephesians 1:10

Everything in the universe will be headed up in Christ. Christianity, fatally ignorant of this truth, teaches the opposite. Christianity actually believes (I can hardly say it) that God has no choice but to give up the greater part of His universe, for eternity, into the hands of Satan. Although God sent His Son to die for all sin, the enterprise flopped. Apparently, Christ died for every sin except one (unbelief), and this sin will ultimately—in spite of the cross—eternally ban billions from His presence, they say.

This EPIC FAIL, endorsed by the world's most popular religion, is based on faulty Scripture translations (see my book, *Martin Zender Goes to Hell*).

Teachers and ministers—eager to embrace the poison of eternal torment—foist it onto gullible hearts.

We complete the eras—and Christ

"An administration of the complement of the eras" (Ephesians 1:10). The word translated "complement" here is the Greek word *pleroma,* which means, "that which fills." A complement is the thing that completes something heretofore incomplete. Not only are God's times (His "eras") incomplete without the work that *we* shall do, but Christ Himself is incomplete without His body. Ephesians 1:23 backs up this startling truth: "[God] gives [Christ] as Head over all, to the ecclesia which is His body, *the complement of the One completing the All in all.*"

In the beginning, God gave Christ to be Head over all His creation. God could have done this by Himself, but it pleased Him to do it through a Son. Jesus Christ Himself said, "I came out of the Father" (John 16:28). For what purpose? Through the Son, the Father intended to—and will—reconcile everything ever created to Himself. *Everything.*

> And He is the Head of the body, the ecclesia, who is Sovereign, Firstborn from among the dead, that in all He may be

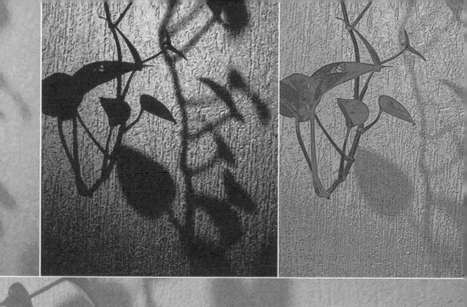

PAST   PRESENT   FUTURE

Colossians 1:16
In Him all is
created.

Colossians 1:20
... through Him all is
reconciled.

Because of
the cross ...
Colossians 1:20

Want the big picture? Here's the secret of Christ,
as explained by Paul. Most Christians
are oblivious of this secret.

becoming first, for in Him the entire complement delights to dwell, and through Him to reconcile all to Him (making peace through the blood of His cross), through Him, whether those on the Earth or those in the heavens.
—Colossians 1:18-20, CLNT

The phrase "All in all" in Ephesians 1:23 ("God gives Him as Head over all, to the ecclesia which is His body, the complement of the One completing the All in all") is vitally important. God's goal: to become All in all, that is, Everything in everybody. This grand purpose, unknown to Israel, and unknown to most of Christianity, is reiterated and confirmed for us in 1 Corinthians 15:28—"Now, whenever all may be subject to Him, then the Son Himself also shall be subjected to Him Who subjects all to Him, that God may be All in all."

This ultra-literal translation yields much treasure.

Christ came into the world to subject all things to His Father, nothing lost, everything in the universe praising Him. The means to this marvel was the cross. *We* will be His fellow-laborers. When the grand subjection eventually transpires, then the Son Himself shall be subject to the One Who subjected everything to Him, namely, His Father.

(God subjected everything to His Son because God knew His Son was more than capable of returning it to Him—richer than when it left. How could creation become richer than the day it departed God's fingertip? By the experience of evil, and the resultant praise and worship, which can come only via practical experience with that black background.)

Christ will not subject Himself, however, until He has subjected all else to His Father.

Let us consult another passage to confirm this truth: In a distant day, everything that came from God shall return to Him.

Romans 11:36—"Out of Him and through Him and into Him is all."

This simple verse wrecks at least three major Christian creeds, and I do love it when that happens. Let God be true, though every human a liar (Romans 3:4).

Let us state Romans 11:36 this way: Everything came out of God; everything exists because of God, and everything returns to God. This truth is so simple, even a child can believe it. Only a hardcore seminary course can beat this much truth and common sense out of a person. *The Message* is eloquent here in its childlike simplicity: "Everything comes from Him; everything happens through Him; everything ends up in Him" (Romans 11:36).

Almost all Christians believe that everything comes from God. A few Christians believe that everything happens through Him (though most Christians attribute all evil things—absolutely speaking—to Satan; never mind that God said, "I create evil" Isaiah 45:7). Hardly anyone believes the last part of Romans 11:36— "Everything ends up in Him."

In his preface to the book of Colossians (*Concordant Literal New Testament*), A. E. Knoch writes:

> The Son of God, the Firstborn of Creation, is the satisfactory solution to all questions which concern creation. Creation did not begin in chaos but in Christ. [Creation] will not end in ruin wrought by humans but in universal reconciliation wrought by the blood of the cross.

Again, Christ is the Agent for this marvelous work of reconciliation. For this purpose, Christ came out of God, becoming His visible image (Colossians 1:15), and dying on the cross. Everything that God was, filled Christ. Thus, in Christ "the entire complement (filling of the Deity) delights to dwell" (Colossians 1:20).

Christ came out of God, and He completes—for us, for our poor, wanting senses—everything that God is. Now, an even more astounding thing: From Christ comes His body, and *we* complete everything that *Christ* is.

Again, in Ephesians 1:23—"[God] gives Him as Head over

It takes a hardcore seminary course to beat this much common sense out of a person.

ROMA
11:3

THE FIRST IDIOT IN HEAVEN

all, to the ecclesia which is His body, the complement of the One completing the All in all."

Read it slowly: His body (this refers to us, the body of Christ) is the complement of (it completes) the One completing the All in all—referring to Christ, for Christ is the One in 1 Corinthians 15:28 who makes God everything (All) to everybody (all).

Try it this way: The One Who completes everything is Christ, and we complete the One Who completes everything. *We complete Christ.* In other words, Christ is incomplete without us. Without us, He is a body-less Head. This incomplete state of Christ keeps the universe from completion. Thus, the created universe awaits *us.* Sentient beings—even animals—subconsciously anticipate our change into glorious, heavenly beings. They somehow subconsciously realize that we are the key to their deliverance:

"For the premonition of the creation is awaiting the unveiling of the sons of God" (Romans 8:19).

I know how unbelievable and unlikely this must seem, but it delights God to do this, and it delights Christ. None of us dreamed this up. Who could have? Do you think you cannot wait to see Christ? Your longing for Him pales in comparison to His longing for you. Christ will not begin completing the universe without us.

These eras—the times segregated by God for carrying out this purpose—need to be completed. Again, from Ephesians 1:10: God's purpose for us is "to have an administration of the complement [the completion] of the eras, to head up all in the Christ—both that in the heavens and that on the Earth."

When all is headed up in Christ (Who will in turn give it all to God), then the times, the eras, which God set apart for this work, will finally be complete. To complete these eras, God predesignates an administration. God is orderly. Yes, He could do everything with a single wave of a magic wand, but He chooses not to. Rather, it delights Him to call out a specific group of people and direct them through a specific period of time for a specific purpose—to bring all creation to a satisfying conclusion.

This is our glorious task—not Israel's.

An administration is "the management of any office." Christ has an office, that is, He has a duty: To bring the entire creation in glorious and happy subjection to the feet of His Father. "Christ" is not His last name, but a title, which says what He does: He is anointed ("christ" means "anointed") to carry out a purpose.

Therefore, we are called to administrate (manage), in heaven, Christ's office (duty) to reconcile all creation to His Father.

Israel does not complete this duty, nor this office. To Israel belongs the Earth. Photographs from the Hubble telescope assure us that Earth is a mere speck of the universe. When considering the future operating field of Christ's body, we are considering—not just a dusty piece of real estate in the Middle East, but—the realm of every spinning galaxy ever made. Israel can't see past Jerusalem. Fine. Let them have it.

To us belongs all else.

ONE MORE CURTAIN CALL: PAUL

Every administration needs an administrator. Peter was administrator of the gospel of the Circumcision. Our administrator is the apostle Paul. He, and he alone, was granted the grace to administrate the administration that will head up the universe in Christ, for God. I will let Paul tell you about it in his own words:

> On this behalf, I Paul, the prisoner of Christ Jesus for you, the nations—since you surely hear of the administration of the grace of God that is given to me for you, for by revelation the secret is made known to me ... in spirit the nations are to be joint enjoyers of an allotment, and a joint body, and joint partakers of the promise in Christ Jesus, through the evangel of which I became the dispenser, in accord with the gratuity of the grace of God, which is granted to me in accord with His powerful operations.

> To me, less than the least of all the saints, was granted
> this grace: to bring the evangel of the untraceable riches of
> Christ to the nations, and to enlighten all as to what is the
> administration of the secret, which has been concealed from
> the eons in God, Who creates all, that now may be made
> known to the sovereignties and the authorities among the
> celestials, through the ecclesia, the multifarious wisdom
> of God, in accord with the purpose of the eons, which He
> makes in Christ Jesus, our Lord.
>
> —Ephesians 3:1-3; 6-11, CLNT

These words are among the highest revelations ever given to
humankind. The red letters of Christ, in Matthew, Mark, Luke,
and John, pale before them. These words in Ephesians are also the
words of Christ, albeit the words of the glorified Christ, transmitted to us via His chosen messenger: Paul.

Not until Paul wrote Ephesians had the words "among the
celestials" appeared in any Scripture. The blessings of Israel were
always heavenly in character, but never in location. Yet now:

> God, being rich in mercy, because of His vast love with
> which He loves us (we also being dead to the offenses and
> the lusts), vivifies us together in Christ (in grace are you
> saved!) and rouses us together *and seats us together among
> the celestials, in Christ Jesus,* that in the oncoming eons, He
> should be displaying the transcendent riches of His grace
> in His kindness to us in Christ Jesus.
>
> —Ephesians 2:4-7, CLNT

Our task, in future eons, will be to make known to celestial
dignitaries, both good and evil, the transcendent riches of God's
grace. What better way for God to transmit these riches, than by
granting such unworthy people as us the highest honors of divine
favor?

The only way we can grasp the height and depth and breadth of this calling is for God Himself to give us a spirit of revelation concerning it. Therefore, my prayer for you is also the prayer Paul prayed on behalf of every member of the body of Christ:

> Therefore, I also, on hearing of this faith of yours in the Lord Jesus, and that for all the saints, do not cease giving thanks for you, making mention in my prayers that the God of our Lord Jesus Christ, the Father of glory, may be giving you a spirit of wisdom and revelation in the realization of Him, the eyes of your heart having been enlightened, for you to perceive what is the expectation of His calling and what the riches of the glory of the enjoyment of His allotment among the saints;

> And what the transcendent greatness of His power for us who are believing, in accord with the operation of the might of His strength, which is operative in the Christ, rousing Him from among the dead and seating Him at His right hand among the celestials, up over every sovereignty and authority and power and lordship, and every name that is named, not only in this eon, but also in that which is impending: and subjects all under His feet, and gives Him, as Head over all, *to the ecclesia which is His body*, the complement of the One completing the All in all.
>   —Ephesians 1:15-23, CLNT

13.
THE KEY DIFFERENCES

THE KEY DIFFERENCES

The accompanying chart lists thirty-one differences between the bride of the Lamb and the body of Christ, between the gospel of the Circumcision and the gospel of the Uncircumcision. In the pages that follow, each of these points is briefly explained. Before we launch, however, allow me to cement for you the importance of the word "of" in Galatians 2:7, and why this two-letter word proves that Peter's and Paul's gospels are, indeed, two separate and distinct messages.

SILVER BULLET

For those needing a single "silver bullet" verse proving that Paul's message was distinct from Peter's, that verse would be Galatians 2:7. From the *Concordant Literal New Testament*:

"I have been entrusted with the evangel of the Uncircumcision, according as Peter of the Circumcision."

Not even the *King James Version* managed to mess it up:

"The gospel of the Uncircumcision was committed unto me, as the gospel of the Circumcision was unto Peter."

The *New International Version*, however (I call this the "New Inconsistent Version"), *has* screwed it up:

"I had been given the task of preaching the gospel to the Gentiles, just as Peter had been given the task of preaching the gospel to the Jews."

The big difference? The NIV has "to" rather than "of," as in, "the gospel *to* the Gentiles." I will explain the significance of this momentarily.

The *New American Standard Bible* also botched it, but unaccountably lists the correct reading in the margin. Here's the text:

"I had been entrusted with the gospel to the uncircumcised, just as Peter had been to the circumcised."

Next to the phrase, "to the uncircumcised," however, the NASB has a footnote: "*of* the Circumcision."

Why didn't they put that in the text? The difference between "of" and "to" could not be more profound. "Of" acquaints us with character, "to" with location. If I play the music *of* the Japanese and you play the music *of* the Mexicans, we are playing different music. But if I play the music *to* the Japanese and you play the music *to* the Mexicans, we may very well be playing the same music.

Prepare yourself now for a brief lesson in Greek.

It's all Greek to me

In First Century Greek, the genitive case ("of," that is, the character of a thing) is indicated (in the feminine singular) by adding the letters eyta (H) and sigma (C) to the end of an article, while the dative case ("to," that is, the location of a thing) omits the sigma. Each of the three oldest Greek manuscripts (Sinaiticus, Vaticanus, and Alexandrinus) clearly indicates the genitive case in Galatians 2:7. As already noted, the *King James Version* translates

3 1 DIFFERENCES

Evangel of the
Circumcision
..... Galatians 2:7 ......

Evangel of the
Uncircumcision

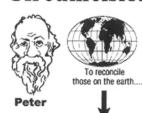

Peter

To reconcile
those on the earth....

In accord with prophets
Acts 3:24-25
↓

Jesus Christ
"Through Him, to
reconcile all to Him
(making peace through
the blood of His cross),
through Him, whether
those on the earth
or those in the
heavens."

Colossians 1:20

Paul

To reconcile
those in the heavens....

A secret until Paul
Ephesians 3:8-10
↓

TRADITIONAL

Servant of the
Circumcision ...... *Rom. 15:8*

Col. 1:15 ...... ## Firstborn of
Every Creature

UNHEARD-OF

Reign on earth → Revelation 5:10

Reign among celestials → Ephesians 2:6-7

Peter called in Israel (Mt. 4:18)	Paul called outside Israel (Acts 9:3)
Proclaimed among Israelites (Js. 1:1; 1 Pet. 1:1)	Proclaimed among the nations (Eph. 3:8)
Salvation *because of* Israel (Acts 10:30-32)	Salvation *in spite of* Israel (Acts 13:6-12; Rom. 11:15)
Saints termed the bride of the Lambkin (Jn. 3:29; Rev. 21:9)	Saints termed the body of Christ (Eph. 5:30)
Glory of the terrestrial (1 Cor. 15:40; Jn. 3:12)	Glory of the celestial (1 Cor. 15:40; Jn. 3:12)
Racial distinctions important (Mt. 19:28; Rev. 21:12)	Racial distinctions irrelevant (1 Cor. 12:13; Gal. 3:28)
Believers known *from* the disruption of the world (Rev. 17:8)	Believers known *before* the disruption of the world (Eph. 1:4)
Believers called first, then chosen (Mt. 22:14)	Believers chosen first, then called (Rom. 8:30)
Will keep law (Mic. 4:2)	Not under law (Rom. 6:14)
Water baptism required (Ac. 2:38)	Water baptism not required (1 Cor. 1:17; 12:13)
Must be *begotten* anew ("born again"–Jn. 3:3)	Are a *new creation* (2 Cor. 5:17)
Pardoned of guilt (that is, *forgiven*–Lk. 11:4)	Not even guilty (that is, *justified*–Rom. 5:1)
The irreverent are condemned (2 Pet. 2:5-6)	The irreverent are justified (Rom. 4:5)
Must have works, or faith is dead (Js. 2:20)	Must *not* be working, only having faith (Rom. 4:5)
Must be an overcomer to avoid second death (Rev. 2:11)	Saved from second death by grace alone (Eph. 2:8-9)
Must forgive others for God to forgive them (Mt. 6:15)	Deal graciously with others as God has dealt graciously (Eph. 4:32)
Expecting grace (1 Pet. 1:13)	Standing in grace (Rom. 5:2)
Not yet manifested what they shall be (1 Jn. 3:2)	Are mirroring the Lord's glory (2 Cor. 3:18)
His manifestation is their change (1 Jn. 3:2)	His manifestation is their manifestation (Col. 3:4)
Exhorted to toss worry on Him (1 Pet. 5:7)	Exhorted not to worry about anything (Php. 4:6)
Exhorted to remain in Him (1 Jn. 2:28)	Died with Him; He cannot disown Himself (2 Tim. 2:11,13)
Tend to have difficulty apprehending Paul (2 Pet. 3:15-16)	Tend to apprehend both evangels (2 Cor. 12:11)
Must be watching (Lk. 12:37; Heb. 9:28)	Watching *or* drowsing (1 Thess. 5:10)
Can be put to shame at His presence (1 Jn. 2:28)	Will be changed at His presence (1 Thess. 4:15-17; 1 Cor. 15:52)
Will go through day of indignation (Rev. 7:1-17)	Not appointed to indignation (1 Thess. 1:10; 5:9)
Will receive Christ on earth (Acts 1:11-12; Zech 14:4)	Will meet Christ in air (1 Thess. 4:17)
Saved left, unsaved taken out (Mt. 24:38-41)	Saved taken out, unsaved left (1 Thess. 4:17)
To be a kingdom of priests over nations (Rev. 2:26-27; Is 61:6)	To have an allotment among the celestials (Eph. 2:6)
Will fill earth with knowledge of God's glory (Hab. 2:14)	Will dispense God's wisdom among the celestials (Eph. 3:10-12)
Will judge twelve tribes of Israel (Mt. 19:28)	Will judge angels (1 Cor. 6:3)
Will have access to temple courts (Rev. 7:15)	Have access to the Father Himself (Eph. 2:18)

this correctly, as does the *Concordant Literal New Testament*. The NIV translators mistakenly use the word "to," even though they properly translate the same word in a similarly constructed passage (Romans 4:11—"And [Abraham] received the sign *of* circumcision"), using "of."

Thanks for your kind attention. Your Greek lesson has concluded.

Here, then, are thirty-one key differences between the gospel of the Circumcision and the gospel of the Uncircumcision, and a brief explanation of each. All verses in this section (except where otherwise noted) are from the *Concordant Literal New Testament*.

1. Gospel of Circumcision, Peter's gospel: Peter called in Israel (Matthew 4:18)

> Now, walking beside the sea of Galilee, He perceived two brothers, Simon, termed Peter, and Andrew, his brother, casting a purse net into the sea, for they were fishers.

Obviously, the Sea of Galilee is in Israel. Why emphasize that Peter, the key holder of the earthly kingdom, first met Jesus Christ in Israel? To make the contrast:

Gospel of Uncircumcision, Paul's gospel: Paul called outside Israel (Acts 9:3)

> Now in his going he came to be nearing Damascus. Suddenly a light out of heaven flashes about him.

The glorified Christ waited until Paul was outside the land of his forefathers before arresting him. There are no accidents in God's earthly arrangements. Paul's divine task was to minister a new gospel to the nations. Therefore, what better place for his wake-up call than among the nations?

2. Gospel of Circumcision, Peter's gospel:
Proclaimed among Israelites (James 1:1; 1 Peter 1:1)

▶ James, a slave of God and of the Lord Jesus Christ, to
the twelve tribes in the dispersion.
▶ Peter, an apostle of Jesus Christ, to the chosen expatriates of the dispersion of Pontus, Galatia, Cappadocia, the
province of Asia, and Bithynia.

Once one realizes that in the New Testament there are two
different gospels being broadcast to two different groups of people,
things that were never obvious before suddenly jump from the
text. For instance: "James to the twelve tribes." Are you reading
someone else's mail and applying it to yourself? All Scripture is for
us, but not all of it is to us.

Gospel of Uncircumcision, Paul's gospel:
Proclaimed among the nations (Ephesians 3:8)

To me, less than the least of all saints, was granted this
grace: to bring the evangel of the untraceable riches of
Christ to the nations.

Paul writes to Romans and Galatians and folks from Philippi.
While it's true you are no more a Philippian than I am, these folks
receiving Paul's letters have one thing in common: They are all
Gentiles, non-Israelites. Concerning messages of salvation, to God
there are only two groups of people: Israelites and non-Israelites;
Circumcision and Uncircumcision. Besides this, the rest is details.

3. Gospel of Circumcision, Peter's gospel:
Salvation *because of* Israel (Acts 10:30-32)

And Cornelius averred, "Four days ago unto this hour was

I fasting, and at the ninth, praying in my house, and lo! a man stood before me in splendid attire, and is averring, "Cornelius, your prayer is hearkened to, and your alms are brought to remembrance in God's sight. Send, then, into Joppa, and call for Simon, who is surnamed Peter. He is lodging in the house of Simon, a tanner, beside the sea."

Without Peter, Cornelius is sunk. Peter belonged to the nation that God called, "A royal priesthood." A priest is a go-between, a channel. On Earth, Israel will always be the channel between God and the nations. Here's how it will work in the earthly kingdom:

Man from nations: I need saved!
Bystander: Quick! Somebody fetch an Israelite!

Sound far-fetched? Read Zechariah 8:23—

> Thus says Yahweh of hosts: In those days ten mortals, from all the languages of the nations, will take fast hold. And they will take fast hold of the hem of a man, a Jew, saying, "We will go with you, for we hear that God is with you."

Gospel of Uncircumcision, Paul's gospel:
   Salvation *in spite of* Israel (Acts 13:6-12; Romans 11:15)

> Now, passing through the whole island up to Paphos, they found a certain man, a magician, a false prophet, a Jew, whose name was Bar-Jesus, who was with the proconsul Sergius Paulus, an intelligent man. He, calling to him Barnabas and Saul, seeks to hear the Word of God. Now Elymas, the "Magician" (for thus is his name construed), withstood them, seeking to pervert the proconsul from the faith. Now Saul, who is also Paul, being filled with Holy Spirit, looking intently at him, said, "O, full of all guile and all knavery, son of the Adversary, enemy of all righteousness, will you not cease perverting the straight ways of the Lord?

And now, lo! the hand of the Lord is on you, and you shall be blind, not observing the sun until the appointed time." Now instantly there falls on him a fog and darkness, and, going about, he sought someone to lead him by the hand. Then the proconsul, perceiving what has occurred, believes, being astonished at the teaching of the Lord.

Here we have a Gentile man seeking salvation, and an Israelite waiting in the wings. Sounds like the perfect set-up, right? Not this time. With Paul's gospel, the presence of a law-loving nation (Israel) hinders a message of grace. The Gentile proconsul Sergius Paulus isn't saved because of an Israelite, but rather in spite of one. Can you say: "God just made a point"?

> For if their casting away is the conciliation of the world, what will their taking back be if not life from among the dead?
>
> —Romans 11:15

Before Paul, the mere mention of the phrase, "the casting away of Israel," would have spelled despair to both Gentile and Jew. Strangely, the casting away of Israel is *good* news here. God withholds full-orbed grace until law comes off the table. Another way of saying it: Until God hardens Israel and temporarily sets her aside, the depths of His grace wait in the wings. Two things keep us from grasping grace: 1) flesh, and 2) law. (In other words: Israel.) If fleshly distinctions matter—where is grace? If one has to obey law or else—where is grace? God will fulfill what He started with Israel, but only after He calls out the last member of the body of Christ and closes this era of the nations.

4. Gospel of Circumcision, Peter's gospel:
Saints termed the bride of the Lambkin (John 3:29; Revelation 21:9)

He Who has the bride is the Bridegroom. Yet the friend of

the Bridegroom, who stands and is hearing Him, is rejoicing with joy because of the Bridegroom's voice. This, my joy, then, has been fulfilled.

I used to think that the closest a person could get to Christ was to be His bride. I mean, doesn't the bride stand only a foot away from the groom? Aren't they holding hands? Then I discovered I was a member of the body of Christ. I was not to be married to Him, I was part of Him. Our relationship to Christ is far more intimate than Israel's. They stand a foot away from Him; that's fantastic, and who would say it isn't? But we *are* Him.

> And one of the seven messengers who have the seven bowls brimming with the last seven calamities came, and he speaks with me, saying, "Hither! I shall be showing you the bride, the wife of the Lambkin."
>
> —Revelation 21:9

Again, the phrase "bride of Christ" does not appear in Scripture. The term is a Frankenstein, like taking the head of a goldfish and putting it on a gerbil. "Christ" is the term associated with our Savior's celestial glories and His call of Paul for the nations. "Bride," on the other hand, was, and always will be, Israel's relationship to Him.

Gospel of Uncircumcision, Paul's gospel: Saints termed the body of Christ (Ephesians 5:29-30)

> For no one at any time hates his own flesh, but is nurturing and cherishing it, according as Christ also the ecclesia, for we are members of His body.

God never spoke of the Gentile nations as being His bride. Rather, members of the nations (and those Israelites who heard the call and forsook their national identity) became members of His body: a much closer relationship. Let us differentiate what God differentiates. We ought not feel guilty that we out-glory Israel. This isn't our plan, but God's. In God's glorious plan, everyone will be satisfied with their respective glories. God delivers what He promises—this for Israel, and that for the nations.

5. Gospel of Circumcision, Peter's gospel:
Glory of the terrestrial (1 Corinthians 15:40; John 3:12)

> There are bodies celestial as well as bodies terrestrial. But a different glory, indeed, is that of the celestial, yet a different that of the terrestrial.

Paul uses creation as an example of differing glories. Paul's use of "celestial" and "terrestrial" points out the differences between the two gospels and the two groups of saints made immortal. Note that the common word is "glory." Israel will not envy the body of Christ, and the body of Christ will not envy Israel. Each will say: "Behold our glory!" and will give God glory for it.

Note, too, the use of the word "body." Bride-of-the-Lamb saints and body-of-Christ saints both have bodies. Bride saints will have bodies constituted like the body of the resurrected Jesus when He appeared to the disciples in Luke 24:36-43 and ate fish with them. They thought He was a spirit, but He said to them: "Handle Me and perceive, for a spirit has not flesh and bones according as you behold Me having." The bodies of celestial saints, however, will resemble the body in which Christ appeared to Saul on the road to Damascus. It was still Christ, but He was no longer a *Jewish* Christ. He was, as Paul later testified, "a light from heaven, above the brightness of the sun" (Acts 26:13).

> If I told you of the terrestrial and you are not believing, how shall you be believing if I should be telling you of the celestial?
>
> —John 3:12

not a Jew

Jew

Paul told the nations of both the terrestrial and the celestial, whereas the earthbound Christ, ministering only to Israelites, withheld from them celestial secrets. Why? Members of the bride of the Lambkin, of course, will be terrestrial, not celestial saints. Israel didn't need to know about the heavens, and Jesus Himself said they wouldn't believe it, anyway.

Gospel of Uncircumcision, Paul's gospel:
Glory of the celestial (1 Corinthians 15:40-41; John 3:12)

> There are bodies celestial as well as bodies terrestrial. But a different glory, indeed, is that of the celestial, yet a different that of the terrestrial, another glory of the sun, and another glory of the moon, and another glory of the stars, for star is excelling star in glory. Thus also is the resurrection of the dead.

Even among those in the body of Christ, bodies differ in glory. To illustrate this, Paul uses the sun, moon, and stars. Each is a celestial body, yes? Yet each has a different glory: The glory of the sun eclipses that of the moon. Someone may say, "I'm a star." Yet even among these, there is differing glory. There are dwarf stars, neutron stars, and blue supergiants. With God's ingenious arrangement, there will be no room for boasting, one star over another. Each will be filled to capacity with the glory of God. Again, the common denominator is: Glory.

> If I told you of the terrestrial and you are not believing, how shall you be believing if I should be telling you of the celestial?
>
> —John 3:12

Historically, Israel has a faith problem. They were unable to grasp even terrestrial truth, let alone truth belonging to the celestial sphere. I do not mean to disparage Israel. They are stuck in a God-inspired hardness (Romans 9:18;11:7-8) and won't emerge until God finishes calling His celestial saints.

6. Gospel of Circumcision, Peter's gospel:
Racial distinctions important (Matthew 19:28; Revelation 21:10-12)

> Yet Jesus said to them, "Verily, I am saying to you, that you who follow Me, in the renascence whenever the Son of Mankind should be seated on the throne of His glory, you also shall sit on twelve thrones, judging the twelve tribes of Israel.

The number twelve always speaks of Israel, and Israel always speaks of fleshly distinction. In this gospel, there is room for boasting. Genealogies are all about boasting. Unless you could trace your ancestry, you were out-of-luck for rulership in the kingdom, and you sure as heck weren't going to sit on one of those twelve thrones.

I was shocked to discover that fleshly distinctions will still exist in the earthly kingdom, that is, the 1,000 years of peace.

Do you imagine that fleshly distinctions belong only in the Old Testament—or only in the four gospel accounts? Is Israel recognized only on this present Earth? Well, watch, as the New Jerusalem descends out of heaven to settle upon the New Earth:

> And I perceived a new heaven and a New Earth, for the former heaven and the former Earth pass away, and the sea is no more. And I perceived the holy city, *New Jerusalem*, descending out of heaven from God, made ready as a bride adorned for her husband. And I hear a loud voice out of the throne saying, "Lo! the tabernacle of God is with humankind, and He will be tabernacling with them, and they will be His people, and God Himself will be with them."
> —Revelation 21:1-2

Even on the New Earth, fleshly distinctions (that's what Jerusalem is all about) hold sway and Israel reigns supreme. Whenever you hear the word "Earth" (whether new or old), understand that Israelites will be on top. On the New Earth, the priesthood of Israel retires (there is no temple there—Revelation 21:22), but she will still be a nation of kings. Note the recurrence of the number twelve (referring to Israel) in the following passage concerning the New Earth:

> And he carries me away, in spirit, on a mountain, huge and high, and shows me the holy city, Jerusalem, as it is descending out of heaven from God, having the glory from God. Her luminosity is like a stone most precious, as a crystalline jasper gem, having a wall, huge and high, having twelve portals, and at the portals twelve messengers, and their names inscribed, which are the names of the twelve tribes of the sons of Israel.
>
> —Revelation 21:10-12

In the meantime, what is going on in heaven?

Gospel of Uncircumcision, Paul's gospel:
Racial distinctions irrelevant (1 Corinthians 12:13; Galatians 3:27-28)

> For in one spirit also we all are baptized into one body, whether Jews or Greeks, whether slaves or free, and all are made to imbibe one spirit.

The body of Christ becomes one body. In this body, no one will say, "He is a Jew," or "She is a Greek."

Israelites can be part of the body of Christ, but, in spirit, they forsake their national identity. Paul was the first member of the body of Christ. He once boasted in his racial distinction, but membership in Christ's body moved him to revoke that in Philippians 3:4-7—

> And am even I having confidence in flesh, also? If any other
> one is presuming to have confidence in flesh, I rather: in
> circumcision the eighth day, of the race of Israel, of the
> tribe of Benjamin, a Hebrew of Hebrews, in relation to
> law, a Pharisee, in relation to zeal, persecuting the ecclesia,
> in relation to the righteousness which is in law, becoming
> blameless. But things which were gain to me, these I have
> deemed a forfeit because of Christ.

Peter could never have said this. For Peter, it was vital to be
a Jew, so he could sit on one of those twelve thrones, where Jesus
promised he would be.

> For whoever are baptized into Christ, put on Christ, in
> Whom there is no Jew nor yet Greek, there is no slave nor
> yet free, there is no male and female, for you all are one in
> Christ Jesus.
>
> —Galatians 3:27-28

In light of what I just said about Peter, it's astonishing to learn
that Peter was not baptized into Christ. That's right. Peter is not
a member of the body of Christ. He is a member of the bride of
the Lambkin. He is an Israelite, and has every reason to boast in
his flesh. When Peter lines up for the kingdom, he will be able to
present his card that says, "Israelite." That will get him in. If this
is not a fleshly distinction, what is?

What a good time to tell you the difference between "Christ
Jesus" and "Jesus Christ." Watch this:

In 1 Peter 1:1, Peter calls himself "an apostle of Jesus Christ."
In Ephesians 1:1, however, Paul calls himself "an apostle of Christ
Jesus." Is this an accident? A minor detail? No. There are no accidents in God's Word. There *are* minor details, but this isn't one
of them. Let us review:

1 Peter 1:1

Peter, an apostle of Jesus Christ, to the chosen

expatriates of the dispersion …

Ephesians 1:1
Paul, an apostle of Christ Jesus through the will of God, to all the saints …

On Earth, our Lord's name was Jesus. The name Jesus Christ, therefore, acquaints us first with His earthly experience. Apparently, "Jesus" was one of the most common names of those times. "Christ," we know, is not Jesus' last name. It is His exalted title; it means "anointed." Thus, the name "Christ Jesus" brings immediately to our mind His exalted status and station.

Remarkably, Paul is the only New Testament writer who uses the name "Christ Jesus"; he does it approximately ninety times. The Circumcision writers (Matthew, Mark, Luke, John, James, Peter, and Jude) use "Christ Jesus" zero times; that's *zero* times. Let us review:

Paul's use of "Christ Jesus": 90
Everyone else's use of "Christ Jesus": 0

What about the name "Jesus Christ?" The Circumcision writers use it, by my count, fourteen times. Does Paul use the title "Jesus Christ" also? Yes. Around twenty times. Why does only Paul interchange the titles? Like the other writers, Paul does refer to the person of Jesus Christ. But, again, only Paul uses the unique combination: Christ Jesus, for only Paul received the truth that a select number of human beings will share the title "Christ." Human beings who eventually do this are known in Paul's letters as "members of the body of Christ." The Circumcision saints, by contrast, are not members of the body of Christ; again, they are the bride of the Lambkin (Revelation 19:7-8), associated with the name "Jesus," the primary name our Lord assumed on Earth.

A.E. Knoch writes in *Studies in Colossians*:

"Christ Jesus" and "Jesus Christ"—what a vast difference between these two titles, though one is merely a transposition of the other. Jesus Christ is the humble, despised, rejected, crucified Messiah. His glories wait until the future, at the time of His return to Earth. At present He has no place down here. But Christ Jesus! Already He is highest in the heavens. Seated at the right hand of God, there is no dignity to equal His.

All might and power, all sovereignty and authority among the celestials is centered in Him. There He is not humbled, but honored. There He is not despised, but praised. There He is not rejected, but acclaimed. There He is not crucified, but glorified. We hail Him, not only as the coming King upon the Earth, but as the present Head of all celestial might and majesty. Hail! Christ Jesus!

7. Gospel of Circumcision, Peter's gospel:
Believers known *from* the disruption of the world (Revelation 17:8)

The wild beast which you perceived was, and is not, and is about to be ascending out of the submerged chaos, and to be going away into destruction. And marvel shall those dwelling on the Earth, whose names are not written on the scroll of life from the disruption of the world, when they observe the wild beast, seeing that it was, and is not, and will be present.

In the common versions, "the disruption of the world" was mistranslated "the foundation of the world." Between the creation of the heavens and Earth in Genesis 1:1, and the re-creation of these beginning in verse 3, a gigantic cataclysm occurred. Genesis 1:1, from the *Concordant Version of the Old Testament*, reads, "In a beginning, God created the heavens and the Earth." So far, so good. Then we read in verse 2: "As for the Earth, it came to be a chaos and vacant." It *became* that way. *The King James Version* mistakenly says God created it that way ("In the beginning God created the heavens and the Earth. And the Earth was without form, and void"), but that's impossible: Isaiah 45:18 says He formed the Earth to be inhabited.

Sin's entrance into the world did not begin with Adam. Sin's entrance began with the disruption of the world way back in Genesis 1:2, long before Adam wandered Eden. Obviously, then, it was some sort of spiritual rebellion. Why does this matter?

Israel is always dealing with sin. The law came, purportedly, to deal with sin. A nation strongly reliant on flesh (Israel) naturally fights flesh. Most Christians are in this place of struggle; they constantly battle their fleshly tendencies. Thus, the call of Israel "from" the disruption of the world makes sense. As soon as sin entered the world, the battle against sin began. This perfectly fits the call of Israel. What is the Old Testament all about? Sin, sin, and more sin.

Gospel of Uncircumcision, Paul's gospel:
Believers known *before* the disruption of the world (Ephesians 1:3-4)

> Blessed be the God and Father of our Lord Jesus Christ, Who blesses us with every spiritual blessing among the celestials, in Christ, according as He chooses us in Him before the disruption of the world, we to be holy and flawless in His sight ...

Appreciate the wonder of this. There are no accidental words or phrases in God's revelation. What a difference between "from" and "before." We were called in Christ before sin even entered the world. In other words, we were secure in Him *before* such things as failure or screw-ups even existed. Thus, neither failure nor screw-ups can remove us from Christ. Nothing can separate us from the love of God (Romans 8:38-39). (That's why believers who follow Paul are so happy, and people who get all "Israel" on you and follow law are so miserable and condemning and self-righteous.)

Allow me to say this again: Because God chose us before the entrance of sin into the world, the subsequent entrance of sin cannot ruin what we have in Christ. (Talk about the assurance of the believer, which Israel does not have.) Paul writes to Timothy in 2 Timothy 1:8-9—

> Suffer evil with the evangel in accord with the power of God, Who saves us and calls us with a holy calling, *not in accord with our acts*, but in accord with His own purpose and the grace which is given to us in Christ Jesus ...

Our calling is not in accord with our acts. Why? We were chosen in Christ before we'd committed any acts. More startling yet, we were chosen in Christ before unsavory acts were even invented.

Why in the world would you want to be an Israelite? Do you like fighting sin? Do you like being on probation? I'm afraid a lot of people do. (Hallmark should have sympathy cards that say: "I hear you want to be an Israelite." Inside, there's a picture of some guy lying inert under a pile of rocks, with the caption: "Good luck with that.")

8. Gospel of Circumcision, Peter's gospel: Believers called first, then chosen (Matthew 22:14)

> For many are the called, yet few are the chosen.

The gospel of the Circumcision is presented as an "if/then" proposition. That is, "If you answer My call, then I will choose you." Thus, Jesus says in Revelation 3:20—

> Lo! I stand at the door and am knocking. If ever anyone should be hearing My voice and opening the door, I will also be coming in to him and dining with him, and he with Me.

Keep in mind this is the relative perspective. Absolutely speak-

Do you like fighting sin? I'm afraid a lot of people do.

ing, no one can respond to Jesus Christ unless God first gives him or her ability to do so. For Jesus also testified, "No one can come to Me if ever the Father Who sends Me should not be drawing him" (John 6:44). God presented the Circumcision gospel as an "if/then" proposition: as a mixture of law and grace. Relatively speaking, it requires human cooperation. God wanted it presented this way. The initial purpose was to demonstrate human failure. God needed a people convinced that they could justify themselves by works of law, so He could later point to those people—utter failures—and say, "See? By works of law no flesh at all shall be justified" (Romans 3:20).

(Remember, Israel was a gigantic demonstration of the failure of flesh: Christianity hasn't got the message and ignorantly—as well as anachronistically—still attempts to follow law.)

Does God cast Israel away now that she has fulfilled her mission as a bad example? No. God is merciful and true to Himself. He will fulfill the promises He made to Israel; He, Himself, will give her a new heart (Jeremiah 31:33).

In the meantime ...

Gospel of Uncircumcision, Paul's gospel: Believers chosen first, then called (Romans 8:30)

> Now whom He designates beforehand, these He calls also, and whom He calls, these He justifies also; now whom He justifies, these He glorifies also.

Having temporarily set Israel aside (read Romans, chapter 11), God was ready to launch an evangel that was presented—from the start—as a message of total grace. Hence Paul's radical language. With Paul, salvation is presented as a done deal—a fact—rather than an "if/then" proposition. It's not something you accept for it to be true; it is something true that you accept. Look at it this way:

Circumcision gospel: "This can be yours—if the price

is right."

Uncircumcision gospel: "The price was right (Christ's sacrifice)—look what you now have."

Anyone who has been chosen by God and designated beforehand for membership in the body of Christ will—at some point during the course of his or her life in this age—hear and heed the truth. The truth *will* be presented to those destined beforehand for this glorious calling, according to Romans 8:29-30—

> Whom He foreknew, He designates beforehand, also, to be conformed to the image of His Son, for Him to be Firstborn among many brethren. Now whom He designates beforehand, these He calls also, and whom He calls, these He justifies also; now whom He justifies, these He glorifies also.

How in the world could this be construed as a challenge to faith? If anything, it's a challenge to God to fulfill what He determined beforehand to accomplish. If a member of the body of Christ—designated eons before that person's birth—is not acquainted, in this lifetime, with his or her call, then the failure is God's, not the person's. After all, Who controls every circumstance in the universe? God, of course (Ephesians 1:11; Colossians 1:20).

The Circumcision gospel is presented as a challenge; this is why works-oriented people like it. The Uncircumcision gospel is nothing but relaxation and total reliance on God; this is why *I* like it.

9. Gospel of Circumcision, Peter's gospel: Will keep law (Micah 4:2)

> And many nations go and say: Go, and we will ascend to the Mount of Yahweh, and to the house of the Elohim of Jacob, and He will direct us in His ways, and we will go in His paths. For from Zion *shall* fare forth the law, and the Word of Yahweh from Jerusalem.

People who read other peoples' mail and apply it to themselves get all sorts of erroneous ideas. Christians read this verse from Micah 4:2 and use it to say, "See? See? We're supposed to do law." This is just as preposterous as pointing to God's instructions to Noah (Genesis, chapter 6), and saying, "See? See? We're supposed to build an ark." In Micah, it's not even a matter of Israel's duty to keep the law. She was already supposed to, and didn't. This is a promise of God: "For from Zion *shall* fare forth the law ..." How can God be so certain of that? He, Himself, will write the law on the corporate heart of Israel.

Gospel of Uncircumcision, Paul's gospel:
Not under law (Romans 6:14)

> For sin shall not be lording it over you, for you are not under law, but under grace.

No wonder people get confused when they read the Bible: They mix it all up. Because, honestly, how do you reconcile Micah 4:2 with Romans 6:14? Here's the secret that will change the way you read Scripture: You *don't* reconcile them. They were not meant to be reconciled. They are two different messages meant for two distinct groups of people. As soon as you learn and live this truth, passages of Scripture that confused and frustrated you will fall into their proper places. Now you no longer have to dilute grace to make it fit with law. (As if that were even possible.) Now you no longer have to try to elevate law to the status of grace.

10. Gospel of Circumcision, Peter's gospel:
Water baptism required (Acts 2:38)

> Now Peter is averring to them, "Repent and be baptized each of you in the name of Jesus Christ for the pardon of your sins, and you shall be obtaining the gratuity of the Holy Spirit."

I'll never forget a bumper sticker I saw one day, while minding my own business and living happily in the grace of God. The driver was obviously a religious person who mixed the two gospels and purchased this bumper sticker from a standard-issue Christian bumper-sticker company that *also* mixed the two gospels. The bumper sticker said: "Obey Acts 2:38."

If I hadn't known better, this depressing, anachronistic command would have ruined my day. Instead, I shook my head, felt sorry for the person, and continued reveling in the grace of God—without having to get wet.

Yes, there was a day when water baptism was required. There was also a day when it was required of you to lead your little lamb to Jerusalem and watch while its little throat was slit. Smearing blood on your doorpost was also, during a particular era now past, required of you. There was a day when you had to circumcise all male offspring on the eight day after birth—and God help you if you did it on the ninth day.

Acts 2:38 was a call for repentance broadcast to a people freshly guilty of killing their own Messiah. The "repent" of the context meant becoming sorry as hell for killing the Christ. Did *you* crucify the Messiah of Israel? I didn't. So skip trying to obey Acts 2:38 and revel in the grace of God instead.

Gospel of Uncircumcision, Paul's gospel: Water baptism not required (1 Corinthians 1:17; 12:13)

> For Christ does not commission me to be baptizing, but to be bringing the evangel, not in wisdom of word, lest the cross of Christ may be made void.

Literal baptism cleanses and unites ceremonially by means of water. Figurative baptism cleanses and unites by means of spirit. It accomplishes what water baptism accomplished, minus the towel. Today, we are baptized into Christ's death (Romans 6:3-4). We have total identification with Christ—his death, entombment, resurrection, and glorification. Water baptism was the shadow, and total identification with Christ is the substance. Now that we have the substance, it's foolish to return to the shadow. Much like an adult sucking a pacifier.

Again, there was a day when baptism saved. Does this mean that repentance and baptism are necessary today? Should we be preaching the message that the cross of Christ saves us from sin, or that salvation comes from Christ plus baptism and repentance? Isn't the answer to this question something we should know for sure? Maybe we ought to be asking ourselves: What has God said about baptism *lately?* Ignoring what God has said lately about any important topic could cause a person to build an ark, circumcise for salvation, or sacrifice sheep.

> For in one spirit also we all are baptized into one body, whether Jews or Greeks, whether slaves or free, and all are made to imbibe one spirit.
> —1 Corinthians 12:13

Paul brought a new message to the nations, and, yes, Paul did baptize a few people early on—not into John's baptism, but into the name of the Lord Jesus. Remember, baptism is a generic rite that ceremonially cleanses people and unites them to a common cause.

Here's the key concerning Paul: His ministry went "from glory to glory" (2 Corinthians 3:18). In other words, the Paul of the middle of Acts is not the Paul of Ephesians. Paul gradually removed all rites and ceremonies from his message, so it eventually and finally became a message of pure grace. And that's where it stands today. Today, there is only one baptism (Ephesians 4:5), and it isn't water.

> Or are you ignorant that whoever are baptized into Christ Jesus, are baptized into His death? We, then, were entombed together with Him through baptism into death, that even as

Christ was roused from among the dead through the glory of
the Father, thus we also should be walking in newness of life.
                                                —Romans 6:3-4

When people ask if I've been baptized, I have the opportunity to herald Christ and say: "Yes. I was baptized 2,000 years
ago." Baptizing in water today denies the great truth of baptism
into Christ's death. Might as well return to killing lambs for the
forgiveness of sins.

11. Gospel of Circumcision, Peter's gospel:
Must be begotten anew ("born again"—John 3:3)

Jesus answered and said to him, "Verily, verily, I am saying
to you, If anyone should not be begotten anew, he can not
perceive the kingdom of God."

Christ alluded to Isaiah 66:8—a nation would be born in one
day. Nicodemus (the man to whom Jesus was speaking) should have
known about it. "Begotten anew" means bringing forth a new thing
from an old thing. The old thing is Israel, and the new thing is an
Israel with a heart of flesh rather than of stone. We're still talking
about the same raw material: Israel. Christianity makes much to
do of being "born again," little realizing that being "born again" is
a national revival of Israel, not an individual revival of non-Jews.

The new birth is not a good Israelite here, and a good Israelite
there. Individuals are not born again; a nation is to be born again.
(Not one person, as I write, has ever been born again.) Of course,
the nation consists of individuals, so every Israelite destined for
the kingdom gets born again simultaneously when God gives to
the conglomerate nation a new heart.

The 1,000-year kingdom will employ this same Earth. In the
1,000-year kingdom, this same oblate-spheroid we now sit upon
will be regenerated. God will remove the curse from it and revital-
ize its fruit-bearing capabilities. So, in a sense, this Earth will be

"born again," right along with Israel. As with Israel, it will be the same raw material, revitalized.

Gospel of Uncircumcision, Paul's gospel:
Are a new creation (2 Corinthians 5:17)

> So that, if anyone is in Christ, there is a new creation: the primitive passed by. Lo! there has come new!

A new creation is far more radical than a new birth. Again, a new birth is regeneration. A new birth takes the same raw material and makes it into something new. Paul is not talking about that, here. In Christ, God has wiped out the old humanity. The deepest message of the cross is: *God has started from scratch.* This isn't Israel's message. With Israel's message (the gospel of the Circumcision), Israel still matters. With Israel's message, the old humanity remains intact, becoming reformed, not destroyed.

Peter never expounded upon the depths of the cross. Peter never taught that the cross wiped out the old humanity—he didn't know it: Jesus didn't give it to him. The glorified Christ gave this message to Paul alone. So Paul eliminated fleshly distinction and said, in Christ, there is "neither Jew nor Greek" (Galatians 3:28). Peter never said this, and neither could he. Peter has to be an Israelite to rule in the kingdom.

The Circumcision gospel appeals to fleshly people. Christians and Jews alike love to work on their flesh; they're fleshly people. They love the idea of reformation. They love self-improvement programs.

We, however, who have tasted the deepest depths of the cross, are not interested in reformation. We look at ourselves and say, "Forget it!" That's the Martin Zender definition of the new creation. New creation looks at old creation and says, "Forget it!" Why? It's too far gone to save. I don't want to work on it—I want to start from scratch. The new creation lets me do that. Or, should I say, the new creation has already done it. All that remains for me is to realize it. "The primitive passed by. Lo! There has come new!" (2 Corinthians 5:17). I don't know about you, but this is some of the best news I have ever heard.

This is you—now—in spirit. You are brand new. So forget worrying about your flesh. Reckon it as dead (Romans 6:5-11) and get on with worshipping Christ with peace and joy of spirit.

12. Gospel of Circumcision, Peter's gospel: Pardoned of guilt (that is, *forgiven*—Luke 11:4)

> And pardon us our sins, for we ourselves also are pardoning everyone who is owing us. And mayest Thou not bring us into trial, but rescue us from the wicked one.

Above is a quote from the world-famous "Lord's Prayer." (It's not called that in the Bible. Rather, it's the prayer Jesus gave to His disciples. Technically, it's the Disciples' Prayer.) The verse above, commonly translated, reads: "Forgive us our trespasses as we forgive those who trespass against us."

Forgiveness assumes guilt. Forgiveness says, "You did wrong, but I will pretend you didn't. There's a penalty for your crime, but I will overlook it for now and let you off the hook."

The English elements of the Greek word for "forgive"—*aphi-emi*—are "from-let." Forgiveness is letting someone off *from* the penalty of whatever crime they committed.

As wonderful as forgiveness and pardon are, the nasty little truth is that a pardon can be revoked. We see this in Matthew 18:23-35, in the parable of the 10,000-talent debtor. Though the master remitted his slave's gigantic debt, the pardon was recalled when that slave refused to extend the same forgiveness to *his* servant. Thus, the permanence of pardon depends on the conduct of the one receiving it.

Human conduct comes and goes. Therefore, so does pardon: A pardon can be withdrawn. Israelites (and Christians who are Circumcision-gospel believers), therefore, have to be constantly on guard for their salvation. Sound like fun? Again, fleshly people like the challenge, and they like to self-righteously condemn other people who, to them, aren't making the grade.

Me? I would rather be justified and mind my own business.

Gospel of Uncircumcision, Paul's gospel:
Not even guilty (that is, *justified*—Romans 5:1)

> Being, then, justified by faith, we may be having peace toward God, through our Lord, Jesus Christ.

No court in the land would have found Richard Nixon not guilty of wrongdoing. Richard Nixon was forgiven, therefore, not justified. He did wrong, but Gerald Ford forgave, or pardoned, him. Realize how radical it is to be justified. The root word of "justified" is "just." And "just" means, "right." Being justified means being pronounced: "Not guilty!"

How can a person who's not guilty be forgiven? It's impossible.

"You are not guilty of this crime. You did no wrong. In fact, you acted rightly. Therefore, we are going to overlook the penalty."

That's ludicrous. No one "overlooks the penalty" of a justified person, because a justified person never was subject to a penalty in the first place.

"Justification" has been degraded to a little-understood theological term. And yet it's no more complicated than the "right-margin justification" function on your word-processing program. This function takes all your text and aligns it to a standard. Right? Very well then: Now you understand justification. God does this with us. His standard is Christ, and He aligns us with Christ. Does He do this based on our behavior? No. If He did, we could never be justified. He bases this on the work of His Son, Jesus Christ. We are "justified gratuitously in His grace, through the deliverance which is in Christ Jesus" (Romans 3:24). According to Paul: "We are reckoning a human to be justified by faith apart from works of law" (Romans 3:28).

This man was pardoned, not justified.

So stop begging God for forgiveness every day. This insults Him. He's tired of hearing it. If you were an Israelite, God could tolerate it. But He's revealed to you the depths of the cross. He's revealed to you that the awful sufferings of Christ have made you right with Him. So when you roll on the floor all weepy that you can never please Him, and you spend your day begging Him to forgive you and be nice to you, He just rolls His eyes and sighs a heavy sigh. Your groveling actually insults what God accomplished through His Son on that horrible cross. The cross was horrible for a reason—wasn't it?

How would you like to give someone a Christmas present, and watch them writhe on the floor and tell you how unworthy they are, and that they could not possibly accept your gift, because they're such a bad, rotten person? Wouldn't that just about frost you? Wouldn't it be the ultimate insult?

Whether we live in the reality of it or not, God has justified us. So you can either live in reality: God sees you through the Person and work of Christ, or else you can roll on the floor, spending your days in self-consumption (religious self-consumption is the ugliest kind), unnecessarily weeping and begging God to do something about your poor flesh that He already did 2,000 years ago.

You're a new creation in Christ.

Wake up and smell the justification.

13. Gospel of Circumcision, Peter's gospel:
The irreverent are condemned (2 Peter 2:4-6)

> For if God spares not sinning messengers [angels], but thrusting them into the gloomy caverns of Tartarus, gives them up to be kept for chastening judging; and spares not the ancient world, but guards Noah, an eighth, a herald of righteousness, bringing a deluge on the world of the irreverent; and condemns the cities of Sodom and Gomorrah, reducing them to cinders by an overthrow, having placed them as an example for those about to be irreverent ...

Are you irreverent under the gospel of the Circumcision? Then you'd better duck for cover.

Gospel of Uncircumcision, Paul's gospel:
The irreverent are justified (Romans 4:5)

> Yet to him who is not working, yet is believing on Him Who is justifying the irreverent, his faith is reckoned for righteousness.

Are you irreverent under the gospel of the Uncircumcision? Congratulations. You meet all the qualifications for justification.

14. Gospel of Circumcision, Peter's gospel:
Must have works, or faith is dead (James 2:20)

> Now are you wanting to know, O empty human, that faith apart from works is dead?

Watching religious people and Christian theologians trying to reconcile James and Paul amuses me. I once watched a chimp at a zoo trying to put a square peg into a round hole and was similarly entertained.

Simple fact: In the Circumcision gospel, faith is not enough. It must be accompanied by works, or you're dead.

Gospel of Uncircumcision, Paul's gospel:
Must *not* be working, only having faith (Romans 4:5)

> Yet to him who is not working, yet is believing on Him Who is justifying the irreverent, his faith is reckoned for righteousness.

In the gospel of the Uncircumcision, works actually insult

faith. Why? Our faith is a gift (Romans 12:3), which acquaints us with the complete work of Christ on the cross. (Read, "believing on Him," above.) The Circumcision folks believe on Him *and* themselves. The salvation of the Circumcision is a cooperative salvation. Not ours.

15. Gospel of Circumcision, Peter's gospel:
Must be an overcomer to avoid second death (Revelation 2:11)

> Who has an ear, let him hear what the spirit is saying to the ecclesias. The one who is conquering may under no circumstances be injured by the second death.

The *King James Version* reads: "He that hath an ear, let him hear what the spirit saith unto the churches; He that overcometh shall not be hurt of the second death."

Many ministries today are based on "overcoming." In fact, this is a buzz-word in many Israel-wannabe camps. Everyone wants to "overcome." Those who do become, of all things, "Overcomers." Nothing beats this, because only one who overcomes avoids the second death. Not only this, but only Overcomers get to eat of the tree of life, according to Revelation 2:7 (KJV):

> He that hath an ear, let him hear what the Spirit saith unto the churches; To him that overcometh will I give to eat of the tree of life, which is in the midst of the Paradise of God.

This call to overcome-or-else fits perfectly with James, who writes that faith without works is dead. In the book of Revelation, faith without works gets you the second death.

Again, this kind of thing appeals to fleshly, religious people. (I am including Jews here, and Christians, who are for the most part wannabe Israelites.) Religious people are excited by the call to overcome. This way, the religious person can overcome and feel superior to other people who are not overcoming. Again, the call of Israel is all about feeling superior; Israel *is* superior. Israel must come to realize the source of her superiority—the Messiah—but still. It feels kinda good to be overcoming while other people are being cast into the lake of fire, which is the (literal) second death.

Christians and Jews mistakenly assume their call is the ultimate. They point to the book of Revelation and, to them, this is the ultimate: To be an Overcomer and eat of the tree of life and miss out on the second death. They cannot imagine anything better. Some of them seem self-righteous and arrogant, because they are. What these people need is: a clue, concerning a better calling and expectation. Here's the big clue, from Paul's letter to the Ephesians:

Gospel of Uncircumcision, Paul's gospel:
   Saved from second death by grace alone (Ephesians 2:8-9)

> For in grace, through faith, are you saved, and this is not out of you; it is God's approach present, not of works, lest anyone should be boasting.

Neither Christians nor Jews actually believe in salvation by grace alone (members of the body of Christ, however, do believe it). In fact, salvation by total grace disgusts most people. It eliminates all fleshly advantage. It does away with one person overcoming and another person not overcoming. It's much more fun and feels much better to wear a T-shirt that says, "Overcomer," rather than one which says, "I have avoided the second death through no merit of my own." Boy, I would hate to be a salesperson selling *that* T-shirt. I'd go broke.

Remember that scene in the movie *Raiders of the Lost Ark* when Harrison Ford encounters that martial arts guru at the airfield brandishing his samurai sword? The guy makes all sorts of figure-eights with his sword, trying to intimidate Indy. Indy tolerates the show for awhile, then just shrugs and shoots the guy.

When Overcomers try to lord it over me, I put up with it for awhile, but then I pull out Ephesians 2:8-9 and just kind of shoot them with it. Either they get it, or they hit the ground like a sack of beets. Either way, I walk away satisfied.

16. Gospel of Circumcision, Peter's gospel: Must forgive others for God to forgive them (Matthew 6:15)

> Yet if you should not be forgiving humans their offenses, neither will your Father be forgiving your offenses.

This hearkens back to the previous section on forgiveness versus justification.

I'll never forget hearing an audio tape of a talk given by Corrie ten Boom, the famous Dutch concentration camp survivor. During her speech at a church, Corrie referenced this verse. She said she had to forgive her German persecutors, or else God would not forgive her. Here's a quote from that tape I'll always remember: "Well? Jesus said it, so it must be true."

Oh, Corrie. It *is* true. But Jesus didn't say it to *you*. God also told Noah to build an ark. "Well, God said it, so it must be true." Yes, it's true. True for Noah, not for us.

Something in Corrie's tone suggested tired resignation, as if Corrie deep down wished what she was saying weren't true. Or maybe she knew this verse clashed with other verses extolling grace. I'm not saying Corrie didn't want to forgive her persecutors. I'm just suggesting she was spiritually cognizant enough to wonder why God was still presenting a "do this, or else" message to a heart bent on grace.

The thing is, He isn't. Yes, I know the verse is plainly there in the red letters that Jesus spoke, but the resurrected Christ said a new thing to hearts yearning for grace—a higher thing spiritually than the words recorded in red. The words of the Man from

Galilee were the words of a minister of the Circumcision gospel (Romans 15:8).

I ask people who think Matthew 6:15 applies to them (instead of only to Jews and Israelite wannabes) if they really believe it. I ask them if they truly believe that if they died today not having forgiven someone for something—anything—if God would send them to the Christian version of "hell." They don't know what to say. That's because, on the topic of forgiveness versus justification, they are confused as hell.

Gospel of Uncircumcision, Paul's gospel:
Deal graciously with others as God has dealt graciously (Ephesians 4:31-32)

> Let all bitterness and fury and anger and clamor and calumny be taken away from you with all malice, yet become kind to one another, tenderly compassionate, dealing graciously among yourselves, according as God also, in Christ, deals graciously with you.

Forgiving others as God has forgiven us is no way for us to behave. Why? God has not forgiven us; He has justified us. He has justified us "gratuitously" (Romans 3:24), that is, by grace. Being thus lauded with grace, we are to extend that same grace to others. Grace is not based on behavior. If it were, it wouldn't be grace. Rather, grace thrives in the absence of good behavior, because sin—and only sin—gives grace its meaning. When sin disappears, so does grace.

17. Gospel of Circumcision, Peter's gospel:
Expecting grace (1 Peter 1:13)

> Wherefore, girding up the loins of your comprehension, being sober, expect perfectly the grace which is being brought to you at the unveiling of Jesus Christ.

Circumcision believers are always looking forward to things that we, in spirit, already have. Spiritually, we have hopped, skipped, and jumped over Israel. Don't feel bad about it; it wasn't your idea. Quit worrying, and revel in it.

Gospel of Uncircumcision, Paul's gospel: Standing in grace (Romans 5:1-2)

> Being, then, justified by faith, we may be having peace toward God, through our Lord, Jesus Christ, through Whom we have the access also, by faith, into this grace in which we stand, and we may be glorying in expectation of the glory of God.

See? Whereas Israel is still expecting grace, we are said to be standing in it. Now. God wants us to live and to bask in the gifts He has given us. I know it's confusing when there are so many apparently conflicting exhortations in Scripture. But now you know these exhortations do not conflict at all. Rather, they are perfectly suited to the people to whom they were written. As John Wycliffe so famously said, and I quoted earlier:

> *It shall greatly help you to understand Scripture if you mark not only what is spoken or written, but of whom, and to whom, with what words, at what time, where, to what intent, with what circumstances, considering what goes before and what follows.*

"It shall greatly help you"? What an understatement.

18. Gospel of Circumcision, Peter's gospel: Not yet manifested what they shall be (1 John 3:2)

> Beloved, now are we children of God, and it was not as yet manifested what we shall be. We are aware that, if He

should be manifested, we shall be like Him, for we shall
see Him according as He is.

There's always one more step to the Circumcision gospel than
to the gospel of the Uncircumcision. The manifestation of Christ,
to the Circumcision saints, precedes their becoming like Him.
Sounds great. What could be better? Our gift:

Gospel of Uncircumcision, Paul's gospel:
Are mirroring the Lord's glory (2 Corinthians 3:18)

Now we all, with uncovered face, mirroring the Lord's glory,
are being transformed into the same image, from glory to
glory, even as from the Lord, the spirit.

Right now, we are mirroring the Lord's glory. Christ speaks
with us—not in parables as He did with Israel, but—face-to-face.
As we come to realize the deepest realities of the cross, we are
transformed into the same image as Christ. Which helps explain
the following:

19. Gospel of Circumcision, Peter's gospel:
His manifestation is their change (1 John 3:2)

Beloved, now are we children of God, and it was not as
yet manifested what we shall be. We are aware that, if He
should be manifested, we shall be like Him, for we shall
see Him according as He is.

Again, here's a one-two process. When He is manifested to
Israel, then they shall be like Him.

Gospel of Uncircumcision, Paul's gospel:
His manifestation is their manifestation (Colossians
3:4)

Whenever Christ, our Life, should be manifested, then you
also shall be manifested together with Him in glory.

With the body of Christ, His manifestation is our manifestation: We are His body, not His bride. When He appears, we cannot
help but appear, for we are one with Him. We have simultaneous
reality, not a one-two process. It's not Christ showing up, then
us. It's: CHRIST. (For we are members of His body. We, too, are
enchristed, that is, anointed.)

20. Gospel of Circumcision, Peter's gospel:
Exhorted to toss worry on Him (1 Peter 5:6-7)

Be humbled, then, under the mighty hand of God, that He
should be exalting you in season, tossing your entire worry
on Him, for He is caring concerning you.

Just when you think tossing your worry upon Christ is the
sweetest thing going, the radical Paul comes along, and we are:

Gospel of Uncircumcision, Paul's gospel:
Exhorted to not worry about anything (Philippians
4:6)

Do not worry about anything, but in everything, by prayer
and petition, with thanksgiving, let your requests be made
known to God …

I once heard the preacher Ray Prinzing describe how he dealt
with his flesh. Whenever he sinned, he said, he pictured himself
stabbing the sin with a fork, and offering it up to God. I used to
think this was a good analogy.

As I became familiar with the truths of justification, however,
I realized that Prinzing was forwarding a two-step process: 1)
recognize sin, 2) offer it. Understanding justification taught me

that God does not even impute sin to my account. Astounding as such truth seems to the ear, Paul clearly writes this in Romans 4:8— "Happy the human to whom the Lord by no means should be reckoning sin!"

So if God no longer reckons sin against me, how can I stab it with a fork and offer it to Him? Before I stab anything with a fork, I have to reckon it as so. But Paul tells me to reckon it as not so. Paul says: "Put away the fork, Zender."

Likewise with worry. Peter says, in essence, "Stab your worry with a fork, and offer it to God!" Sounds like the ultimate spiritual exercise until we hear Paul saying, in essence, "Don't even worry. With Christ, worry shouldn't even exist. If you're stabbing your worry with a fork, you haven't understood the grace of God. Drop the fork, folks, and don't worry about anything."

21. Gospel of Circumcision, Peter's gospel: Exhorted to remain in Him (1 John 2:28)

> And now, little children, remain in Him, that, if He should be manifested, we should be having boldness and not be put to shame by Him in His presence.

Again, this illustrates the difference between being *with* Christ, and being a member of His body. If Christ is there and you are here, you'd better stay close, or you risk being put to shame by His presence. But if you are a part of His body, how can you not be where He is? Do you need exhorted to "remain" with yourself? Of course not. Thus also, us and Christ: It's impossible for us to be put to shame by His presence.

Gospel of Uncircumcision, Paul's gospel: Died with Him; He cannot disown Himself (2 Timothy 2:11,13)

> Faithful is the saying: "For if we died together, we shall be

living together also ... if we are disbelieving, He is remaining faithful—He cannot disown Himself."

There you go. "He cannot disown Himself." Why not? Christ identifies us *with* Himself. If He disowns us, He disowns Himself. Note how Paul relates the pronoun "we" with "Himself": If *we* are disbelieving, He is remaining faithful. Why? He cannot disown *Himself.*

We = Himself.

You will not find this truth in the four gospels, nor in any other of the Circumcision writings. It's only in Paul. Israel is always one step away from it. Again, they're the bride, not the body.

In that last passage from 2 Timothy, Paul references his own writing, practically quoting from his letter to the Romans. A key passage explains our identification with Christ, Romans 6:5-11. Note the repetition of the word, "together"—a key word of this key passage:

> For if we have become planted *together* in the likeness of His death, nevertheless we shall be of the resurrection also, knowing this, that our old humanity was crucified *together* with Him, that the body of sin may be nullified, for us by no means to be still slaving for sin, for one who dies has been justified from sin. Now if we died *together* with Christ, we believe that we shall be living *together* with Him also, having perceived that Christ, being roused from among the dead, is no longer dying.
>
> Death is lording it over Him no longer, for in that He died, He died to sin once for all time, yet in that He is living, He is living to God. Thus you also, be reckoning yourselves to be dead, indeed, to sin, yet living to God in Christ Jesus, our Lord.

22. Gospel of Circumcision, Peter's gospel:
Tend to have difficulty apprehending Paul's evangel (2 Peter 3:15-16)

And be deeming the patience of our Lord salvation, according as our beloved brother Paul also writes to you, according to the wisdom given to him, as also in all the epistles, speaking in them concerning these things, in which are some things hard to apprehend, which the unlearned and unstable are twisting, as the rest of the Scriptures also, to their own destruction.

Poor Peter. He didn't quite get Paul. It was easier for a person of the nations to get Paul, than for Peter. Peter had all that Israelite baggage. A person of the nations hears about total grace and says, "Oh. Okay. Cool." An Israelite hears it (or a religious Christian—same thing) and says, "Huh? That can't be! There are so many things we must do to please God!"

People steeped in religion from birth have a very difficult time grasping grace. I used to try talking to pastors about the grace of God, thinking that if I could get them to see the distinctions of Paul's gospel, then they could tell their congregants. Well, talking to a trained seminarian about the grace of God is like trying to describe a nuclear submarine to a deep-sea mollusk. They just don't get it. They are too steeped in law and works.

These days, I would much rather teach grace to untrained people who still command their own brains and haven't joined the cult of Christianity. I tell these folks about Paul and grace, and they say, "Really? That's awesome!"

Nothing makes religious Christians angrier than mere neophytes excelling them in spiritual freedom. They hate to hear about people getting blessed apart from works. Why? They've worked their brains out to get where they are. They've sweated and worried and fumed—so by God, other people better be sweating and worrying and fuming as well.

One of these sweaty, religious, fuming people once complained to me: "Zender, you make salvation too easy!"

My response: "I do? Oh, wow. My mistake. I misspoke. I didn't

Talking to a trained seminarian about the grace of God is like trying to describe a nuclear submarine to a deep-sea mollusk.

mean to say it's easy—I meant to say it's free."

Gospel of Uncircumcision, Paul's gospel:
Tend to apprehend both evangels (2 Corinthians 12:11)

I have become imprudent; you compel me. For I ought to be commended by you, for I am not deficient in anything pertaining to the paramount apostles, even if I am nothing.

Paul had the edge on Peter because he understood both Peter's gospel and his own. How? Paul was raised in Peter's gospel. Paul was one of those rare Israelites who could let go of his ancestral baggage and grab ahold of the grace train. Paul grasped both messages; therefore he could argue successfully on matters of Christ against anyone—Jew or Greek. Whenever a Circumcisionist came up against Paul, however, the Circumcisionist got quickly buried, knowing only his own gospel and not Paul's.

Grace understands both evangels, because the joy of grace is generally founded upon a history of working and failing. One who is tutored only in the law, however, has never tasted transcendent grace. Therefore, the law person has only one viewpoint from which to argue.

23. Gospel of Circumcision, Peter's gospel:
Must be watching (Luke 12:37; Hebrews 9:27-28)

Happy are those slaves, whom the Lord, coming, will be finding watching. Verily, I am saying to you that He will be girding Himself about and causing them to recline, and, coming by, will be serving them.

I love this. That is, I love that I don't have to do it. The above relates to the "Overcomer" theme. In Israel, you had to watch for signs, and God help you if you didn't. You constantly had to be on your guard, as our Lord's parable about the ten virgins illustrated

(Matthew 25:1-12). If your lamp lacked oil when the Bridegroom showed up, you missed the wedding. The last thing you wanted was to be scrambling for oil when you heard His approaching footsteps. No one knows the hour of His appearing, so you have to be constantly checking your oil levels—and I don't mean in your car.

> And, in as much as it is reserved to a human to be dying once, yet after this a judging, thus Christ also, being offered once for the bearing of the sins of many, will be seen a second time, by those awaiting Him, apart from sin, for salvation, through faith.
> —Hebrews 9:27-28

For Israel, He is coming to those awaiting Him. And the one with the most oil, wins.

Gospel of Uncircumcision, Paul's gospel: Watching *or* drowsing (1 Thessalonians 5:9-10)

> For God did not appoint us to Indignation, but to the procuring of salvation through our Lord Jesus Christ, Who died for our sakes, that, whether we may be watching or drowsing, we should be living at the same time together with Him.

I'm only half joking when I say: Paul's gospel is the lazy person's gospel. If you have believed Christ in accord with Paul's gospel, then salvation is yours whether you are watching *or* drowsing. I never would have believed this without the testimony of this verse. Are you watching carefully for Christ? Great; you're saved. Are you more worried about the Pittsburgh Steelers than about the Savior's coming? Well, that's not so great—but the result is the same: You are saved from Indignation. With Paul's gospel, salvation is based upon grace—not upon forsaking your favorite football team.

Christians and Jews absolutely hate this message. The Steelers don't much care for it, either.

24. Gospel of Circumcision, Peter's gospel: Can be put to shame at His presence (1 John 2:28)

And now, little children, remain in Him, that, if He should be manifested, we should be having boldness and not be put to shame by Him in His presence.

This truth relates to the previous. If you don't have five quarts of oil in your reservoir (that is, if you're not "remaining in Him"), then you could be highly embarrassed when He shows up. Imagine being one of those ten virgins, hearing the Bridegroom approach. Instead of looking all sexy on a couch with your full lamp—as you're supposed to—you're running around sans make-up, with rollers in your hair, saying, "Now where did I put that lousy oil?" What is the Groom going to think about *that?*

Gospel of Uncircumcision, Paul's gospel: Will be changed at His presence (1 Thessalonians 4:15-17; 1 Corinthians 15:51-52)

For this we are saying to you by the Word of the Lord, that we, the living, who are surviving to the presence of the Lord, should by no means outstrip those who are put to repose, for the Lord Himself will be descending from heaven with a shout of command, with the voice of the Chief Messenger, and with the trumpet of God, and the dead in Christ shall be rising first.

Thereupon we, the living who are surviving, shall at the same time be snatched away together with them in clouds, to meet the Lord in the air. And thus shall we always be together with the Lord.

Lo! a secret to you am I telling! We all, indeed, shall not be put to repose, yet we all shall be changed, in an instant, in the twinkle of an eye, at the last trump. For He will be trumpeting, and the dead will be roused incorruptible, and we shall be changed.

For us, the Lord's presence brings joy, not worry. Pure joy. Joy and relaxation and expectation of glory.

25. Gospel of Circumcision, Peter's gospel: Will go through Day of Indignation (Revelation 7:1-17)

And after this I perceived four messengers standing at the four corners of the Earth, holding the four winds of the Earth, that the wind may not be blowing on the land, nor on the sea, nor on any tree. And I perceived another messenger ascending from the Orient, having the seal of the living God. And he cries with a loud voice to the four messengers to whom it was given for them to injure the land and the sea, saying, "You shall not be injuring the land, nor yet the sea, nor yet the trees, until we should be sealing the slaves of our God on their foreheads." And I hear the number of those sealed: a hundred forty-four thousand. Sealed out of every tribe of the sons of Israel are: out of the tribe of Judah twelve thousand are sealed; out of the tribe of Reuben twelve thousand; out of the tribe of Gad twelve thousand; out of the tribe of Asher twelve thousand; out of the tribe of Naphtali twelve thousand; out of the tribe of Manasseh twelve thousand; out of the tribe of Simeon twelve thousand; out of the tribe of Levi twelve thousand; out of the tribe of Issachar twelve thousand; out of the tribe of Zebulon twelve thousand; out of the tribe of Joseph twelve thousand; out of the tribe of Benjamin twelve thousand are sealed. After these things I perceived, and lo! a vast throng which no one was able to number, out of every nation and out of the tribes and peoples and languages, standing before the throne and before the Lambkin, clothed in white robes and with palm fronds in their hands. And they are crying with a loud voice, saying, "Salvation be our God's, Who is sitting on the throne, And the Lambkin's!" And all the messengers stood around the throne and the elders and the four animals. And they fall on their faces before the throne and worship God, saying, "Amen! Blessing and glory and wisdom and thanks and honor and power and strength be our God's for the eons of the eons. Amen!" And one of the elders answered, saying to me, "These clothed in white robes, who are they, and whence came they?" And I have declared to him: "My lord, you are aware." And he said to me, "These are those coming out of the great affliction [Tribulation/Indignation]. And they rinse their robes, and they whiten them in the blood of the Lambkin. Therefore they are before the throne of God and are offering divine service to Him day and night in His temple. And He Who is sitting on the throne will be tabernacling over them. They shall not be hungering longer, nor yet shall they be thirsting any longer; no, neither should the sun be falling on them, nor any heat, seeing that the throne-centered Lambkin shall be shepherding them, and shall be guiding them to living springs of water, and every tear shall God be brushing away from their eyes."

Sorry for the large chunk of paragraph there, but I wanted to make it uncomfortable for you to read, so maybe you'd skip it.

Israelites and Circumcision believers (most Christians) have been appointed to go through the coming Tribulation, as I've already spoken of earlier. Israel's place of business during the 1,000 years will be on Earth, so there's no need to remove them from Earth. The new birth requires much labor pain. That's what the Tribulation is: labor pain.

Some Israelites and proselytes of Judaism will be Overcomers, and they will make it through the Tribulation. Some Jews and Christians will overcome by being sealed on their foreheads and living through it; some will overcome by being martyred for the sake of the truth. Either way, nothing will be easy. And yet to be able to say, "Been there, done that, got my Overcomer T-shirt," will be a great thing for an Israelite, or a proselyte of Israel, in that day.

Gospel of Uncircumcision, Paul's gospel:
Not appointed to Indignation (1 Thessalonians 1:9-10; 5:9)

> For they are reporting concerning us, what kind of an en-
> trance we have had to you, and how you turn back to God
> from idols, to be slaving for the living and true God, and
> to be waiting for His Son out of the heavens, Whom He
> rouses from among the dead, Jesus, our Rescuer out of the
> coming Indignation. ...
>
> For God did not appoint us to Indignation, but to the
> procuring of salvation through our Lord Jesus Christ ...

As members of the body of Christ, we are not appointed to
Indignation. Rather, we are ambassadors of God's peace.

God will soon declare war on the world. The coming de-
struction described in the book of Revelation will make Steven
Spielberg's *War of the Worlds* look like a Tom Cruise movie (Oh,
wait—it *is* a Tom Cruise movie). Many members of the body of
Christ still write me to ask whether or not they will be called
upon to endure the terrors described in the book of Revelation.
They won't be. Neither will you be, reader, if you are a member of
Christ's body. Here's one reason:

> All is of God, Who conciliates us to Himself through
> Christ, and is giving us the dispensation of the concilia-
> tion, how that God was in Christ, conciliating the world to
> Himself, not reckoning their offenses to them, and placing
> in us the word of the conciliation. For Christ, then, are
> we ambassadors, as of God entreating through us. We are
> beseeching for Christ's sake, "Be conciliated to God!"
> —2 Corinthians 5:18-20

We are living in an era wherein God implores humanity to be
at peace with Him. Being the strong, silent type, God speaks now

only through the members of the body of Christ. What is God's "diplomatic solution" to a world that hates Him? Ever since the cross, God refuses to recognize conflict. The world can spit in God's face, flip Him the middle finger, and call His Son every name in the book. His reaction? He smiles and says, "I am conciliated to you."

He will not always come across this way.

God will soon change His tactics. You say, "Martin, God does not change." True. God will change His tactics, not His character. God's tactics will appear changed only from the relative vantage point of humans on Earth. From the absolute perspective, God has planned to "change tactics" for a long time.

Back in the day, the United States tried to make nice with Iraq. They wouldn't listen, so we rattled their windows a little bit. The result? They listened after that. Basically, this is what God does, except His reasons and goals are far loftier. There will come a time when this present era of grace will end, and God will use alternative means to bring the world in worship to His feet.

God disciplines. If you don't believe that, read Hebrews, chapter 12.

Back to Iraq. Before the United States—or any nation—declares war on another nation, that nation withdraws its ambassadors. The reason is self-evident, but I will state it anyway: The warring nation does not want to blow up its own ambassadors. We are ambassadors of peace, not war. Our mission is to declare conciliation. When God places that conciliation on the back burner, we will be more out of place here than SpongeBob SquarePants in a Jackie Chan movie.

The U.S. military relieves conscientious objectors of military service because killing other humans compromises the objectors' belief system. God's plan to kill a third of humankind (Revelation 9:18) compromises *our* belief system because our belief system is the gospel of grace as found in 2 Corinthians 5:18-20. Hence, the need for us to be snatched away beforehand (1 Thessalonians 4:17).

Even *God's* eras come to an end. Paul said in Romans 11:25— "Callousness, in part, on Israel has come, *until the complement of the nations may be entering.*" There are a finite number of people in the body of Christ. When that last member enters, this present window of grace closes.

So teach grace while you still can. In the meantime—prepare to be evacuated.

26. Gospel of Circumcision, Peter's gospel:
Will receive Christ on Earth (Acts 1:10-12; Zechariah 14:4)

> And as they were looking intently into heaven at His go-ing, lo! two men stand beside them in white attire, who say also, "Men! Galileans! Why do you stand, looking into heaven? This Jesus Who is being taken up from you into heaven shall come thus, in the manner in which you gaze at Him going into heaven." Then they return into Jerusalem from the Mount called Olivet, which is near Jerusalem a Sabbath's journey.

People usually mix up the snatching away (the so-called Christian "rapture") with the coming of Christ for Israel. These are two separate events. The resurrection of the worthy saints in Israel—when Christ returns to the Mount of Olives—was foretold by Daniel in Daniel 12:1-3. When Paul talks about the snatching away ("rapture") in 1 Corinthians 15:50-53, he calls it "a secret" (verse 51). As I said earlier, because it was a secret up until the time Paul wrote this, then this resurrection cannot be the resurrection described centuries before by Daniel.

Christian expositors don't get this, because they don't grasp the difference between the two gospels. In fact, one website I've looked at declares: "This false doctrine on the secret rapture is contradic-tory to the words of Jesus." Classic. A classic example of mixing the two gospels. These expositors are always pitting the words of the earthbound Jesus against the words of Paul, either trying to make them fit or thinking they are making some stupendous point about how one, or the other, passage must be false. As you ought to realize by now, these disparate passages don't fit, and neither were they meant to. Both verses are true in their respective places.

> And His feet shall stand in that day on the Mount of Olives, which is adjoining Jerusalem on the east.
> —Zechariah 14:4

Jesus Christ will literally touch down upon Earth, at the precise geographical location identified above. Here's the problem, then, for those trying to make Paul's "secret rapture" fit with "the words of Jesus":

Gospel of Uncircumcision, Paul's gospel: Will meet Christ in air (1 Thessalonians 4:17)

> Thereupon we, the living who are surviving, shall at the same time be snatched away together with them in clouds, to meet the Lord in the air.

We don't wait for Christ's feet to descend to Earth, to the Mount of Olives. In fact, we are not meeting Him on Earth; we are meeting Him "in the air." These two passages cannot be harmonized. They are deliberately different. They describe two different comings of Christ: one coming for the body of Christ; and one coming for the saints of Israel (and other Circumcision-gospel believers). Unless one grasps the difference between the gospel of the Uncircumcision and the gospel of the Circumcision (Galatians 2:7), one will either attempt to water down the snatching away to make it fit the Mount of Olives appearance, or one will elevate the Olivet experience to some ill-suited celestial sphere.

How wonderful to have the key of the two evangels. With this key, we can believe *all* of Scripture, keeping each passage in its proper place.

27. Gospel of Circumcision, Peter's gospel:
Saved left, unsaved taken out (Matthew 24:38-41)

> For as they were in those days before the deluge [flood],
> masticating and drinking and marrying and taking in mar-
> riage until the day on which Noah entered into the ark, and
> did not know till the deluge came and takes them all away,
> thus shall be the presence of the Son of Mankind. Then two
> shall be in the field; one is taken along and one left: two
> grinding at the millstone; one is taken along and one left.

This verse has often been presented to me as proof there's no
such thing as a "secret rapture." These people say: "See? You say the
righteous will be taken away. But Jesus says the righteous are the
ones left; in the example of Noah, the sinners were taken away."
For body-of-Christ saints, however, the opposite occurs.

Gospel of Uncircumcision, Paul's gospel:
Saved taken out, unsaved left (1 Thessalonians 4:17)

> Thereupon we, the living who are surviving, shall at the
> same time be snatched away together with them in clouds,
> to meet the Lord in the air.

These people don't realize they're making my argument for
me. In fact, I use these two verses to prove that the snatching away
and the coming for Israel are two different events. They point to
these verses and say, "See? Your verse from Paul isn't true." I use
it to say: "Both of these verses have to be true. There are two different things happening here to two different groups of believers."
When you try to harmonize verses that are deliberately opposed,
you have to either water down one verse, or elevate the other one.
Understanding the difference between the two evangels puts
you in the enviable position of believing these statements as they
stand. In the Circumcision gospel, the unsaved are taken away, yes.
In the gospel of the Uncircumcision, however, the unsaved are left

on Earth (as well as believing Israelites and Christians who believe the Circumcision gospel: Christ returns for them *after* the Tribulation). Which isn't proof that Paul is wrong and Jesus is right. It's proof that Paul and Jesus are saying two different things.

28. Gospel of Circumcision, Peter's gospel:
To be a kingdom of priests over nations (Revelation 2:26-27; Isaiah 61:6)

> And to the one who is conquering and keeping My acts until the consummation, to him will I be giving authority over the nations; and he shall be shepherding them with an iron club, as vessels of pottery are being crushed, as I also have obtained from My Father.

Another "Overcomer" verse, from the *Concordant Literal New Testament*. (Whereas the CLNT has "to the one who is conquering," the KJV has "he that overcometh.") Another opportunity to get a T-shirt, but here the rewards for doing so are spelled out: Whoever overcomes will shepherd the nations with a rod of iron. Sound familiar? That's the call of Israel.

> Yet you shall be called "Priests of Jehovah"; "Ministers of our Elohim," it will be said of you. The estate of nations you shall eat, and in their glory you shall vaunt.
> —Isaiah 61:6

Non-Israelites are never called "Priests of Jehovah" in the Scriptures. But do religious folks ever love priesthood. The Anglican, Catholic, Episcopalian, and other churches exist because people love the pomp and circumstance of dressing-up their priests and ministers. In the old days of Israel, there was much pomp and circumstance—but that was when a priest was divinely appointed and necessary. (If you have never seen the costuming God demanded of the priesthood in that day, Google "Israelite priest.")

We humans love our religious costuming. Some of us are upset to be robbed of frilly, colorful vestments. Therefore, a substantial segment of the human race currently "plays Israel." The Lutheran, Catholic, Greek Orthodox, and other religions are falsifications of a priesthood that God will properly re-instigate once this era of the Gentiles wraps up. (The priesthood of Israel will resume—with a new heart—when Christ returns to the Mount of Olives and resurrects the twelve apostles and the other saints of Israel.) Imitating priesthood now, during this administration of the grace of God, is a grievous mistake—out of timing with God's purpose.

Gospel of Uncircumcision, Paul's gospel:
To have an allotment among the celestials (Ephesians 2:6)

> God ... rouses us together and seats us together among the celestials, in Christ Jesus ...

Priesthood, like Israel, belongs on Earth. Among the celestials, fleshly distinctions vanish and there is no priesthood. For Israel, priesthood finally vanishes on the New Earth (after the 1,000-year reign of Christ on this present Earth), where John saw no temple. For the body of Christ, there never will be a priest between us and the throne of heaven.

29. Gospel of Circumcision, Peter's gospel:
Will fill Earth with knowledge of God's glory (Habakkuk 2:14)

> For the Earth shall be filled with the knowledge of Yahweh's glory, as the waters are covering over the sea.

Israel's call is wonderful. Israel has been pining for a long time to be the agents by whom God reconciles the Earth. I, for one, will be happy for her when this finally happens. I will be happy for the inhabitants of Earth as well. I will be happy for God—needless

Some of us
are upset to be
robbed of frilly,
colorful
vestments.

to say. And yet I will not be on Earth enabling all this happiness. Rather, I ...

Gospel of Uncircumcision, Paul's gospel:
Will dispense God's wisdom among the celestials (Ephesians 3:10-12)

> That now may be made known to the sovereignties and the authorities among the celestials, through the ecclesia, the multifarious wisdom of God, in accord with the purpose of the eons, which He makes in Christ Jesus, our Lord; in Whom we have boldness and access with confidence, through His faith.

In the beginning, God created the heavens and the Earth. God's goal, through the cross of Christ, is to reconcile both the heavens and the Earth (Colossians 1:20) to Himself. Israel will be His means of reconciling the Earth, and the body of Christ His means of reconciling the heavens. This for this, and that for that. No need to dilute or ignore one calling in order to believe another. Both are true. Israel will be doing her thing, and I will be doing mine.

Praise and glory to God for both.

30. Gospel of Circumcision, Peter's gospel:
Will judge twelve tribes of Israel (Matthew 19:28)

> Yet Jesus said to them, "Verily, I am saying to you, that you who follow Me, in the renascence [regeneration of the world] whenever the Son of Mankind should be seated on the throne of His glory, you also shall sit on twelve thrones, judging the twelve tribes of Israel.

Jesus' prophecy applied to Peter and the other eleven. They are the select Israelites who will be judging all the other Israelites. What a wonderful, glorious calling! Yet, we ...

Gospel of Uncircumcision, Paul's gospel:
Will judge angels (1 Corinthians 6:3)

> Are you not aware that we shall be judging angels, not to mention life's affairs?

What an obvious point of contrast between the gospel of the Circumcision, and that of the Uncircumcision. It speaks for itself.

31. Gospel of Circumcision, Peter's gospel:
Will have access to temple courts (Revelation 7:15)

> Therefore they are before the throne of God and are offering divine service to Him day and night in His temple. And He Who is sitting on the throne will be tabernacling over them.

Yet another example of Israel being one step removed from the glory we enjoy as members of Christ's body. To have access to the temple courts and to stand before the throne of God was the highest and most intimate contact with God that an Israelite could hope for on Earth. Just when you think that nothing could eclipse it in glory, you read that we ...

Gospel of Uncircumcision, Paul's gospel:
Will have access to the Father Himself (Ephesians 2:18)

> For through Him we both have had the access, in one spirit, to the Father.

I bow my head in worship.

14.
EMBRACE THE NEW MESSAGE

EMBRACE THE NEW MESSAGE

In the '90s, a man named Jory Brooks was pastor of the Restoration Bible Church near downtown Detroit. This church loved Israel and the law. None of the congregants, however, were Orthodox Jews. None of the men wore beards (at least not down to their chests). Few of the women wore head scarves.

Even so, these pleasant people tacked maps of the Holy Land on their vestibule walls, and spoke with relish (and other condiments) of the Jewish feast days. They believed the Anglo-Saxon peoples were the Lost Ten Tribes, so they lived continually conscious of their "Israelite heritage." One congregant, Edna, was sure she was of the tribe of Ephraim—an Ephraimite. Another, Ed, claimed to be a Reubenite. Still another said, "I am a Benjamite."

"What are *you?*" one of them asked me.

"A parasite," I said.

Pastor Brooks heard from a friend that "this guy in Ohio" believed in the successful saving power of Christ and could speak intelligently on it. That's how I arrived at the RBC in the spring of 1997.

You see, this church also believed in the eventual salvation of the world through Christ's sacrifice. On my first three ventures north, I spoke on topics related to the grand victory of Christ's cross. Everyone liked me; I was a big hit. Only one problem: On the eve of my fourth visit, I lay awake wrestling with the fabulously exciting and dangerous prospect of teaching the congregation the beautiful truth concerning justification apart from works of law.

I knew from conversations with several members that the very concept of "apart from works of law" (Romans 3:28) vexed them like a Jesus parable. They could not imagine life without Moses and large rocks. What finally convinced me to carry out my plan was that I was getting tired of driving all the way to Detroit every third Sunday.

I showed up looking like one of them—in my suit and tie. Thus attired, I started in. I said, "I believe the truths of the scattered tribes of Israel as described in Amos 9:9. I *know* who you are." Many smiles radiated up from the pews; they loved my italic placement. But then I said, "And here is one good reason why it doesn't matter."

So much for upturned mouths, then. And yet, I soldiered on. I spoke of the reasons why the apostle Paul himself renounced his Israelite citizenship—considering the title "Benjamite" to be so much refuse (Philippians 3:4-8)—for the excellencies of Christ. I said that, in Christ, there was neither Jew nor Greek (Galatians 3:28). I told them that justification by faith could only exist in an absence of law, because, "by works of law, no flesh at all shall be justified" (Romans 3:20).

Forty minutes later—after detailing the differences between forgiveness and justification, between law and grace—I finished in a sheen of forehead sweat.

Ordinarily, after I'd spoken here, people would come up to me and tell me how much they'd enjoyed my address. They would come up to "Mazel Tov" me, and offer to take me out for ritually slaughtered lamb. This day, however, there was no *Mazel*, and not a single *Tov*. If anyone cared a whit for my hunger, none made me aware of it.

But then, *she* came.

I was still at the podium dabbing my forehead when I noted her approach. It was one of the younger women. I turned to greet her, preparing for the worst. The look on her face was, to me, unintelligible. There was a glaze to it. Either she was completely happy, or completely ready to stone me. I detected nothing in-between either of these possible poles.

Fixing her eyes intently upon me, she said (her voice quavering), "I have been coming to this church for three years ..." She now looked as if she were going to cry.

"And I have never, in my life ..."—Oh, boy, here it came—

"I have never, in my life, heard what you spoke of today. Today, Mr. Zender, *I have heard my gospel for the first time!*"

For the next hour, I acquainted her—in full, glorious detail—with the gospel of Paul. God caused her to realize the truth, and she became—then and there—a member of the body of Christ.

Since this encounter fifteen years ago, God has given me an analogy that I often use to describe the phenomenon of authentic, God-given belief in the face of two coexistent yet disparate gospels.

ALL THE HITS, ALL THE TIME

Imagine, if you will, that the gospel of Paul is a radio signal that broadcasts at a frequency of 92.1 FM. The gospel of the Uncircumcision is, indeed, a specific message, containing specific facts, concerning a specific act at Calvary, accomplished by a specific Man, namely, the Savior of the World, our Lord Jesus Christ.

Now imagine that the gospel of the Circumcision, which is also a specific message, containing specific *different* facts, concerning a specific act at Calvary, accomplished by a specific Man, namely, the Messiah of Israel, is broadcast at a completely different frequency, namely, 1400 AM. This shouldn't be difficult to imagine, as we have just noted thirty-one key differences between these two gospels;

they cannot be broadcasting at the same frequency.

We learned in the last chapter that Israel was foreknown *from* the disruption of the world, while members of the body of Christ were foreknown *before* the disruption of the world. In both cases, God knows beforehand who are His—long before the individual believers are born. Therefore, God has preappointed each believer for what he or she will believe—or whether he or she will believe at all in this life.

For a long time, only one gospel existed in the world: the gospel of the Circumcision. If you wanted to know God, there was only one frequency to tune to: 1400 AM. The flagship station, of course, was Israel. There was not much confusion, then. After all, if there is only one restaurant in town, no one argues about where to go.

We know the world contains both believers and those to whom God has simply not granted faith. So in the days before the calling of Saul on the road to Damascus, either a person was given a receiver with an antenna set to receive 1400 AM, or they had no antenna for spiritual matters whatsoever. It was an either/or proposition. Either you were an Israelite, or a proselyte of Israel. There was no other source of truth, and no other means of salvation.

The only other option was unbelief.

Along this line of spiritual antennas, consider the Ethiopian eunuch of Acts 8:26-39. Please, bear with this lengthy passage; you'll be glad you did. From *The Message*:

> Later God's angel spoke to Philip: "At noon today I want you to walk over to that desolate road that goes from Jerusalem down to Gaza." He got up and went. He met an Ethiopian eunuch coming down the road. The eunuch had been on a pilgrimage to Jerusalem and was returning to Ethiopia, where he was minister in charge of all the finances of Candace, queen of the Ethiopians. He was riding in a chariot and reading the prophet Isaiah.
>
> The Spirit told Philip, "Climb into the chariot." Running up alongside, Philip heard the eunuch reading Isaiah and asked,

"Do you understand what you're reading?" He answered, "How can I without some help?" and invited Philip into the chariot with him. The passage he was reading was this:

> *As a sheep led to slaughter,*
> *and quiet as a lamb being sheared,*
> *He was silent, saying nothing.*
> *He was mocked and put down,*
> *never got a fair trial.*
> *But who now can count His kin*
> *since He's been taken from the Earth?*

The eunuch said, "Tell me, who is the prophet talking about: himself or some other?" Philip grabbed his chance. Using this passage as his text, he preached Jesus to him. As they continued down the road, they came to a stream of water. The eunuch said, "Here's water. Why can't I be baptized?"

He ordered the chariot to stop. They both went down to the water, and Philip baptized him on the spot. When they came up out of the water, the Spirit of God suddenly took Philip off, and that was the last the eunuch saw of him. But he didn't mind. He had what he'd come for and went on down the road as happy as he could be.

Think of when you've been tuned to your favorite radio station, but you can't hear it because you're out of signal-range. All you get is static. The nearer you get to the station, however, the clearer the signal becomes. Two dozen miles out, you begin to hear bits and pieces of music and talk. The static still hisses, but not so much. As you continue on, recognizable sound emerges as the static dissipates.

The Ethiopian eunuch got a first-century dose of this. In the womb, God had placed within the man an antenna preprogrammed to 1400 AM. In all his years on that dark continent, that specific amplitude modulation never went forth. Then one day he got ahold

of the Hebrew Scriptures. Static in his head gave way to bits of
signal. In came voices, and snippets of beautiful music. Just when
a particular chord would grab him, however, the signal faded and
static once again overcame and blurred his apprehension.

Lucky for him, Queen Candace sent him to Jerusalem on
official business. There he was, in his chariot, wrestling with the
book of Isaiah for the umpteenth time, and up came a man *radiat-
ing* 1400 AM: Philip. Standing near Philip was like straddling the
freaking broadcast tower. Suddenly, the eunuch's antenna starting
smoking like a lightning rod, and a message started coming in—
loud and clear. The result? "He had what he'd come for and went
on down the road as happy as he could be" (Acts 8:39).

Consider Paul, now. Consider him when he was still Saul
the Pharisee. The man obviously had an antenna for the above-
mentioned frequency—he was born with it. In addition to this,
God caused him to be born in Israel, where the programming was,
"All Israel, all the time." Naturally, Saul received and accepted the
gospel of the Circumcision.

But this man, Saul, was also implanted, from birth, with another antenna. This other antenna was designated beforehand by
God to pick up a frequency that had never before been broadcast
in the history of the known world. In fact, in those days, if you
had even mentioned "92.1 FM" (i.e., Gospel of the Uncircumcision), the men in white (if that's what psychiatric professionals wore
back then) would have whisked you off to your new home. For
one thing, no one even knew of the existence of another "band,"
let alone that odd combination of numbers "92.1," let alone the
potency of those numbers.

On the day Saul traveled east on that now-famous road to
Damascus, the undreamed-of frequency came beaming from
heaven in an unseen surge of power. Paul's receiver went bonkers;
the Pharisee was now hearing something resonating so powerfully
within him that the strength and clarity of the signal knocked
him off his feet.

We have glorified the first men who set foot on the moon. This human milestone is dwarfed, in comparison, by that moment in history when the first human being received the first broadcast—direct from celestial realms—of the 92.1 FM frequency.

The same day God called Saul, other humans wandered the planet possessing the identical means as Paul of receiving a signal they had neither heard of nor could have imagined. Oblivious to their gift, they went about their business. Their only means of discerning the signal was to be in range of a transmitter broadcasting it.

Something else happened that day which has not happened since: The 92.1 signal came directly from the celestial world. Subsequently, the signal has come only from those humans prepared by God to broadcast it:

> Whoever should be invoking the name of the Lord, shall be saved. How, then, should they be invoking One in Whom they do not believe? Yet how should they be believing One of Whom they do not hear? Yet how should they be hearing apart from one heralding? Yet how should they be heralding if ever they should not be commissioned? According as it is written: How beautiful are the feet of those bringing an evangel of good!
>
> —Romans 10:13-15, CLNT

Thus Paul tells Timothy in 2 Timothy 2:2—"And what things you hear from me through many witnesses, these commit to faithful humans, who shall be competent to teach others also."

At that moment in time, subsequent to the heavenly broadcast, there was only one human transmitter of the 92.1 frequency on the face of the planet: Saul.

Now let us consider the case of the apostle Peter. This man, like Saul, was born with the 1400 AM receiver/antenna. And yet, unlike Saul, Peter was not given the means of receiving 92.1 FM.

Remarkably, the men who traveled to Damascus with Saul saw the light from heaven, but did not hear the voice: "Now those who are with me gaze, indeed, at the light, yet they hear not the voice of Him Who is speaking to me" (Acts 22:9).

We know from Galatians 2:1-2 that Peter heard Paul's message:

> Fourteen years after that first visit, Barnabas and I went up
> to Jerusalem and took Titus with us. I went to clarify with
> them what had been revealed to me. At that time I placed
> before them exactly what I was preaching to the non-Jews.
> I did this in private with the leaders ...
> *—The Message*

And yet Peter's antenna did not receive Paul's message. We know this for two reasons:

    1)   Peter's own testimony in 2 Peter 3:16—

> Some things Paul writes are difficult to understand. Ir-
> responsible people who don't know what they are talking
> about twist them every which way.
> *—The Message*

    2)   Our Lord's testimony concerning Peter in Matthew
        19:27-28—

> Peter chimed in, "We left everything and followed you.
> What do we get out of it?" Jesus replied, "Yes, you have
> followed me. In the [regeneration] of the world, when the
> Son of Man will rule gloriously, you who have followed
> me will also rule, starting with the twelve tribes of Israel."
> *—The Message*

If Peter had received the new frequency to the extent Paul did, he would have denounced his Israelite heritage, as Paul did (Philippians 3:4-9).

Yet, he did not.

Paul is a member of the body of Christ; Peter is not. Peter has a throne in the Millennial kingdom; Paul doesn't.

Back to Michigan.

Here at the Restoration Bible Church, I became a part of what I considered first-century drama. I was in a room, full of either actual Israelites or Israelite wannabes (proselytes), where the leaders broadcast continually at 1400 AM. I was the first person ever at that church to broadcast on the 92.1 FM frequency.

A certain woman in that congregation had either a single antenna preset to receive 92.1 (in which case she sat in that pew miserable for years, failing to truly grasp a word of what was said), or two antennas, one for each frequency (in which case she understood what she heard all those years, but it failed to resonate to the degree that the new frequency did).

I have to hand it to the Restoration Bible Church for keeping grace away from their law. The church simply did not teach grace. Thus, they were consistent. The church taught a pure Israelite message, and never even pretended that anyone was saved apart from works.

This cannot be said of most Christian churches. Most Christian churches teach a non-evangel. A non-evangel, according to Paul, is an evangel that "distorts the evangel of Christ."

In Galatians 1:6-9, from *The Message*, Paul says:

> I can't believe your fickleness—how easily you have turned traitor to Him who called you by the grace of Christ by embracing a variant message! It is not a minor variation, you know; it is completely other, an alien message, a no-message, a lie about God. Those who are provoking this agitation among you are turning the message of Christ on its head.

> Let me be blunt: If one of us—even if an angel from heaven!—were to preach something other than what we preached originally, let him be cursed. I said it once; I'll say it again: If anyone, regardless of reputation or credentials, preaches something other than what you received originally,

let him be cursed.

The "completely other" message Paul mentions here—the "variant" message, the "alien" message, the "no-message," the "lie about God," was *not* the evangel of the Circumcision. (How could Paul have called the evangel of the Circumcision any of these things, when the evangel of the Circumcision, taught by Peter and the others in Jerusalem, was the evangel given by Jesus Himself? Jesus is the Messiah, and faith in Him—accompanied by works—will lead Israel into her prophesied Millennial kingdom, where she will rule the world.)

No, Paul was not referring to the Circumcision evangel here. Rather, he was referring to an "evangel" (I put it in quotes because it was a false evangel) that was "turning the message of Christ on its head." The *Concordant Literal New Testament* says, "distorting the evangel of Christ."

What was the message—or the evangel—of Christ? Salvation by the grace of God, apart from works, as taught by Paul. (Remember? Paul's the one who constantly referred to Him as "*Christ* Jesus.")

What was turning it on its head? Introduction of a foreign element, namely, the law.

Paul zeroes in on the Galatian problem in chapter 3, verses 1-4:

> You crazy Galatians! Did someone put a hex on you? Have you taken leave of your senses? Something crazy has happened, for it's obvious that you no longer have the crucified Jesus in clear focus in your lives. His sacrifice on the cross was certainly set before you clearly enough. Let me put this question to you: How did your new life begin? Was it by working your heads off to please God? Or was it by responding to God's message to you?
>
> Are you going to continue this craziness? For only crazy people would think they could complete by their own efforts

what was begun by God. If you weren't smart enough or strong enough to begin it, how do you suppose you could perfect it? Did you go through this whole painful learning process for nothing? It is not yet a total loss, but it certainly will be if you keep this up!

—*The Message*

The modern Christian message is even worse. At least the Galatians realized their new life began in the strength of Christ crucified. The modern Christian message, however, insists that new life in God begins by the free, uninfluenced exercise of the human will (a euphemism for "salvation by human willpower") and the power of that will to "accept Jesus." So the thing that Paul calls down curses upon in Galatians, chapter 1—mixing the evangel of grace with elements of law—he would pronounce a double curse upon today. Today, the clergy fail to even start people with a pure message—and then they add law ("obey the Ten Commandments") after that.

The modern Christian church fails to recognize the difference between the gospel of the Circumcision and that of the Uncircumcision. Thus, it produces a bastardized gospel—a mixed message—the very gospel Paul condemns in chapter 1 of Galatians as being a "non-gospel" and, in fact, a lie about God:

> Let me be blunt: If one of us—even if an angel from heaven!—were to preach something other than what we preached originally, let him be cursed. I said it once; I'll say it again: If anyone, regardless of reputation or credentials, preaches something other than what you received originally, let him be cursed.
>
> —Galatians 1:7-9, *The Message*

Christianity brags of its credentials, how many people it attracts, and the scholarly attainments of its teachers and pastors. Paul cares nothing for theological achievements. In fact, he says, "If *anyone* ... preaches something other than what you received originally, let him be cursed" (Galatians 1:9).

By Paul's definition, the modern Christian church and its preachers are cursed. Paul even predicted that religion would deteriorate into satanic lies: "In subsequent eras, some will be withdrawing from the faith, giving heed to *deceiving spirits and the teachings of demons*" (1 Timothy 4:1).

Disguised as an angel of light (2 Corinthians 11:14), Satan deceives people with the cloak of religion. Satan doesn't deceive people in nightclubs—that would be too obvious. No, Satan cleverly fools people within religion—the place where people think they're learning about God. Instead, Satan sees to it that they are fed lies about God and His plans for humanity.

This is a serious matter. Organized religion is doomed to destruction. Religion's message is an alien, variant, no-message lie about God—a hodgepodge of disparate elements that honors neither the gospel of the Circumcision nor that of the Uncircumcision. Rather, it mixes the two to produce an unpalatable, unrecognizable mess that Paul himself would spit from his mouth.

WHICH EVANGEL IS YOURS?

Many times, I have been in the presence of those who hear Paul's message but don't understand him. They even say, "I don't get Paul." I speak to these folks of: "our identification with Christ," being "complete in Christ," being "crucified with Christ," "transcendent grace," of God "reconciling the heavens and the Earth to Himself," of "the conciliation of the world," of the God Who is "operating all in accord with the counsel of His own will," of, "one died for the sake of all, consequently all died," of the "new creation," and of, "as in Adam all are dying, thus also in Christ shall all be vivified." What do I get in return? Blank stares. Furrowed brows. Sighs of exasperation.

Yet another person will approach and speak to these same folks of: "Israel," "law," "Ten Commandments," "Hebrews," "Jesus,"

God's *latest* frequency will change your life.

"sin," "worthy," "temple," "lamb of God," "priesthood," "Matthew," "Mark," "Luke," "John," "James," "Peter," "Passover," "baptism," "Jesus the Nazarene," "Overcomer," "Revelation," and "144,000."

And they just about lose their minds with happiness.

The people hearing *these* things become transformed. A light goes on inside them. They love all things Israel. They love the idea of being worthy of salvation. They love the idea of working. They love the idea of law. They love the idea of priesthood and ceremony and a people set above all other people. They love the brown-haired, bearded, sandaled Jesus. They love Jerusalem; many of them want to visit the Holy Land, or be baptized in the Jordan River. The rite of baptism fascinates them; they can't wait to get wet. They love ceremony. They love candles and angels and burning incense.

Again, try bringing Paul to them, and it's like speaking Japanese to a Frenchman. Truly, they don't get Paul. Paul is "too hard." Paul is "too intellectual."

Thing is, they can't make grace jive with law. If truly given the choice between law and grace, they will choose law every time. Why in the world would anyone do that? Religious humans love the idea of outperforming other humans. Law allows this. The Israelite message makes room for fleshly distinction and accomplishment.

Like Israel, many of these religious folks are self-righteous. They don't realize—as even an Israelite must eventually realize—that even fleshly advantage is ultimately a gift of God. Like Israel, they will need a whack upside the head to awaken them to this fact. For those bride-of-the-Lamb saints who are alive when the Tribulation begins, this is precisely what will happen. Not being members of the body of Christ, they will not be snatched away ("raptured"), and will surely go through those terrible days.

That's why I say the snatching away of the body of Christ will be a small, unnoticed event—quite opposite of the *Left Behind* scenario. Most people on the planet are unbelievers or Israelites or Christians who believe in Israel's Circumcision gospel.

I used to write off modern-day Circumcision believers. I used to think, "Why are these people responding to Israel's message? Don't they know that Paul's is the active evangel?" Finally, I realized: Even though the Circumcision evangel is an evangel "in-waiting," it can still be heard and embraced, even by non-Israelites who nevertheless wish to associate themselves with that holy nation. I am speaking of proselytes such as Cornelius of Acts, chapter 10.

I no longer condemn these folks. It's apparent they simply are not in the body of Christ. This does not mean they're not saved, but they're not saved in accord with Paul's gospel. Rather, they are saved in accord with Peter's gospel. They will have a place in that earthly kingdom—but only if they are faithful and endure to the end of the Tribulation.

THE SPECIFICS OF PAUL'S EVANGEL

The three criteria for belief in Paul's message are found in 1 Corinthians 15:1-4 (CLNT):

> Now I am making known to you, brethren, the evangel which I bring to you, which also you accepted, in which also you stand, through which also you are saved (if you are retaining what I said in bringing the evangel to you, outside and except you believe feignedly).

> For I give over to you among the first what also I accepted, that [1] *Christ died for our sins* according to the Scriptures, and that [2] *He was entombed*, and that [3] *He has been roused the third day* according to the Scriptures ...

All an Israelite needs to believe to be saved is that Jesus Christ is the Messiah, come to save Israel. Nowhere is an Israelite exhorted (as body-of-Christ believers are) to believe in the cross and all it accomplished—in the matter of sin—apart from any human "free will." (Remember, Israelites were exhorted to believe in their Messiah even before Jesus had died on the cross.)

Israelites don't even have to believe (as body-of-Christ believers do) that Jesus Christ was actually stone-cold dead for three days. (Jesus was not gallivanting with God in heaven during those three days. If He had been with God [instead of dead], then Jesus didn't actually die for our sins and none of us are saved. The truth is that if God, the Father of Christ, hadn't raised His Son—Jesus would still be dead today.)

All that Israelites need to believe for salvation is what Peter confessed in Matthew 16:16—"Thou art the Christ, the son of the living God," and the realization that, "flesh and blood does not reveal it to you, but My Father Who is in the heavens" (Matthew 16:17). (Even an Israelite, though, must unhand the self-righteous insistence that saving faith comes from within a person, instead of from God's spirit.)

Once a person gets that ironed out, it's just a matter of backing it up with good works.

There now. Do you believe that Jesus is the Messiah? Do you back up your faith with good works? Does Paul drive you crazy? Do you love to read James and Jude? The four gospels? Do you love the law, including the Ten Commandments? Are you just *certain* that you need dunked or sprinkled with water to be saved?

Welcome to the earthly, 1,000-year kingdom. Please, bring your offering to the new temple, three times a year. As for me, I will be looking in on you from heaven, marveling at your glory, but thankful to God to be a part of His celestial kingdom.

Everything comes out in the wash. At the consummation (end) of the eons (described in 1 Corinthians 15:20-28), God will become "All in all." There is coming a time, true, when no fleshly distinction will matter anymore—not to you—the proselyte of Israel—and not to God.

That time has not arrived, yet. Until then, we must recognize distinctions. Picture an automobile plant, and imagine that the body of the car and the engine are manufactured at the same plant.

Imagine two assembly lines: one for the body, one for the engine. Unless these lines are kept distinct, confusion reigns and there's no car. At the end of the line—and at the end only—we at last have a finished product. At that point, all distinctions vanish. Before then, distinctions are essential to the final success.

Therefore, Paul exhorts us, through Timothy, in 2 Timothy 1:13—"Have a *pattern* of sound words, which you hear from me"; and in 2 Timothy 2:15—"Endeavor to present yourself to God qualified, an unashamed worker, *rightly dividing the Word of truth.*"

MY MESSAGE

If you're like me, the words of Christ written in blood red in your Bible always kind of scared you. I wanted to be like Jesus when I was a kid, but Jesus kept setting the bar just a little too high. He didn't seem to have much of a sense of humor, either. When people asked Him a question, Jesus seldom gave a straight answer. Instead, He answered questions in a roundabout way. Ask Jesus what time dinner was, and He would tell you a parable about Jonah. Get comfortable for a second, and He would predict His death. Ask Him when things would finally be good again, and He would say, "Woe to those suckling children in those days" (Luke 21:23).

I'm not saying Paul was Mr. Pin-the-Tail-on-the-Donkey, but the dark cloud that seemed to surround Jesus—in my mind—disappeared with Paul. Paul was like, "Grace and peace. How about a little fruit of the spirit in your life? But anyway, we're all justified." Paul seemed really scatterbrained to me—the man clearly had no clue how to punctuate a sentence—but the dark cloud was gone. I pictured him short and just a little bit chubby. Paul was the kind of guy who would drink beer on a boat and say, "Are we there yet? I'd like to see Antioch before the second coming."

From Abraham to Moses to Paul, God unveils His heart. The law of Moses was not meant to portray God's innermost heart. Rather, the law prepared the way for Christ. Jesus Christ was

Relax and don't worry; that's for me.

God's image, but even Jesus was a minister of the Circumcision gospel (Romans 15:8), intentionally concealing the depths of His Father's grace while He was on Earth.

The message of God's deepest grace was saved for a little lunatic from Tarsus en route to Damascus to kill Christians.

Paul's message is: RELAX AND DON'T WORRY. Does that resonate as much with you as it does with me? That's *my* message.

WHY WE CAN'T LIVE LIKE JESUS

Most of our lives, we've been told we have to live like Jesus. After much trial and error, we've discovered it's not even possible to live like Jesus. Why? By now, you should be able to guess the answer. The obvious answer is that Jesus is the Son of God, and you are not: Jesus Christ was a sinless being, and some days you can barely put your socks on straight. The less obvious answer is that Jesus Christ, on Earth, was a minister of the Circumcision, and conducted Himself accordingly. He tithed, refused to eat pork chops, and kept the Sabbath day holy. Oh—and Jesus suffered and died on a cross to take away the sins of the world.

These days, those poor souls who try to "walk in His steps" must be very tired by now, frustrated at their inability to raise the dead, think up parables, and take away their own sin, let alone that of the world. And yet they persist. That's why they're so hard to be around. We call them "religious people."

If we're not supposed to live like Jesus, who *are* we supposed to live like? The answer should not surprise you:

> For if you should be having ten thousand escorts in Christ, nevertheless not many fathers, for in Christ Jesus, through the evangel, I beget you. I am entreating you, then, *become imitators of me.*
>
> —1 Corinthians 4:15-16, CLNT

How could Paul have the audacity to tell people to imitate him instead of Jesus? Paul never knew the Jewish Messiah, Who did everything in accord with Mosaic law. Otherwise, Paul could have retained the law, pointed to it, and told us: "Do this." But Paul is the one telling us that we are justified apart from works of law. He can't, then, set forth the earthly Jesus for us to copy. Appropriately, Paul leaves that job to Peter:

> For this were you called, seeing that Christ also suffered for your sakes, leaving you a copy, that you should be following up in the footprints of Him Who does no sin, neither was guile found in His mouth.
>
> —1 Peter 2:21-22

Tell me again why you want to be an Israelite? Not even Israelites can fully follow the footprints of Christ, until Christ imparts to them a new spirit. But still, they have to give it the old Israelite try. All while remaining humble. All while acknowledging that every righteous act comes from above, not below.

Where does this leave us? While it may not seem so on the surface, Paul also tells us—members of the body of Christ—to imitate our Savior. Yet we are to imitate Christ in His new capacity as ruler of the universe, seated at the right hand of God.

For real?

If the Jews can barely imitate the earthly Jesus, how are we supposed to imitate the glorified Christ? Thank God that the glorified Christ has graciously shown the kind of lifestyle He wants from us through a human being who is just like us, only worse: the apostle Paul.

The former Saul of Tarsus was a murderer, an enemy of God. ... An idiot. To the one deserving the direst doom, Christ bestowed the greatest grace. In light of such love, Paul lived his life in service and giving thanks—perfectly in accord with the evangel he heralded. This, then, is how we are to live our lives: In service and thanks.

What a change from worry and work.

WHAT'S NEXT?

Some of you want to believe what I'm saying, but you're not sure. You may feel that traveling with Paul means abandoning Jesus. You have an emotional attachment to Jesus, having spent most of your life reading Matthew, Mark, Luke, and John. You're drawn to Paul, but you feel guilty whenever you're not working hard or sacrificing something.

WWJD?

Jesus would want you to turn to Paul. Why wouldn't He? Jesus commissioned Paul. Ultimately, you are honoring the Savior by turning from the letters in red to the latest, greatest revelation given to humans.

Embrace the new message.

EPILOGUE

Now you know of God's intention to become All in all, through the cross of His Son. At the end of a series of time periods known as "eons," God will return everything ever created in heaven and Earth to Himself. Yet that glorious consummation, spoken of by Paul in 1 Corinthians 15:21-28, is a long way off. In the meantime, difficult times lie ahead. There will come a time—soon, I believe—of which our Lord said, "Then shall be great affliction, such as has not occurred from the beginning of the world till now" (Matthew 24:21). We've come to know this as "the Tribulation," but our apostle Paul calls it, "the coming Indignation" (1 Thessalonians 1:10).

The Indignation will be the birth pangs that bring Israel, finally, into the kingdom. The Indignation will be the catalyst that once-and-for-all breaks this godless world of its pride, preparing it for the reign of Christ.

No one wants to live through the coming Indignation. But many will. And many will die during it. Jesus compared our day to the days of Noah:

> For even as the days of Noah, thus shall be the presence of
> the Son of Mankind. For as they were in those days before
> the deluge, eating and drinking and marrying and taking
> in marriage until the day on which Noah entered into the
> ark, and did not know till the deluge came and took them
> all away, thus shall be the presence of the Son of Mankind.
> —Matthew 24:37-39

In the days of Noah, however, God provided a lifeboat. God instructed Noah to build a shelter for those few He intended to save from mass destruction. That shelter was the ark.

Likewise, today, Paul's gospel is the lifeboat from mass destruction, a modern-day ark. The gospel of God's grace is the shelter, built by God, that will spare those who believe Paul's message from the coming Indignation, delivering them into the glories of heaven. The Circumcision message will *not* do this, for those who believe *that* gospel to Israel will go *through* the day of Indignation and remain on Earth (Revelation 7:9-14).

For the body of Christ, this deliverance out of Indignation will be nothing short of a rescue. Paul wrote to the Thessalonians:

> You turn back to God from idols, to be slaving for the liv-
> ing and true God, and to be waiting for His Son out of the
> heavens, Whom He rouses from among the dead, Jesus, our
> Rescuer out of the coming Indignation.
> —1 Thessalonians 1:9-10

Please, remember this key point: All humans will eventually be saved; yet only those who hear and heed Paul's message will be delivered out of the coming Indignation (as members of Christ's body) and taken to heaven. This is the meaning of 1 Timothy 4:10, which is otherwise a mystery to most people: "We rely on the living God, Who is the Savior of all humankind, especially of believers." How can God save everyone, but *especially* believers? Like this: He saves everyone *eventually*—eons from now. But those to whom He gives belief in this life (belief in the gospel of Paul) come in early—*way* early. Everyone eventually gets glory, but believers in Paul's Uncircumcision evangel get super-excessive glory—and they get it sooner (before the day of Indignation even begins).

Of course, God knows beforehand those who are His in *this* lifetime. God knows, but we don't. That's why we herald. Those who have been chosen beforehand for membership into the body of Christ, will be called (Romans 8:30). They will hear Paul's message of grace through heralds (Romans 10:4).

I am a herald.

Satan despises and even fears the reality of a select group of human beings becoming members of the body of Christ. Satan fears this because he currently reigns over significant sectors of heaven, where *we* are headed to rule and reign. Satan is called, "The chief of the jurisdiction of the air" (Ephesians 2:2), and when our bodies are changed, we will rise "to meet the Lord in the air" (1 Thessalonians 4:17). In other words, we will usurp not only Satan's reign, but his realm. His territory. Fearing this, Satan has placed ingenious trip wires before every essential element (belief) of Paul's gospel. These are known as "teachings of demons" (1 Timothy 4:1).

In the last chapter of this book, I gave you the essential elements of Paul's gospel, namely, the death of Christ for all sins, His entombment, and His resurrection. These ought to be simple beliefs, yet they've been deviously twisted. There are three major Christian creeds (introduced by Satan, via human councils and religious conclaves) that effectively keep millions from believing in the gospel of Paul. I am not talking about worldly people now, but Christians—sincere, but severely misguided Christians. These false teachings not only deny the death of Christ for sins, but deny the death of Christ itself.

In order for you to learn more about these satanic teachings—the most prevalent teachings in Christianity—and how they effectually keep good people from believing in the gospel of the grace of God, I have written a special report: "WHAT IS A BELIEVER?"

I am offering this report free of charge, because I want you to

MARTIN ZENDER

be saved from the coming Indignation and not be duped by the prevailing religious apostasy, nor suffer God's judgment upon it—a judgment that shall usher millions into destruction and death.

Sign up at my website at www.martinzender.com to receive your free download of, "WHAT IS A BELIEVER?" (If you have no Internet access, then send $9.95 to cover printing, shipping, and handling, to Starke & Hartmann, Inc., P.O. Box 6473, Canton, OH, 44706.)

This report contains vital information for your peace today, and your future tomorrow.

God bless you,

Martin

SPECIAL REPORT

WHAT IS A BELIEVER?

www.martinzender.com

This book is dedicated to my father-in-law, Jakim Harry Tonn, who died in December of 2008. He loved the Scriptures, and especially the writings of the apostle Paul. Most importantly, he believed the writings of the apostle Paul.

Jakim spent several decades promoting the God of peace he found in Paul's letters. During his final years, he translated *The Gospel of God's Reconciliation of All in Christ*, by E. F. Stroeter, from German to English.

For his service to his Lord, he shall someday be richly rewarded. Rebecca and I look forward to that day. Weeping may endure for the night, but joy comes in the morning. See you in the morning, dear Jakim.

For further information:

www.martinzender.com
www.concordant.org

If you liked this book, please leave your comments at:

www.thefirstidiotinheaven.com

Additional books by Martin Zender:

Flawed by Design
How to be Free From Sin While Smoking a Cigarette
How to Quit Church Without Quitting God
Martin Zender Goes to Hell
Martin Zender's Guide to Intelligent Prayer
The Really Bad Thing About Free Will

 www.facebook.com/zendermeister

PHOTO CREDITS
Cover: © Can Stock Photo Inc. / dundanim
Pg. 7: wwarby; pg. 38: Brenda-Starr; pg. 42: NASA Goddard Photo and Video (galaxy), and USFWS Pacific Southwest Region (desert scene); pg. 45: Rebecca Tonn; pg. 49: kevin dooley; pg. 70: mckay-savage; pg. 73: johannakl; pg. 80: Casey David; pg. 87: Christiano Betta; pg. 99: KaDeWeGirl; pg. 110: p22earl; pg. 125: 85mm.ch; pg. 135: LuzA; pg. 151: edoardocosta; pg. 157: 85mm.ch; pg. 162: nick@; pg. 167: McWilliams Graphics; pg. 186: bazylek100; pg. 195: altemark; pg. 209: kimrose; pg. 221: radiant guy; pg. 240: Chris Eden (sunburst), and Martin Barland (sandaled foot); pg. 249: Perfecto Insecto; pg. 259: Associated Press; pg. 272: Alex Bellink; pg. 285: 50 Watts; pg. 303: © Can Stock Photo Inc. / stillfx; pg. 308: Rebecca Tonn; pg. 321: Rebecca Tonn/Ian W. Scott; pg. 344: Dan Scott Whitcomb. All photos except cover photo and pages 45, 259, 303, 308, 321, and 344: *Creative Commons License: Attribution*

Martin Zender is known as The World's Most Outspoken Bible Scholar. He is an essayist, conference speaker, radio personality, humorist, and author of seven books on spiritual freedom. His essays have appeared in the *Chicago Tribune*, the *Atlanta Journal-Constitution*, the *Cleveland Plain Dealer*, and other newspapers. He has hosted the Grace Cafe radio program at WCCD in Cleveland, and the syndicated Zender/Sheridan Show at flagship station WBRI in Indianapolis.

Zender's unique mix of scholarship and entertainment has gained him an enthusiastic following world-wide. A champion of Scriptural integrity, Zender heralds truth over tradition, faith over fear, and plain speech over theological jargon. He lives with his wife Rebecca Tonn in Colorado Springs.

What if God made you the way you are on purpose?

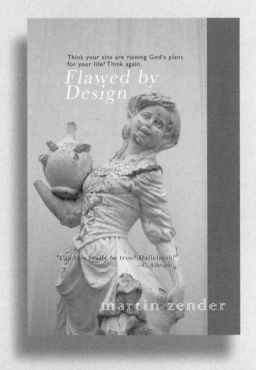

Flawed by Design

EXCERPT
FLAWED BY DESIGN

Pages 11-13

Awoman crashes into the home of Simon the Pharisee. The town sinner, she neither knocks nor removes her sandals. Whoredom is fresh on her clothes, yet something belying this rests angelically upon her face. Only one person here can appreciate the transformation. The woman hurries to the feet of the Master.

An unusual thing had occurred in the early morning hours of that day, after the last man (the last client) had slipped into the Jerusalem night. As she looked about her cubicle, a dread of the future gripped her. Why should she feel this now? Why tonight? No immediate answer came, yet a vision of her final hours flickered in the flame of her one remaining candle. She would die in this room; which night, she did not know. It would be soon, though. Death would come slowly in a pool of blood, released onto the floor by her own hand. Her sister Mariba would find her. Mariba would scream, there would be a funeral—thirty days of mourning—then it would all be over.

The walls closed in. Stars twinkled outside these walls, somewhere. A sun shone on the other side of Earth, though not for her. For her there was only the shadow cast by her burning piece of wax, a leather ghost running from her feet to a corner, up a wall, across the ceiling, then back to her naked feet. Nothing could escape the cubicle. Floor, wall, ceiling, then back to engulf her. Her hands went to her face now; she was crying.

She had to get out.

Not one other soul occupied the side street where she burst from her home. Urgency along this void of humanity became her silent scream. She would not break down in the city.

Outside the Essene gate, down the valley of Hinnom, up over the aqueduct, then west toward the Bethlehem Road; this brought her to the field. Recently gleaned, dead and quiet, the soil sent coolness into her legs. From above, the heavens lay frozen and mute. Between these two voids she fell to her knees to gather a piece of Earth. Instead, she found a stone, for God had placed it there centuries ago, for her to find. Now it would become her means of hating Him. She picked up the stone as a man would grasp it, then found her feet. Her left eye was already trained into the heavens, right wrist cocked toward the throne room.

All agonies now shifted to the act of throwing. Every sinew, muscle, joint, and fragment of despair made ready the rock for the face of God. She would hit Him, yes. And her tongue, too, lay poised with the forbidden question, "What have You *made* me?!"

The stone traveled a little way into space, propelled by the impetus of the word "made." But then it returned to Earth, though she never heard where.

She had missed.

The forbidden question, however, had not missed at all. In fact, it had hit squarely, and she knew it. Something had happened. Now she felt millions of invisible eyes. She had unmistakably commanded something, perhaps everything. The field was now a stage. With knowledge of this came a liberating rush of boldness. What happened next happened too quickly to stop.

Pages 29-30

Frustrated with your failures? Feeling condemned? Can't overcome a bad habit? I've got great news for you:

"Now we have this treasure in earthen vessels, that the transcendence of the power may be of God and not of us" (2 Corinthians 4:7).

Your humble little vessel of sin is made that way on purpose. We are clay pots by design, not because we have gone afoul of God's intention for us. Let this revelation soothe the exhausted self-improver. Retire, Christian soldier! You fail by design, not because you are a failure. God wants you cognizant of the source of your power, and He has many creative ways of driving this home. One of these is sin.

Wouldn't some of us love to shed our earthenware now and still walk among mortals? Our sins keep us from producing a perfect walk, and we mourn this. What we do not understand is that an imperfect walk is the main idea of this life. God puts the treasure of His spirit in earthen vessels now to keep the vessels from situating themselves upon high places. A perfect walk is not what we need right now. Who could live with us? Could we stand ourselves? Humility is a blessed thing this side of resurrection. Vessels on high shelves sit poised, ready to topple and shatter upon hard floors. Pride is burdensome and is known for preceding falls. Can it be so bad to be delivered of this?

Thank God for the comfort of mistakes. Mistakes remind us of our clayhood and drive us toward Christ. When we finally quit chasing perfection and accept these vessels of clay, we will become happier. When we forget about ourselves, peace will ensue. The happy acceptance of imperfection is the beginning of easy breathing. Because, really, how can you be peaceful and flogging yourself simultaneously? You can't. That's why no one in a religion is truly happy. People in religions act happy because they're expected to, but they're only one step away from disappointing their deity and suffering his wrath. How happy can they truly be?

Pages 34-36

In the Bible, God is always getting humans into scrapes so that He can get them out of the scrapes and show His power. You say, "No, Martin. God isn't getting the humans into the scrapes. The humans are getting themselves into the scrapes." Well, that theory works fine until you consider accounts such as the hardening of Pharaoh's heart. And we're going to do that shortly. But first I want to show you how God delights in making things humanly impossible before He sets to work.

Remember the story of the blind man Christ healed? What is the first thing the Lord does? He spits on the ground, makes mud, and then smears the mud on the man's eyes. Then He tells the man to go wash in the Pool of Siloam. The guy comes back reading *The Jerusalem Post*. Just when you think God is crazy with this mud business, you start to wonder, *Maybe God is making a point. Maybe mud on top of blindness is God's way of compounding a problem.*

Consider 1 Kings, chapter 18, when Elijah challenged the prophets of the false god Baal to a contest, to see which God was real. Elijah and the prophets of Baal would each set up an altar. Each would pray to their God to send fire down to their respective altars. The God who sent fire down would be the true God. The prophets of Baal went first.

According to verse 26 of that chapter, the prophets of Baal "called on the name of Baal from morning until noon, saying, 'O Baal, answer us.' But there was no voice and no one answered. And they leaped about the altar which they made."

No Baal. It was Elijah's turn.

Notice the curious thing Elijah does to his altar. I'm quoting from verses 33-35. Elijah said, "'Fill four pitchers with water and pour it on the burnt offering and on the wood.' And he said, 'Do it a second time,' and they did it a second time. And he said, 'Do it a third time,' and they did it a third time. And the water flowed around the altar, and he also filled the trench with water."

With the dousing of the altar, Elijah, through the spirit of God, was setting up a field of "impossibility" on which God would demonstrate His power.

Is God making some things impossible for you? Is God dousing your life with water? And when you seem about to recover, is He dousing you a second time? Then a third time? Is there running water in the trenches of your life? Are you getting ready to put on your swimsuit, sit down, and stare at your insurmountable trials? Good. The sooner you do that, the better off you'll be. God has purposely dampened your life with impossibilities, in order to bring you to the end of yourself. The result is that you will be in a relaxed position (flat on your back, for instance, or on your face) to hear and see His new plan for your life. ■

Martin,

I heard you on a radio show in Chattanooga, TN about a year ago. You debated a Baptist minister. The host sent me one of your books: *Flawed by Design*. I had been a Baptist from a young age until about twenty. Then there were too many questions that didn't add up, so I became mostly an atheist.

When I read your book, I nearly went deaf because of all the clicking sounds. Those were the sounds of all those things in the Bible that didn't add up, clicking into place. I credit your book as the means God used to allow faith in Him to return to me. I now realize that Christ died on the cross for all our sins and His grace is sufficient to save us. —*John P.*

martin zender
The book for people with weaknesses

HOW TO BE FREE FROM SIN
WHILE SMOKING A CIGARETTE

EXCERPT

How to be Free From Sin While Smoking a Cigarette

I don't smoke, but I sometimes wish I did. I have other questionable habits that I won't burden you with. But I can picture myself holding a cigarette, or letting it hang cock-eyed out of my mouth like Humphrey Bogart used to do. Whenever I talked—mumbled, I mean—the cigarette would bounce up and down. Then I'd squint and say something devilish to Lauren Bacall.

In this fantasy of mine, I know smoking is bad for me. I know it's wrong. I know I'm sinning, even while I'm doing it. But I do it anyway because it's cool, because life has been unfair to me, because Bacall has great legs, and because if I don't do *something*, I'll lose my mind. It's the worse kind of sin: knowing it's bad, but doing it anyway.

Preachers today lower their voices when speaking of such bad-ness. They'll talk all sing-songy about stock sins like anger, jealousy, and pride. I call these stock sins because they're a dime a dozen. I'm not saying they're not bad, but I find myself doing them without even thinking. The sins I'm talking about—the sins that make the preachers furrow their eyebrows and talk like Vincent Price—are the ones where the wretched sinner says, "Yes, this would be a sin, all right," then does it anyway.

According to the clergy, there's no refuge for this. It's not like it's an accidental sin. It's not like it's a one-time deal. It's more like, "We're sorry, Lord, for what we did today. And we're sorry, too, that we're probably going to do it again tomorrow. And the day after that. And the day after that." The only comfort from the pulpit for this kind of badness is the remote possibility of a Sno-cone stand in hell. So no matter what your particular weakness is—

Well, hold on a minute. It just occurred to me that maybe you don't have a weakness. This is something I had not considered until now, and it changes everything. This project is shot if most of my readers don't have a weakness. If you don't have a weakness, how can I let you waste your time reading a book about weaknesses and how to deal with them? If you don't have a weakness, then please accept my apology, return this book to your bookseller, and use the money you saved to send a real sinner to Bible camp.

This book is written only for those who know what they're supposed to do but sometimes don't do it. It's written for those who think that their own particular weakness keeps God from completely liking them. It's written for those who just can't shake a bad habit. This book is written for the wretched souls who totter between their passion life and their desire for God, not realizing that in order to have a desire for God they must also be dogged by at least one nagging passion that keeps them humble and needing Him. It was wrong of me to assume the worst of you. So forgive me, please, and have a blessed day.

For those who do have a weakness—or two—welcome to paragraph seven. It appears that we've lost a few of the religious folks. At least now we can speak honestly among ourselves.

We're believers. Or we're seekers. Some of us love Jesus Christ already; others aren't sure if we want to or not. In either case, there are bad things we all do occasionally (or continually, perhaps) that dismantle our happiness in front of God. They've got a term for this dismantling that is so weighty and terrible it deserves its own paragraph.

The term is guilt.

Is it possible to be free from sin, even while sinning? Is it possible to be free from sin and the guilt associated with it, even while narrowing your eyes at Bacall and leaning toward her match?

I know what religion has told you. Religion has told you that freedom from sin means you don't sin anymore. But is this God's thought? If this is God's thought, then no one today can be free from sin—at least none of the honest people who made it past paragraph six. But I generally find that God's thoughts and the thoughts of orthodox religion are two different things. I'm happy to report it's also the case here.

This book is written and dedicated to all the poor sinners in the world who can't stop sinning, but who love or want to love the Lord, Jesus Christ. Here's the good news: *You have already been freed from sin.*

Thanks for hanging on. God's Word is about to deliver you from discouragement, condemnation and guilt, without asking you to change a thing you're doing. On second thought, you may have to change one thing. If you've been beating yourself over the head trying not to sin, you're going to have to quit that. Stop assaulting your head.

You still here? Great. That last paragraph wasn't a joke. I would never joke about something as serious as sin. How could I possibly tell you to quit pummeling yourself over it? Because this monumental effort—and the repeated failures and inevitable guilt trips that follow—is ruining your opinion of yourself, taking away your peace, and robbing you of the affection due Christ. You're working so hard trying to *impress* Him that you're not paying enough attention *to* Him.

"But if I let down my guard for even a second," you say, *"I'll sin like a crazy person."*

Hold on. That's what religion has told you, and I just suggested that religion is usually wrong. It's wrong here, for sure. Religion supposes that by keeping a moral watchdog chained to your flesh, you'll stop sinning. You've probably already disproved this theory with many a botched New Year's resolution. The Pharisees disproved it 2,000 years ago.

Pages 19-20

Before his trial, Scripture describes Job as "flawless and upright." This is verse 1 of chapter 1. But then Job loses his family, his wealth, and his health. Now listen to him in chapter 10, verse 1: "My soul is disgusted with my life; let me give free rein to myself and my concern; let me speak in the bitterness of my soul." Ah, there's the real Job, the mess of a man that was seething beneath that skin all along. But before he could understand his weakness, Job had to be broken. Can you imagine your Christian brother or sister even thinking Job's "blasphemous" words? No one would invite the real Job to the Wednesday prayer meeting, at least not without asking him to comb his hair and keep his scabby mouth shut.

George Bernard Shaw was a genius. It was he who said: "Virtue is insufficient temptation." Many times, those who appear virtuous have not been sufficiently tempted. Their virtue is Hollywood-wall virtue, propped up with half a dozen two-by-fours and a New Year's resolution. It's self-control untested. The world can spot phony Christian virtue ten miles away. Christians can't see it because they are too busy admiring themselves in the mirror.

Real human virtue is being broken by trial and lying like a pile of lumber in the wake of a hurricane. That's when the good stuff starts; it's when God goes to work. Real human virtue is helplessness before God. Helplessness before God is the beginning of a true spirituality that stands strong when the wind blows. Well, it has no place to go but up.

Page 28

Romans 5:8—"Yet God is commending this love of His to us, seeing that, while we are still sinners, Christ died for our sakes."

God went out of His way here to say, in effect, "I did not justify you in your Sunday clothes. I did not justify you while you were loving your neighbor as yourself, or praying to Me in the quietness of your room. Instead, I justified you while you were yelling at your children, running up your credit card, stuffing yourself with donuts—and worse. I did this for you on your worst day, not your best. I did it this way so that you could thank Me the rest of your life instead of wasting your time trying to figure out how to downplay your faults and impress Me."

What did you say, God? Our robes were rustling.

When God justifies us this way, we're finished before we start. Since He did His best for us at our worst, what can we do now to improve the relationship? Act better? But He already did His best for us while we were acting our worst. What can we do now to blow our relationship with Him? Sin? But He already maxed out on His love for us while we were sinning like crazy people. ■

Dear Martin,

I stumbled across your book at the library while researching other faiths and was instantly intrigued. As I read, I could literally feel the guilt falling off of me. I swear I feel 10 pounds lighter each day because I no longer pack my sins around with me. I feel the love of God more clearly now than ever. The reality of God's grace is beautiful. The pure logic of it is so obvious now, but was so hidden before. Thanks be to Him, and to you for voicing it. The only regret I have is that it took so long for me to truly experience the power of the cross.   —*Susan R.*

"God used this small book to change my life. After fifteen years in the pulpit, I finally understand what hell is. Better late than never."

-J. Marcus Oglesby, M.Div.

MARTIN ZENDER
GOES TO HELL

MARTIN ZENDER
Author of "How to Quit Church Without Quitting God"

At last. Here are the facts.

EXCERPT

MARTIN ZENDER GOES TO HELL

Pages 27-31

When Adam sinned, what was the consequence? Go and see. Here was the worst sin ever. What better time to reveal the ultimate, horrible fate? But it's not there. You'll be driven from the Garden, Adam, and you'll have to hoe like mad to make anything grow. Eve, childbearing will introduce you to pain so severe you'll see white. And today, you begin to die, both of you. It's the penalty of your disobedience. Death and weeds and cramps the color of lightning. And I should mention this as well—I won't be coming around as often.

Bad enough, but not a word about an eternity of torture in flames. I wonder why. Do you?

Along comes Cain then, who murders his brother Abel. Murder is an unknown crime until then, but the worst since the Satan/Eve/ fruit debacle. Now is a good time for God to unveil the Mother of All Punishments, to discourage future lawbreakers. But no, not a word about it. There is judgment, yes, but it's rational and reasonable: Cain's farming labors get cursed—the ground won't produce for him—and he has to wander the Earth as a nomad. We anticipate such phrases as, "Burn forever, murderer," or, "Go to hell, Cain," but they are not here.

I hope no one is disappointed.

What about in the days of Noah? The citizens of that era sinned as a profession. All people thought about back then was: How can we sin with more skill and greater efficiency? They loved their grim occupation and rarely took a break from it. If any people deserved eternal torment, it was these. Burn the blasphemers in hell forever? Surprisingly, no. The sinners merely got wiped out in a flood. Merely? Think about it. One glug and down came your curtain. It couldn't have been pleasant, but it was better than burning forever.

God does sometimes employ fire and brimstone to curtail the careers of professional sinners. Like Lysol, however, fire and brimstone kill germs on contact. (That is, the fire and brimstone do not eternally torment the germs.) Consider the twin cities of Sodom and Gomorrah, cities which today have become synonymous with sexual perversion. When the hour of reckoning arrived, "The Lord rained on Sodom and Gomorrah brimstone and fire from the Lord out of heaven" (Genesis 19:24). The result? God "destroyed the cities of the valley" (verse 29). Note the conspicuous absence of "God began to torment the inhabitants of these cities for eternity."

What about in the days of Moses, when there were laws for everything and a thousand ways to break them? Here's another ideal opportunity for the doctrine of eternal torment to begin "crawling all over Scripture," as I've been told that it is. And yet, it is another opportunity squandered by God and His servant Moses, who could get mad enough to smash rock. All threats in the days of Moses concerned earthly rewards and punishments only. Kill another man's bull, and your bull was killed. Mishandle some point of law, and your crops failed. Tangle with Moses himself, and some terrible thing happened with your wife's hormones. Or an enemy would storm your gates. Or both.

All bad enough, but not crazy. Nothing eternal and not a hint of unending flame. Capital punishment was by stoning then, the worst that could happen. It was nothing you wanted in on, but at least you died. One rock to the head relaxed you enough to dim the finish. No more taxes, tents, scorpions, sand storms, or Moses. For men and women toiling and failing upon an evil planet, death often came as a mercy.

To review, nowhere in the Old Testament does any God-inspired writer mention one word about an eternity of torment for disobeying God. Not one scholar has ever found it, no, not even those who have searched for it desperately. Strange that a doctrine that is "everywhere" has not yet appeared in a segment of the Bible that is, by my reckoning, about three and a half inches thick.

Is it that the amateurs of that delicate era could not shoulder such a responsibility? Then let the Old Testament lightweights stand aside to make way for Someone Who Knows How To Damn. Close the Old Testament books, and make way for genuine terror. Turn one page past Malachi, all ye sinners. To the Gospels! But rejoice not. Rather, fear. For you did not realize how good you had it in the days of old. You are about to pine for those days of flood, famine, and stone. For here, finally, comes One Rising to New Levels of Damnation, a Divine Unveiler of Heretofore Unimaginable Torture. His Good News, in a nutshell, is "Love Me before you die, or my Father will do worse than kill you!" His name?

JESUS CHRIST, SAVIOR.

> The spirit of the Lord is on Me, on account of which He anoints Me to bring the evangel to the poor. He has commissioned Me to heal the crushed heart, to herald to captives a pardon, and to the blind the receiving of sight; to dispatch the oppressed with a pardon, to herald an acceptable year of the Lord...
> —Jesus Christ, Luke 4:18-19

Are you ready now to find out how things *really* are?

Pages 35-38

The most frightening threats Jesus made to the Israelites are probably those found in Matthew 5:29-30 and Mark 9:43-48. Here, Jesus explains how much better it is for an Israelite to pluck out his or her eye, or tear off his or her hand, than to let these members lead one into "the fire of hell." These verses have terrified countless millions over the centuries, people to whom the verses don't even apply. These are Israelite threats for an earthly, Israelite kingdom.

The "fire of hell"? That's bad translating. Jesus never said the word "hell" in His life. He didn't speak English. The word that left His lips was *Gehenna*. That's right. Jesus warned the Israelites about "the fire of Gehenna," not hell, and any concordance will confirm this for you (see word #1067 in Strong's, and page 474 in Young's.) Gehenna is a small valley along the southwest corner of Jerusalem. It's a geographical location, a place you can walk in today. God made sure that some versions of Scripture got this right (the *Concordant Literal New Testament*, *Rotherham's Emphasized Bible*, and *Young's Literal Translation*, to name three).

As any dictionary will tell you, Gehenna is where the Israelites of old dumped their garbage and offered sacrifices to foreign gods. In the old days it was called the Valley of Hinnom. From *The Random House Dictionary*, under the entry *Gehenna*: "The valley of Hinnom, near Jerusalem, where propitiatory sacrifices were made to Molech." It may be a pleasant green valley today, but in the 1,000-year kingdom it will function as a crematorium for the corpses of criminals (Isaiah 66:23-24).

The "fire of hell"? Here is the only instance where the *King James Version* has taken the name of an actual place and made it something else. Watch this: Where the Greek has *Hierousalem*, the KJV translates "Jerusalem"—every time. Where the Greek has *Nazaret*, the KJV makes it "Nazareth"—every time. Where the Greek has *Bethleem*, the KJV has "Bethlehem"—every time. This is sensible. It's an honorable and consistent way of translating. But here, where Jesus says *Gehenna* (another geographical location), the KJV (as well as the *New International Version*—NIV—and *New American Standard Bible*—NASB), makes it "hell." Gee, that's weird. Can you explain it? I can. Ever hear the phrase, "theological bias"?

Pages 43-46

Matthew, chapter 25. Here we find "the Son of Mankind come into His glory, seated on the throne." In front of Him are gathered "all the nations," and "He shall be severing them from one another even as a shepherd is severing the sheep from the goats." This judgment is advertised in your local church as "the final judgment" of "all humankind," when "God's enemies" go to either "heaven or hell," for "all eternity." But no. Each sheep and goat represents a nation, not a person. This is not Uncle Harry standing before Jesus; it is Ethiopia. It is not Aunt Hazel trembling before Him; it is Russia. It is not Jim the milkman; it is Afghanistan.

This judgment occurs at the inauguration of the thousand-year kingdom, in the valley of Jehoshaphat. Like Gehenna, this is a literal, geographical location outside Jerusalem (see map again on page 37). As with Gehenna's fire and worms, this judgment is practical. Jesus returns to find Earth's political alignments amok. Good nations will be low; the evil will sit on high. The Great Judge will cure this. What criteria will He use for judging? Their belief in Him? Their confession of faith? The mode of their baptism? No. It will be that nation's policy toward Israel, nothing more. No one will ask, "What church did you go to?" or, "Why didn't you have more faith?"

To make this the general judgment of all humanity is to slaughter the context. But who cares? The possibility of a near-universal twisting of this judgment, and a vast misrepresentation of God's character, will not bother most people. Why? I will tell you. ∎

> Dear Martin,
> I have just finished *Martin Zender Goes to Hell*. This is one of the best books I have ever read. All anxiety over my loved ones has vanished. Praise God! The facts you present are unassailable. —*Stephen S.*

All my life, since I was about 6, I knew God was not in a box, knew there was freedom. In February of 2009, I heard you and Dan on the radio for the first time. My kids and their friends have always known me to be someone who stuck with God's word and Holy Spirit, rather than with some slick preacher or formal church. I literally cried when I heard you guys for the first time! I wonder if you really realize how dramatic this can be for folks who feel like they have just come home? Thank you for being bold!

—*C.V., San Francisco*

The
MARTINZENDER
DANSHERIDAN
Show

WBRI
indianapolis

 www.martinzender.com

My husband, 2 grown sons and I have been listening to your daily messages for a couple of years now. You are refreshingly different. I've been on a search for truth for about 10 years. We listened to a variety of Internet messages but settled on yours because it's dependable, funny, and best of all is NOT like regular church teaching. The gift you've been given is clarity. It's not a commonly possessed gift! —M.R., *Atlanta*

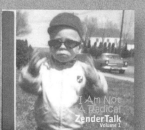

Dear Martin, Please keep the *Clanging Gong News* coming! We are a couple of families living in eastern Iowa, and have been getting together for fellowship for a few years now. You are a breath of fresh air to us! I have been known to read sections of your newsletter out loud, with tears in my eyes. God put you in our lives at *exactly* the right time. Keep doing what you do!

—A.B., *Cedar Rapids*

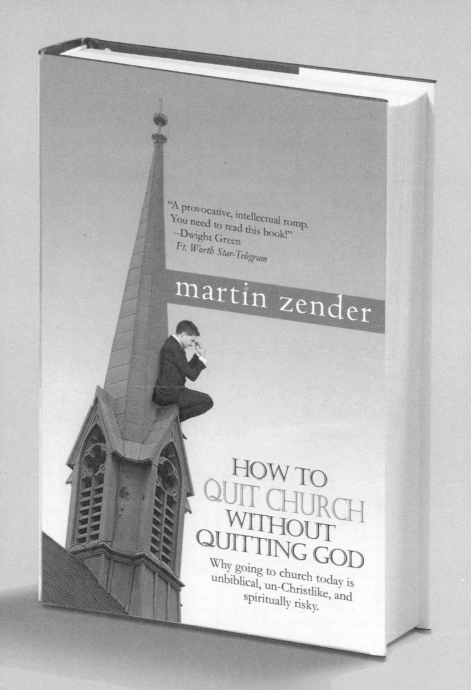

"A provocative, intellectual romp.
You need to read this book!"
—Dwight Green
Ft. Worth Star-Telegram

martin zender

HOW TO
QUIT CHURCH
WITHOUT
QUITTING GOD

Why going to church today is
unbiblical, un-Christlike, and
spiritually risky.

COMING JULY 2012

"OMG!" —*Cynthia F.*

www.youtube.com/zendermeister